"Not It"

An Approach

to Life

LORI REHNELT

Debby

My best to you!

Lori Rehnelt

Endorsements

"What a fun book! Lori got to the heart of what was important
and 'it' in my life and helped me sort out what was 'not it.'
I've often struggled with having too much on my plate, and now
I regularly ask myself, 'Is this part of who I want to be and how
I want to spend my time—or is it, indeed, not it?'"
— Jill Swanson, author of
Out the Door in 15 Minutes: How to Look Fabulous Fast

"*'Not It': An Approach to Life* is a brilliant book that will help you
reach your full potential. It's packed with tips on how to look at
what's not working in your life, and assists with an array of ways
to uncover and discover what makes your heart sing.
A valuable gem, with priceless advice."
— Janice Novak, M.S., founder and president
of ImproveYourPosture.com

"*'Not It': An Approach to Life* will serve as a helpful tool to overcoming obstacles that lead to inefficiencies, slow downs, or even a "shut
down" in life and/or work. My life is now more efficient and organized thanks to the systems she helped me create. I recommend

Lori's book and her coaching skills to help you get past any stumbling block in life—I was able to do it with her help!"
— **Nancy Weatherup**, president of USAdvisors
Wealth Management

"'*Not It': An Approach to Life* is full of useful tips and efficient action steps for every aspect of your life. Lori has done the research so that you can improve your life quicker! She has packed a lifetime of experience in an easy-to-read book."
— **Marlow Felton**, author of *Couples Money:
What Every Couple Should Know about Money and Relationships*

"In '*Not It': An Approach to Life*, Lori Rehnelt helps people reframe the key aspects of their personal and professional lives. This book helps readers hone in on significant life and business challenges, and provides immediate calls to action. '*Not It': An Approach to Life* is an invaluable addition to any library."
— **Laura Reider Novakowski**, founder and president of Positive Power Strategies, Inc.

"Drawing from her personal experience and snippets from many authors and conferences, Lori Rehnelt offers a toolbox of suggestions and exercises for facing, changing, or enhancing your life journey. She has done the homework for us!"
— **Ruth Stricker**, founder and executive director of The Marsh, A Center for Balance and Fitness

Acknowledgments

Thank you to my beloved family and friends for your unconditional love and support, without which this book would not be possible.

A special thank you to Pastor Rance Settle for your Bible study on vocation, which was a springboard resulting in my business consulting and coaching practice, Systems For Change, and this book—*"Not It": An Approach to Life*.

A big thank you to everyone at Beaver's Pond Press for providing a step-by-step process for pulling my first book together, and educating me each step of the way. Even though it wasn't always easy, your wisdom and encouragement guided me through.

ISBN: 978-1-59298-938-6
Library of Congress Control Number: 2014939962

Printed in the United States of America
Designed by Dan Pitts
First Printing: 2014

18 17 16 15 14   5 4 3 2 1
Beaver's Pond Press, Inc.
7108 Ohms Lane
Edina, MN 55439
(952) 829-8818
www.BeaversPondPress.com

Contents

Introduction

Remember playing "not it" when you were a kid?

"Not it, not it, not it!"

In the childhood game, saying "not it" exempts someone from performing a deed, provided he or she is not the last person to call "not it." The last person to call "not it" must perform the deed at hand, *provided he or she lies in the realm of responsibility* (meaning he or she is within hearing distance of what's going on, in the childhood game; or the deed is something he or she can and wants to take on, in adulthood). For example, if a phone is ringing and multiple people could answer it, the last person to say "not it" has to answer the phone.

Just like playing the game of "not it" as a child, when you see a task or situation in your life that you don't want as an adult, you can play "not it," with or without anyone knowing. You could say "not it" when someone else zips into a parking spot you were waiting for, because it's obviously no longer available and you hope a better one will open up. Or say "not it" silently to yourself when the boss is on another rant, to remind you that this job is no longer "it" as you search for a better one. Playing "not it" may not keep you from all the tasks you dislike, yet by identifying them, you can change your situation in the future (so you never have to do those tasks again or can do them in a pleasurable way).

I see excess weight on my body; my skinny jeans are tight; and I say to myself "not it" when a temptation comes my way.

When I see myself tempted to put off something I can do right now, I say "not it" to the temptation of procrastination and do the activity anyway. Maybe missing one fitness class is not a big deal in the grand scheme of things or maybe the bill I received is not due for twenty more days, but in either situation, I feel better saying no to the procrastination and yes to the good feeling of doing things in my life that are right for me.

The "not it" game in life is about discovering choices and deciding what works *for you*. It's about saying NO to what's unhealthy and YES to what works best. "Not it" is a discovery process, a tool in life for when you ask yourself what's next and aren't quite sure. And when you are in the "don't know," ask for clarity. Ask God. Ask the universe. Just ask.

"Not it" provides clarity.

The answer you receive may not be what you expect, or come from the source you're expecting. For example, you ask a friend for help on a project, and instead of getting help from her, your son happens to stop by, and gives you a hand. Maybe you've been asking the universe for a different car and then your mom decides to get a new one and give you hers.

Throughout this book, I'll provide many examples and concepts that have worked well for my clients and me as we chose to live lives we had only previously dreamed of. If one of these examples says "not it" for you, great! Then the example has served its purpose by prompting you to take a look at some area in your life and decide what *is* right for you. The examples are tools—not a how-to-live-your-life-by-these-rules (there are no rules). It's up to you to trust your gut and know in your heart what is right for you.

I was in the boo-hoo stage of my divorce at the time I took a Bible study on vocation with Pastor Rance Settle and, through tears, wrote these notes:

Do what you love...

Do what you are most passionate about...

Don't let your buts get in the way...

Don't let anyone stop you!

Identifying my passions was my first task, and through the months that followed, I jotted down what I loved at work, at home, and for recreation. I had no idea how it would all come together, but God did! I later recognized this as a pivotal point in my life.

Fifteen months later, participating in PSI Seminars and taking coaching classes helped me pull it all together. Since then I have begun to live a life I'd only previously dreamed of. In coaching clients, I learned: when it's "not it" anymore; when life changes; when things that were perfect at one time just aren't anymore...

- My old skinny jeans don't fit because I lost more weight—yeah!
- A relationship turns abusive—definitely "not it."
- This house is too small now that we have children.

The necessary changes are not always as evident as a baggy pair of jeans, an abusive situation you now realize you want to leave, or the home you've outgrown.

I've designed this book to promote health and well-being with tips and tools to show you the way—to health, balancing work and home, good relationships, and more.

Some of what you read in this book may seem elementary, yet in certain situations *we know* we need to do something and *just don't*. Some of us just "don't know what we don't know" because we didn't have someone to show us the way, or we're in a dysfunctional situation, or we don't feel we can learn.

When life is spinning out of control, I ask you to "press pause" and take time to reflect on what's got to change. I will ask you throughout this book to consider possibilities and look at life in a different way than you may have in the past. *Not It: An Approach to Life* is about lessons I've learned along my journey as I've worked on recovering from codependency, and assisted others on their journeys from challenging situations. I have included some Al-Anon twelve-step insights I gained, although this is not an Al-Anon book and does not replace a twelve-step program of any type.

I am a Christian and I wrote this book because I believe God brings things to our awareness, and as I was learning about alternate ways of thinking through coaches' training, I took what fit and let the rest go. I am not writing this to judge anyone; I am sharing concepts that have worked for me and for those I coach and consult. As I share examples with you of how the "not it" concept has worked, there will be times I pull from my faith and times I pull from my training.

I refer to twelve-step programs and the Bible as I share stories of how my faith was a key part of recovering from codependency and growing forward. Say "not it" if you want to in those parts—it's okay if you do not share my beliefs. I hope you find the inspiration and strength to live the life of your dreams whether you share my beliefs or not. This book contains tools for you to use. Some of the tools you may not believe in; some you may consider "woo-woo," but I hope to shed light where I can. I also may share sources I do not believe, though I love their messages.

Some tools may pertain to you now, some in the future, or some maybe never. I am writing to a large audience and about many situations; some tools may not apply to your life. When that is the case, say "not it" and use what resonates with you.

I do not claim to be an expert in everything covered in this book; much of this information has gradually come across my desk during more than twenty-five years of reading, and attending classes and seminars. My goal here is not to be the nutrition or fitness expert; there are enough of them out there. I'm sharing my experiences and those of my clients for the sole purpose of creating coaching tools and examples in various life arenas to encourage you to look at your life and determine what "not it" looks like for you. Perhaps, as you read through the book, you will see things that will work better for you than what you are currently practicing. On the other hand, you may say, "I have no time to do this exercise," and that is fine. If I've gotten you to think about what you are doing, I've met my goal.

At the time I took the Bible study on vocation, I read from the book *Simple Abundance: A Daybook of Comfort and Joy* by Sarah Ban Breathnach, in which I found this quote:

> "Careened between feeling I was frittering my life away
> to feeling that I was sacrificing it on the altar of my own ambitions..."[1]

This struck a chord with me as I was taking stock of what was and wasn't working in my life. I was working the concept of "not it" before I even labeled it. I had always felt a pull between work and home with a strong desire to balance both. I looked back at my life and remembered that as a girl, I would read magazines, newspapers, and cookbooks when visiting my grandparents and share recipes, sayings, tips, and prayers that intrigued me. I worked in the library in my high school, and as a teen, I began a practice of "reading with a pen and scissors," saving whatever struck my fancy it was mainly articles on fashion, nutrition, fitness, and relationships. I clipped pictures and words from these magazines and taped them to my wall, creating a wall of inspiration (now termed a *vision board*). These practices evolved for me along with many other "systems" I share with my clients today.

I knew when my boys were babies that I wanted to write someday. I even borrowed a typewriter for a time. I kept my focus on my boys and career while telling myself "someday" I would write…

> Well, thirty years later, my someday is here!
> All my life, thorny knots of understanding have unraveled themselves on scraps of paper: napkins, newspaper margins, backs of recipe cards, and Post-it notes. Sometimes I have been awakened in the dead of night after a dream by the insistent voice: *Write this down*. I did as I was told . . . [2]

This paragraph resonated with me as I read from the book *Something More: Excavating Your Authentic Self*, by Sarah Ban Breathnach. It's something I've been doing for years and something I encourage my clients to do as they examine their own lives.

When I was waking up from an unfulfilling life and then later, working as a coach, I read a lot of books. Rather than reinvent the wheel, I share many quotes from books, recommended reading, and coaching homework for you here. As I show you how to say "not it" in your own life, I will point out "not it" behaviors I have witnessed. Grab a notepad or journal to capture inspired thoughts you have as you make your way through the chapters.

By sharing stories, concepts, and tools, this book will assist you to live the life of your dreams!

God bless you on your journey.

Getting Started
on Dream Building

To get to the point where you're ready to build your dreams, you have to know what you want. Knowing what you *don't* want can be a first step in knowing what you do. The key point of "not it" is that, once you realize what you don't want, you take your focus to the clarity you have gained and what you do want, totally dismissing the "not it" discovery even when the undesired pops back in.

When a "not it" attempts to pop back into your life (and it will), just like your favorite chip will tempt you on a diet, say, "NO, not it" and refocus on the good you have. You will get more of what you want when you focus on it and appreciate it. As I learned in my training, what you focus your attention on grows; and what you think about, you bring about, and so it is.

Do not get attached to a "not it" thought—just let it swim in and out like a fish (a concept I learned in yoga class). When those

The past should not be a place where we live, but something from which we learn. We are to forget those things which are behind and reach forward to those things which are ahead and we're to press toward the goal for the prize of the upward call of God in Christ Jesus.[3]

- PHILIPPIANS 3:12–14

thoughts do pop in, don't analyze—let them go. It may be a relationship that is decidedly over, so don't get into analysis paralysis over it just because thoughts are popping back in. You don't "need" to rethink it. You don't. You've already decided. Just say "not it," let go, and move on to the next right thing. Think about what is 100 percent right; what is your GREAT? Focus on that, and it will appear.

When I was losing weight and got into a size ten, it was good. I didn't settle and stay there, though. I got to my version of great, which is a size six, and took the size ten while I was on my way to the six.

PRESS PAUSE

When thoughts start spinning out of control, when your life feels unmanageable, press pause (a concept I learned attending a Press Pause Women's Wellness retreat, in a workshop from presenter Mary Marcdante). Take a break with a pen and paper and a favorite beverage, relax, and just start writing. Do a brain dump. Ask yourself what your story is. Ask yourself what does not feel right. What has to change? What has to change immediately, now? What can wait while you take time to work things through? What do you want your life to look like compared to how it looks right now?

Pressing pause is a time for renewal.

Pressing pause is a great tool to use between busy bouts in our lives. Seasons change; big events come our way. When we take time to reflect between the holidays and New Year's, for example, we can set ourselves up for a great new year. We may purposely block off some time at home to regroup, to make plans for the next few months, the next season. Maybe you have put away the Christmas gifts, decorations, and updated your files for the new year to get your house in order.

This is a great time to have a date night with your spouse and decide what your next season will look like. Are there trips you wish to take? Plans to make? Budgeting to decide on? Reorganizing or remodeling to do? Press pause together, bring your calendars, and make it fun! Light the candles, make it romantic, have some fun food and beverages to share, and really connect and enjoy each other. Ask each other, "How can I support you during this time as you are doing...?" Whatever it is (training for a marathon, writing a book, taking a class), support each other and be proactive, so no elephants are in your living room. Communicate and share what you want so there's no acting ugly later on about needs not getting met (see the next chapter for more on that). Of course, there will be a bit of hip-shooting (you may not know how you can support each other specifically until the day arrives) but nonetheless you've communicated in advance—you know what's coming up, so it's no surprise. When you celebrate the event, it's all the sweeter because you worked together as a couple. What a good model for those around you, especially your children!

When you take the time to communicate, clean up, and prepare, your life is saner.

When you've reached a milestone in your life (for example, a child is married and off on his or her honeymoon), you can decide to press pause and go away as a couple to reconnect and say, "Ahhh, we did it; we pulled it off. Now we can relax and look at what's next for us."

From this point on in the book, the "not it" chapters are set up to focus first on your dreams, feelings, and thoughts, and then work outward to your physical well-being, followed by your environment and relationships, then ending with your finances and career, as shown below. Follow along on this journey, deciding what is "it" for you.

So how can I get from where I am today to the life I am dreaming of?

Right now I am dreaming of the day I can retire, living the healthy active lifestyle I currently have, only doing a lot more of it!

What are you dreaming of?

- College degree?
- New car?
- Different home?
- Children?
- Satisfying career?
- Empty nest?
- Travel?
- Gourmet kitchen?
- Boat or RV?
- Cabin?
- More family time?
- Time at the gym?
- Yoga?
- Golf?

I wonder what it is for you. Let's find out.

What? Don't have time? What are you too busy thinking about? What's it costing you?

As Ruth Stricker, founder and executive director of The Marsh in Minnetonka, Minnesota, wrote in a *Marsh Monthly* newsletter:

I want to give you something you didn't know you wanted and

once you get it, can't imagine your life without it. By calling up your inner observer and becoming a noticer, moments of reflection can bring growth, discovery, or even surprise. It may be a sudden realization that we already have a "something" or are progressing toward it. It may mean speeding up to an alert state or slowing down for a pause. For sure it means time for being present and checking in... a 'now that I think about it' time. "When we have it, we don't know what we would do without it" presents gratitude and joy in bits and pieces in our life. Some examples as "a-ha's" that come to mind could be when we realize what it feels like to be fit and healthy, or how to live with a chronic disease or injury, or how we have healed after a trauma, or when we discover more tolerance or empathy. Perhaps we've discovered that joy and humor make us feel better when we share them with others or we reach a hidden goal that we didn't think was very important, or feeling the victory of a competitive goal. It may be how we have accepted a loss, or moved on from disappointment, or how comfortable we have become in our own skin.[4]

MAKING DREAM SHEETS FOR NOW AND THE FUTURE

I ask that you to take a few moments to press pause in your life, to go find a comfy spot to work (this can be done alone or in a group/family setting). Get a big piece of blank paper, colored pencils (or just a spiral notebook and pen), and have fun jotting down everything you want: draw, color, paste photos pulled from magazines. Do it your way and have fun! Don't think about the how or the when; just dream.

I remember doing this back in 1986— on my dream sheet I had an office with my name above the door. I didn't even know what type of office I would have; I was in college and just dreaming. I also had a house and boat in my dream. Later in 2003, I opened an insurance office and did have my name above the door. This dream did "manifest" in my life. Writing a book has been another dream of mine for many years, and here I am, the time is now.

Okay, so we've created our "dream sheets." Now what? Let's look at the components. Break it down. Ask what's already in the works and what's way out there in the future. What do you believe you can have and what is blocking you from attaining it? You may not know what is holding you back, or maybe you do but don't want to admit it; or it's just not time yet—it's a someday thing.

You may have a bucket list for someday, and because you've identified it and think about it, an opportunity may pop up sooner than you expect. Put anything that is a someday dream on a back burner, watch it simmer and see what happens. Like a cake, the ingredients are added separately and may not be great alone. Want to eat raw egg, cocoa, oil, and flour? Alone, each ingredient is, well, yuck! Mix them into your batter and put the cake in the oven. It needs to bake for a while, which means waiting patiently for the marvelous end result. The ingredients are like puzzle pieces coming into your life all at different times; individually they may not make sense. This is not the typical "set a goal, break it down, and put the steps on your calendar." I am all about doing that for the steps we realize we want to take right now, but things on the back burner will show up when the time is right. Keep your eyes open, knowing what you want. Remember: just because something is on a back burner, you don't have to lose your focus or forget about it. Something simmering still needs to be tended to, stirred, and checked on periodically to keep it out there as a possibility. Sometimes a pot needs to be dumped, like a deadbeat boyfriend you decide is "not it" or a job you had your heart set on that landed in someone else's lap.

I wonder what story you're telling yourself about what's on your dream sheet. What are you telling others? Do your words and actions match? Have you ever heard that actions speak louder than words? What if you rewrite your story? The one I hear you telling me now is not a very happy story, when you say you can't do this, or this could never happen for me.

What about the things you are doing right now that just aren't fun, that are dragging you down? I had a job once where I felt like I was swimming in molasses—not fun! If it's not fun, don't do it. Simple. Or if you simply feel that you must do it, and can't delegate it, what can you do to make it fun?

I wanted to exercise. I was running yet felt in a rut because of my environment, the same old treadmill. So I bought new gym clothes and an iPod shuffle and loaded fun music onto it. Things got better. I also began getting outdoors and riding my bike when spring came. Whatever you must do that you cannot delegate, make it fun! I add simple luxuries to my day, such as a new flavor of toothpaste or floss to jazz it up. Maybe for you, it could be a walk, a bubble bath, a clean home and car, tomato soup and a grilled cheese sandwich, or fresh-baked chocolate chip cookies made from healthy ingredients. Whatever you choose doesn't need to be expensive. I use fun cleaning supplies and turn on some music, lighting candles while I dust, having fun snacks as I clean, washing my car inside and out, and rewarding myself with a manicure. If you don't feel good, as noted in *The Secret* by Rhonda Byrne, shift it. Stop what you're doing, notice your feelings, decide what you want to change, and change it. I stop by taking a break, going for a walk, clearing my head, and then getting back to it. Change it up a bit; use colored file folders and fun office supplies instead of basic ones. The bottom line is to feel good now.

> "If you don't design your own life plan, chances are you'll fall into someone else's plan. Guess what they have planned for you? Not much."
>
> **—UNKNOWN**

Do what you can to make your life fun! I don't recommend spending a fortune or being wasteful with what you have. Donate items; swap them. When you feel good, you attract what you desire faster. So know what it is that you want; go for it with all you've got; and look ahead, not back. Feel good.

Ever lose your keys or can't figure out what to do next? I learned of a method from my friend, Dawn. When I search for my keys and just cannot find them, I throw my hands in the air as I inquisitively say, "I wonder where my keys are." Usually after I say this, I find the missing item immediately or very shortly after. Magical. The same goes with the next right move for me in my other choices.

Dare to dream, and trust your inner knowing. Back when I was working in a nursing home business office, a position was created for a nurse who would assess a resident's condition, transmit that information to the state, and ultimately determine the billing codes for the patient. It was called an MDS (Minimum Data Set) coordinator. I knew I could do the coordinator position, but it was closed to me because it was exclusive to nurses. I worked for several more years in long-term care business offices and one day applied for a position titled medical data manager. What I found was the MDS coordinator position delegating the nursing component due to a nursing shortage. I took the job. It was what I had envisioned years before.

You wouldn't get the idea if you couldn't do it!

If you can't consider something possible right now and you really want it, know that it's available to you at some point. If you can dream it, you can do it. Shelly, a client, once told me, "I remember when I was home with my babies I thought going out to a nice restaurant was an impossible dream. Once they grew older, I became a career woman and enjoyed going out for nice food on a consistent, regular basis. Since I love to cook, I appreciate a well-prepared meal served with great presentation and atmosphere. Just a few years of waiting until my little ones grew a bit and my belief that it was possible made it well worth the wait. Now I do everything I ever wanted—especially travel."

TRUSTING BLESSINGS TO COME YOUR WAY

I met motivational speaker and author Zig Ziglar in Dallas, Texas, while attending his Sunday school class at the First Baptist Church and a *See You at the Top* book signing. The scripture of the week for First Baptist was Psalms 139:1–7:

> O Lord, you have examined my heart and know everything about me. You know when I sit or stand. When far away, you know my every thought; you chart the path ahead of me, and tell me where to stop and rest. Every moment you know where I am. You know what I am going to say before I even say it. You both precede and follow me, and place your hand of blessing on my head. This is too glorious too wonderful to believe! I can *never* be lost to your spirit! I can *never* get away from my God![7]

My notes from Zig's Sunday school class included the following:

- Look for the good.
- Set goals.
- Be before Do; Do before Have.
- Focus on one thing at a time.
- When going to work, have a goal when you get there.
- Many people fail at their first attempt, but we are growing! We become new.

Attending this class and meeting Zig influenced me to pursue personal growth and follow my dreams as they unfolded. I learned that

God gives us what we need when we need it, like the old saying, "God doesn't call the equipped, he equips the called." Trusting that did not always come easy to me. When I was a young mom, each time my sons reached a new phase in their lives, I would question myself as their mom. I just wanted to do the right thing for them. Sometimes I did not want to leave my comfort zone, the nice routine we already had. I would resist the changes, like when they outgrew their eight o'clock bedtime.

When we meet resistance, it's not a bad thing. It may feel bad at the moment, but what we are doing is stepping outside the box, stepping outside our norms and comfort zones. It's a good thing to release what is holding us back and use the state of uncomfortableness to propel us forward to that which we are seeking—our dream! Go for it!

Let it go; it's on its way!

If all the puzzle pieces aren't put together yet, we're just seeing evidence of what we want showing up in our lives. It's on its way! Yeah! So don't give up because you can't see the whole picture yet. Be grateful and amazed as you watch the puzzle pieces magically fit into place. Just stay focused on what it is you want and the old will fall away like the skin of an old snake. Resistance is what you feel as you move into the new life you want. Stay focused, have fun, rejoice!

When looking at where we want to be, our desired outcome, we determine what tools we need to get us there: a pen and paper, a checkbook, a map? A dust cloth and vacuum? The classroom? Paint and brush? Get the picture? Who do you want to support and assist you? Ask and be prepared for a no and be open to assistance from someone you do not expect. Mom can't always be there—a friend may be there to help instead.

What does it look like? Your calendar? Your space? What do you need? Time? Money? How many yoga sessions per week? How many days per week would you like to run, lift weights, or swim? How often do you want to visit family? Friends? Be specific about how much time and money is required to accomplish these goals.

The "how" can limit you—you have no idea how.[9]

TRUSTING INSPIRED THOUGHT OR INTUITION

Whether revealing the hard truth about toxic relationships, your exhaustion level, or a thankless job, intuition is always trying to communicate, though you may not hear. It resides in a quiet place obscured by the chatter of everyday thoughts, according to Judith Orloff, author of *Positive Energy*.[10]

While out shopping on the way "up north" to go fishing, a friend and I stopped at a little discount store and ran across insulated bags for about ten dollars each. We chose a red one, but I kept going back to a blue one. But it did not make sense to me at the time to buy two bags, so I dismissed my intuition that said buy it (even though I knew I wanted it). About three weeks later, I bought a new car and it was blue. The blue bag would have been perfect to keep in my new car. I regretted not picking it up, as I use the other bag all the time and could have used a second one. Lesson learned; when I *feel* like that about something, to move forward with it even if it does not make sense at the time. I will learn to trust my intuition.

> "Until a man selects a definite purpose in life, he dissipates his energies and spreads his thoughts over so many subjects and in so many different directions that they lead not to power, but to indecision and weakness."
>
> **—NAPOLEON HILL,**
> *THE LAW OF SUCCESS*[8]

The key is to trust your inner knowing, the whisper you hear from your spirit, from God.

A few years ago, I had an opportunity to move to the Twin Cities from Rochester, Minnesota for a job. While interviewing, it was time to renew the lease on the townhome I was renting. I took a leap of faith and gave the sixty-day notice, trusting my feeling that I would get the job and move. Even though I did not get the offer until four interviews and a few weeks passed, I was grateful I had trusted my intuition, my feelings, and my instincts, and made the move, believing I would find the right home. I did and it all worked out very well.

If you abide in me, and my words abide in you, you will ask what you desire, and it shall be done for you. [11]

- JOHN 15:7

It's fun watching it all unfold.

While writing this book, I had lunch with a friend and opened a fortune cookie that said: "Patience is your ally at the moment. Don't worry! When it comes to inspiration, the sky's the limit!" You never know when words will jump off a page and speak to you. God is guiding us in our day to day. Trust it!

THE STORY OF THE 3RD BRIDGE

I was out hiking and was ready to leave the trail. It was springtime and there had been heavy rains. I kept getting blocked by the water-covered path and rerouted to the "3rd bridge," yet I did not want to go that far. I did not believe I had time. I found new places on the trail because of these wet spots blocking me and had time to pray, to ask about things that were going on in my rapidly changing life. As I kept walking, I kept seeing signs for the "3rd bridge" and finally just surrendered to the fact that I would be going there. It did not take as long as I had anticipated and I learned to trust where I was led, to take the time to pray. I received clarity on what was on my mind, and when I got to the third bridge, it ended right by a road that provided a quicker route than I realized, getting me back to my car and on my way. I was reminded to trust that day, to let go and surrender, and, most importantly to press pause and pray. When I feel my way is blocked, when I feel I am being rerouted in another direction, I remember the third bridge and say, "Okay, God, I surrender; I pray and trust I am being led to a better place than I imagined."

Many times through the personal growth and healing process I ask myself, "How do I incorporate this concept into my behavior? My actions?"

I plan my work and work my plan, as I learned in Al-Anon. After I've prayed about my plan and sought good counsel about the details, I commit myself to following through with whatever I decide is best.

So I say to you, ask, and it will be given to you; seek, and you will find; knock, and it will be opened to you. For everyone who asks receives, and he who seeks, finds, and to him who knocks, it will be opened. If you then, being evil, know how to give good gifts to your children, how much more will your heavenly father give the Holy Spirit to those who ask him![12]

- LUKE 11:9–10, 13

DREAM, BELIEVE, ACHIEVE

Once we get into dream building, we often see blocks to our dreams showing up. I love reading Leo Buscaglia, and in *Living, Loving, and Learning*, he says:

> It's amazing—you may not realize it, but so much of what you are *not* is because you are literally standing in your own

way of becoming. And what I'm pleading with you about is to get the hell out of your way! Fly, life and love is all available to you! And all you have to do is take the responsibility and grasp it. But so many people don't trust themselves. They don't believe in themselves. They don't even like themselves.[13]

In the next two chapters, "Acting Ugly: A Case of Unmet Needs" and "Self-Care: Putting Your Needs First," we will look at various negative blocks to our dreams and ways to overcome them. This is an area in life most of us would rather avoid at all costs, yet addressing the negative will provide the energy you need to zoom toward your dreams. It's not pretty, but it is essential to clear out the old stuff, stop dragging it around, make way for the new—living your dream life! After you eliminate the ugliness that is holding you back, you will jump right back into building your dreams! So hold on through the storm because there's a beautiful rainbow at the other end. Take a deep breath and dive right in...

HOMEWORK

1. Create your dream sheet by yourself, or with a group of coworkers, a group of friends, a Bible study group, or with your family.

2. Look at what's on your dream sheet—does it surprise you? Be inquisitive, curious about your dreams, and ask what you see happening now. What would you want to change to see your dreams come true? You may not have that clarity right away, yet just by putting the questions out there, the answers will start coming to you.

3. Can you identify the steps you need to take to begin the journey toward the life you are dreaming of?

Acting Ugly:
A Case of Unmet Needs

When our needs are met:

- We gain clarity.

- The crazies go away.

- We feel better.

- We draw people to ourselves.

That's what we need to start building the life of our dreams. Acting ugly is the first clue that our needs aren't being met and we need to make a change.

So let's start by determining what I mean by "acting ugly," then identify what needs aren't being met and how you might move forward (more on that in the next chapter). As you start seeing glimpses of what you want, document it.

I will show you how. Let the adventure begin!

Anyone "acting ugly" has an unmet need. Dr. Deborah Kern first introduced me to the concept, while at a Press Pause Women's

Wellness Retreat organized by Franciscan Skemp Medical Center of La Crosse, Wisconsin.

Here are some examples of acting ugly:

- Giving someone "the look"
- Sarcastic comments
- Complaining
- Long looks
- Critical remarks
- Proving a point in not such a nice way, like "barking up someone's tree"
- Belittling others
- Angry blowups
- Road rage
- Scolding
- Sighs, groans, and moans
- Stewing in negative thoughts while letting them seep out to those around you

Get the picture? When we are acting ugly, who wants to be around us? When we are needy, we push people away. Most people want to run—walking on eggshells is no fun!

When we are acting ugly, we can't see beyond what we are acting ugly about.

Acting ugly usually comes from some unmet need. And if you say, "I shouldn't have that [need]," it means you still have an unmet need. When you discount your need, minimize it, or deny it, the need is still unmet, which keeps you stuck.

Maybe you've identified someone in your life who is acting ugly. It's not your job to fix that person or fulfill his or her needs, even if there's an expectation that you will. It's that person's expectation, not your obligation—even if he or she has a little tantrum.

According to David J. Schwartz in *The Magic of Thinking Big*, once the victim of this failure disease has selected a "good" excuse, he sticks to it.[14] Then he relies on the excuse to explain to himself and others why he is not going forward. And each time the victim makes the excuse, the excuse becomes embedded deeper within his subconscious. Thoughts, positive or negative, grow stronger when fertilized with constant repetition. At first the victim of excusitis knows his alibi is more or less a lie. But the more frequently he repeats it, the more convinced he becomes that it is completely true, that the alibis are the real reason for not being a success.

Okay, but what if you find yourself acting ugly? Take five minutes to feel sorry for yourself. I mean REALLY sorry for yourself—exaggerate it to hilarity! Hit a pillow. Exaggerate it to the point of laughter and have a good long belly laugh; let your laugh come from your toes. Then laugh at how silly it is to act this way. Feel better?

Once you've had a good laugh, ask yourself what you were really so angry or in the dumps about.

What's your story? Can you take off the victim's glasses and tell a different story about what's going on? What are the parts of the story that reflect your needs? (See list of needs on page 34.) What jumps out and says "not it"?

When we tell ourselves a story and it conflicts with reality, there is no reason to be upset with someone else who may be involved. Our stories set up the expectation that people should do something for us and when they don't, we can get ugly and they have no idea!

Bad things may happen to you. Suffering is optional; there is no need to drag all the bad stories you have into the future, which has a clean slate. Let go of the past, forgive, and stop being the victim.

NEEDS

- Connection
- Acceptance
- Affection
- Appreciation
- Belonging
- Cooperation
- Communication
- Closeness
- Community
- Companionship
- Compassion
- Consideration
- Consistency
- Empathy
- Inclusion
- Intimacy
- Love
- Mutuality
- Nurturing
- Respect/ self-respect
- Safety
- Security
- Shared reality
- Stability
- Support
- To know and be known
- To see and be seen
- To understand and be understood

- Trust
- Warmth
- Honesty
- Authenticity
- Integrity
- Presence
- Play
- Joy
- Humor
- Peace
- Beauty
- Communion
- Ease
- Equality
- Harmony
- Inspiration
- Order
- Physical well-being
- Air
- Food
- Movement/ exercise
- Rest/sleep
- Sexual expression
- Safety
- Shelter
- Touch
- Water
- Meaning
- Awareness
- Celebration of life

- Challenge
- Clarity
- Competence
- Consciousness
- Contribution
- Creativity
- Discovery
- Efficacy
- Effectiveness
- Growth
- Hope
- Learning
- Mourning
- Participation
- Purpose
- Self-expression
- Stimulation
- To matter
- Understanding
- Autonomy
- Choice
- Freedom
- Independence
- Space
- Spontaneity

—FROM PRESS PAUSE WORKSHOP[21]

FEELINGS WHEN NEEDS ARE NOT MET

- Afraid
- Apprehensive
- Dread
- Fearful
- Foreboding
- Frightened
- Mistrustful
- Panicked
- Petrified
- Scared
- Suspicious
- Terrified
- Wary
- Worried
- Annoyed
- Aggravated
- Dismayed
- Disgruntled
- Displeased
- Exasperated
- Frustrated
- Impatient
- Irritated
- Irked
- Angry
- Enraged
- Furious
- Incensed
- Indignant
- Irate
- Resentful

- Confused
- Ambivalent
- Baffled
- Bewildered
- Dazed
- Hesitant
- Lost
- Mystified
- Perplexed
- Torn
- Disquieted
- Agitated
- Alarmed
- Discombobulated
- Disconcerted
- Disturbed
- Perturbed
- Rattled
- Restless
- Shocked
- Startled
- Surprised
- Troubled
- Turbulent
- Uncomfortable
- Uneasy
- Unnerved
- Unsettled
- Upset
- Embarrassed
- Ashamed

- Chagrined
- Flustered
- Guilty
- Mortified
- Self-conscious
- Fatigued
- Beat
- Burnt out
- Depleted
- Exhausted
- Lethargic
- Listless
- Sleepy
- Tired
- Weary
- Worn out
- Aversion
- Animosity
- Appalled
- Contempt
- Disgusted
- Dislike
- Hate
- Horrified
- Hostile
- Repulsed
- Tense
- Anxious
- Cranky
- Distressed
- Distraught

FEELINGS WHEN NEEDS ARE NOT MET

- Edgy
- Frazzled
- Jittery
- Nervous
- Overwhelmed
- Restless
- Stressed out
- Vulnerable
- Fragile
- Guarded
- Helpless
- Insecure
- Leery
- Reserved
- Sensitive
- Shaky
- Pain
- Agony
- Anguished
- Bereaved
- Devastated
- Grief stricken
- Heartbroken
- Hurt
- Lonely
- Miserable
- Regretful
- Remorseful
- Sad
- Depressed
- Dejected

- Despondent
- Disappointed
- Discouraged
- Disheartened
- Forlorn
- Gloomy
- Heavy hearted
- Hopeless
- Melancholy
- Unhappy
- Wretched
- Disconnected
- Alienated
- Aloof
- Apathetic
- Bored
- Cold
- Detached
- Distant
- Distracted
- Indifferent
- Numb
- Removed
- Withdrawn
- Yearning
- Envious
- Jealous
- Nostalgic
- Pining
- Wistful

—FROM PRESS PAUSE
WORKSHOP[22]

You do not deserve to have additional pain on top of what you've already experienced. By acting ugly, you become unattractive to others and you push people away without even realizing it, causing a downward spiral into further victim mode because not only are you hurting, but no one seems to care.

Having unmet needs is like having an empty bucket or throwing crumbs to a starving cat. Sara, a client, said, "I finally met my dream man and he has a boat! For years I walked along a favorite lake looking out at the boats and wanting to be out there on the lake instead of looking at it." Her bucket had been empty; she was the starving cat. Single at the time, she had no desire to buy a boat, maintain a boat, pull a boat behind a vehicle, let alone drive the boat. All she wanted was to find someone who enjoyed the water as much as she did. Well, she met him! Yeah! It was summer and they had their first boat ride. While on the boat, they had so much fun, they talked of boating at least weekly. Then life happened; they had family events and summer trips to do other things they enjoyed. So what did Sara do when those boating events did not come weekly? She focused on the drip in her empty bucket and acted ugly. She did not have gratitude for what she had—the man of her dreams. The boat was only a very small part of the puzzle, and she was focusing on that very small part of their great life! For years she had wanted the lifestyle of being on the boat so bad, because when she was on the water she felt energized. So she focused on that and felt disappointed. Once she recognized what she was doing, she had to stop telling herself that story, focus on the big picture—the dream life they shared—and STOP ACTING UGLY! She started focusing on gratitude, and they were able to boat that summer. It may not have been exactly as much as she wanted, but she had to remember that she wanted the other pieces of their great life as well. Just think what damage continuing to act ugly could have done based on a story she was telling herself. At some point, it would have ruined their relationship and she could have gone back to being single again. "Not it!"

Imagine you're the parent of adult children and you really want your kids to visit you. When you focus on not getting what you want, you can become ugly by throwing guilt their way, making comments like, "Come back when you can stay longer." You get in a position of resentment, which is not attractive. When I am not attractive, why would my kids want to come over to visit me? I end up pushing them away instead of attracting them to me. I have to stop throwing guilt-ridden comments at them.

The answer is to be grateful for what you do have; in gratitude you are more attractive than a toxic, resentful, needy person. If you notice you aren't getting the things you want, take notice of how you're acting. What is my story? Only I can change it. Only I can become more enjoyable to visit. Instead of a guilt-ridden comment, how about saying, "Thank you for your visit. I really enjoyed seeing you." Or "You made my day"; "Thank you for bringing me _____"; or "Thank you for helping me with _____."

I can change the story I've been telling myself about what's lacking and turn it into a story of how I'm seeing what I want come into my life. I do not need to share this story with anyone. I can just keep it in my "inside voice," inside of my head.

If it's not right, it's not right—move on.

You can try to make it right, but it may not be. Think of an arrow hitting close to a bull's-eye, but not right on target. There may be something in your life that is so close, yet not it, not quite, and it never will be quite right. If you ever feel like you are settling for less, that might be it. It's less; not quite right; almost—which is disappointing. "Bearable, maybe, but a letdown all the same," says a quote from the book *Changing for Good*. "Emotional distress weakens you psychologically, in much the same way a fever weakens you physically."[15]

All the more reason to stay away from negative people. If you see yourself becoming ill, watch out—it's a sign of burnout and will be addressed in the chapter on careers.

One exception to keeping a distance from someone acting ugly is when that person is truly grieving. When we have a loss, we all go through the five stages of grief. Not everyone goes through the stages at the same time. It is different for each person.

All five stages (listed below) must be complete for healing to happen. I recommend compassion and understanding in these cases.

The Five Stages of Grief

Denial: "This isn't happening"—not acknowledging or accepting. Acting as if the lost job, deceased family member, or former spouse is still there. No tears.

Anger: Wanting to get even, fight back, blaming someone else for leaving or changing.

Bargaining: Making deals with God to stop or change the loss. Begging, wishing, and praying for that loss to come back.

Depression: Bitter, hopeless, mourning the loss. Being frustrated, feeling a lack of control, numb, full of self-pity.

Acceptance: A time of personal growth, comfort, healing. Finding the good that can come out of the pain of loss, including fond memories of the person or place. There's a difference between resignation and acceptance. You have to accept the loss, not just bear it quietly. You can realize it takes two to make or break a marriage. You can realize that the person is gone (in death) and it's not their fault—they didn't leave you on purpose. Even in cases of suicide, often the deceased person was not in their right frame of mind.[16]

When you are struggling with grief, get help. There are great support groups out there. You will heal, survive, even if you can't believe that right away. Just know that it is true. To feel pain after loss is normal. It proves we are alive, human. We can't stop living. We become stronger, while not shutting off our feelings for the hope of one day being healed and finding love and happiness again. Helping others through something you have experienced is a wonderful way to facilitate your healing and bring good out of tragedy. And remember if you or someone you love is having suicidal thoughts, don't hesitate to call a suicide hotline or the police.

Maybe you're grieving the loss of a dream or career that went away or a dating relationship that came to an end. There are many situations to grieve over—recognize them and work through them. Being blocked by grief keeps us stuck, unable to move forward.

Also, there's nothing wrong with a little pain, as Leo Buscaglia notes in *Living, Loving, and Learning*:

> I've learned so many wonderful things over the years in painful situations. In fact, sometimes it takes death to teach us about life; it takes misery to teach us about joy. So embrace it when it comes. Say it's a part of life. Put your arms around it. Experience it! Learn to feel again. Don't deny it.
>
> Maybe it does hurt. Say it's okay to hurt. Scream, yell, gnash the walls. Experience the pain. Cry. Bang on the table. Let it come out. And then *forget* it. Otherwise you're going to store it up forever. And you know what happens when you store up pain? It takes its toll on you. You're the one who gets the ulcers and the migraine headaches.[17]

Often while grieving we experience a spiritual death, and we act ugly, we stop feeling, we stuff our feelings. We lack energy to do even the most basic things. Here is a list of some symptoms of spiritual death:

- Detachment
- Sadness
- Disillusionment
- Boredom
- Emptiness
- Loneliness
- Being indifferent
- Lacking interest
- Coolness
- Lessening of gentleness
- Lessening of small courtesies
- Insecurity
- Jealousy
- Ambition
- Feeling misunderstood
- Feeling used
- Feeling in a rut
- Feeling hopeless
- Despair
- Bitterness
- Anger
- Being impatient
- Being irritated
- Nervousness
- Having self-pity

- Lacking wonder
- Feeling isolated
- Mechanical, routine, surface communication
- Neglecting appearance
- Preoccupation with appearance
- Too quick to agree with others
- Taking advantage of others
- Taking others for granted
- Having frequent quarrels
- Saying insults
- Rudeness
- Teasing
- Sarcasm
- Nagging
- Participating in continuous escapes, such as "do-gooding," TV, sports, compulsive socializing, promiscuity, eating, liquor, etc.

See the homework section where I ask you to put a checkmark next to all the symptoms you identify with, and journal about it. Then ask yourself, "Do I have to go on dying in these ways? Do I realize that changing these symptoms is a personal decision? How do I feel about confronting myself with the decisions to change? How can I find a new life? Do I want to? Will I?"

Another way to look at needs, Maslow's Hierarchy of Needs, starts with the basics and moves up from there.

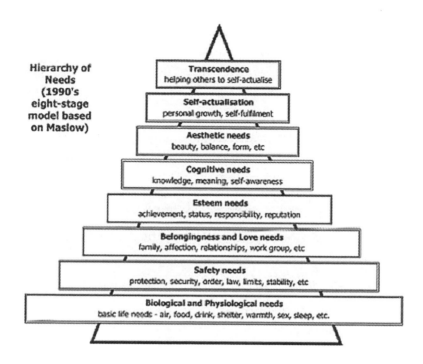

Hierarchy of Needs (1990's eight-stage model based on Maslow)

Transcendence
helping others to self-actualise

Self-actualisation
personal growth, self-fulfilment

Aesthetic needs
beauty, balance, form, etc

Cognitive needs
knowledge, meaning, self-awareness

Esteem needs
achievement, status, responsibility, reputation

Belongingness and Love needs
family, affection, relationships, work group, etc

Safety needs
protection, security, order, law, limits, stability, etc

Biological and Physiological needs
basic life needs - air, food, drink, shelter, warmth, sex, sleep, etc.

The first four levels are considered the deficiency needs. The next four are growth needs. Within the deficiency needs, each lower need must be met before moving to the next higher level. Once each of these needs is satisfied, if at some future time a deficiency is detected, the individual will act to remove the deficiency. According to Maslow, an individual is ready to act upon the growth needs if, and only if, the deficiency needs are met.

What level do I see myself at? Can I identify unmet needs on a certain level? Are those unmet needs holding me back from my dreams? Are they causing me to act ugly?

I love the Bible passage Psalm 107:28–30:

> *Then they cry out to the Lord in their trouble and he brings them out of their distresses. He calms the storm so that its waves are still. Then they are glad because they are quiet so he guides them to their desired haven.*[18]

In other words, *they cry out*: are they acting ugly? Perhaps. He allows them to feel and express their discomfort—to determine "not it"—to determine what they do want. Also:

- *He calms the storms*—supplies their desires.

- *They are glad because they are quiet*—their needs are satisfied and the cries cease.

- He *guides them to their desired haven*—their dream life!

And from Psalm 78:29:

> *So they ate and were filled for he gave them their own desire.*[19]

Finally, from Revelation 21:4:

> *God will wipe away every tear from their eyes; there shall be no more death, nor sorrow, nor crying; and there shall be no more pain, for the former things have passed away.*[20]

A line from Shakespeare's *Antony and Cleopatra* adds to the idea of God supplying our needs, but from a different perspective. It says, "We ignorant of ourselves, beg often our own harms, which the wise powers deny us for our good; so find we profit by losing of our prayers."

Because we cannot see the big picture and have no idea what may come next, we need to trust God and the universe for not supplying our every want, and know he has something better in mind.

OVERCOMING FRUSTRATION AND MOVING BEYOND UGLINESS

Frustration seems to be a sign of the times these days. It's all around us and can infect us with its negativity. Why do we get so frustrated and act ugly? Frustration can be a signal that we're not focusing on what we want, according to the book *You 2: A High Velocity Formula for Multiplying Your Personal Effectiveness in Quantum Leaps* by Price Pritchett. It can also be a simple and reliable sign that what we're doing *isn't* working.

Our tendency then is to bear down and work even harder to try to make it happen—doing the same thing, even harder, and getting little, if any, results.[23]

What's the answer? Look at what you want to change. Do something—ANYTHING—different, and notice whether it works to move you toward what you desire. If it produces a result you want, do it again (and look at ways to "tweak it" to have it work even better).

If it doesn't produce the result you want, then DROP it like a hot potato (after giving enough of your attention and time for a fair trial). What difference would it make to your momentum to change the way you look at frustration? To think of it as a simple signal that what you're doing isn't working and that it's time to do something else?

> "Things still won't always work out as you'd hoped or planned, but that just becomes a fact of life instead of a problem to be solved."
>
> **—MICHAEL NEILL,**
> **AUTHOR OF** *SUPERCOACH*[24]

Remember the old saying about picking yourself up, dusting yourself off, and starting all over again? When life gives you lemons, make lemonade.

Sometimes when we make changes in our lives, we run into people we used to know who maybe haven't been around to see us evolve into who we are today. When we get an award, change careers, run a marathon, open a business, or become successful in some way, shape, or form, there are those dear people in our lives who say, "I did not know that about you," or "I never knew you could or would do that," or even, "You have tried a lot of things."

I remember thinking at those times, "Well, how would you know? You had preconceived notions about who I am, what I've done, and what path you think I'm going down. I have not only tried a lot of things, but I have done a lot of things and those were building blocks. Cut me some slack and give me some credit here. You didn't ever really get to know me; you only assumed things about me based on something you heard or maybe because I am _____ (fill in the blank; example: divorced). Get to know the real me. Be happy the false beliefs have fallen away—they are 'not it.' But I am."

In moving beyond ugliness, realize that not everyone may be receptive to the changes you're making, especially if you decide not to tolerate someone's ugly behavior anymore. As Joel Osteen writes in *Become a Better You*:

> To reduce your stress, be aware of high-maintenance people in your life who are usually controllers... They're not interested in you; they're interested in what you can do for them. They're interested in how you can make their life better. If you fall into the trap of trying to keep them happy, you're going to be frustrated in your own life.[25]

You can recognize issues in others, but you cannot change them, so don't even waste your energy. Accept and adjust your own behavior accordingly by using boundaries. (See homework item number 3 below).

HOMEWORK

1. Are you grieving? Ask yourself, "What stages have I experienced? In what stage do I most frequently find myself? How do I feel about where I am?" Journal. Get it out. Become aware of where you are, and start working on yourself from this point forward to the dream you want so bad.

2. Look at the list on symptoms of a spiritual death. Put a checkmark next to any symptom that applies in any way. Journal about the symptoms you have an emotional charge on, that you have the strongest feelings about. Write in detail expressing your feelings about those symptoms. Get it out of your body and off your mind so you can feel better, deal with it, and move on with your life.

3. Ask yourself, "What have I been putting up with for far too long? Am I feeling overwhelmed? Overcommitted? Overburdened?" What has to change? Brainstorm the options. What part can you change? What can you do right now? Even if it's not solved, I know I'll feel better just doing something to start a ball rolling.

Self-Care: Putting Your Needs First

Remember what you hear when you're about to take off on a plane? The flight attendants instruct you to put your own oxygen mask on before assisting others. The same is true in life. If we don't take care of ourselves, we are not our best selves when caring for or caring about others.

Think back to the graphic in the Introduction (on page 17), which started with an inner circle of dreams, feelings, and thoughts; then expanded to nutrition, fitness, and personal image. Out from there came your environment and relationships, then your finances and career. There are those souls in life who take care of everyone around them first and leave themselves last (if there's any time or energy left, that is). In fact, I have coached people who hardly get themselves to the bathroom in time due to their caring for others!

So I always like to start with an inner circle of care—self-care. Are you taking care of yourself? (Okay, roll your eyes if you must, but there really are people who do not believe they have the time or energy to do this.) Are you brushing your teeth? Exercising? Taking a shower? Getting to your medical appointments? Are you wearing clean clothing? Is your laundry done? How about your

> "Finding a quiet center in which to create and sustain an authentic life has become as essential as breathing... "
> **—SARAH BAN BREATHNACH,**
> *SIMPLE ABUNDANCE: A DAYBOOK OF COMFORT AND JOY* [26]

dishes? Do you have healthy food available? Look for more detail on these topics in the "Your Personal Image" and "Your Home" chapters.

Oftentimes it is not what we *do* that makes us tired; it is the constantly thinking about what we still have *to do* that makes us tired. Thinking about it all the time eats our energy.

Accomplishing things gives us a good feeling and increased energy. We can be physically tired, but feel good about what we have done. When we keep thinking about what we still have left to do, that's when we become mentally exhausted. Keep the focus on what's next, and if you think of another thing, just add it to your list. We are most effective when we do one thing at a time and do it well, rather than multitasking and doing a lot quickly and incompletely.

DEALING WITH LABELS OTHERS ATTACH TO US AND FEELINGS OF URGENCY

My friends call me a tornado and a full-speed-ahead girl. There are positive and negative elements to both terms that describe me and I embrace them all. Tornados can be efficient and also spin out of control. Don't lose sight of the good in being a tornado if you are one. What I have been learning over the years is to slow down—not just because my friends suggest it. I have learned many lessons to be careful and yet embrace the good in being fast-paced and decisive, thinking on my feet, jumping into action, and adjusting where needed. I now know I need to slow down when I take on more than is desirable for me. I am learning to do this, making my life so much more enjoyable.

I almost gave away a sewing machine and serger because, when I did pull them out, it was like I had to relearn the machines. I wanted to mend a couple dresses for a little girl and I was on a deadline; self-imposed, of course. As my frustration level increased, I asked myself why I was in such a hurry. There was nothing pressing on my schedule. Hurrying through my sewing was an old behavior that no longer served me. As soon as I recognized this, I slowed down and did a neat job. I finished my work, admired it, and realized I enjoyed it. I allowed myself to take the time to have fun! Lesson learned.

Having a feeling of urgency is one of the most reliable indicators that what you actually need to do is slow down and take a break. Rather than try to "change your state" when you're feeling low, do your best to center yourself in the present moment, recognizing that no matter how urgent or pressing a course of action may seem,

How to Unwind When Thoughts Go Too Fast

- Press pause and give yourself time to relax ALONE.
- Stretch to relax your body from tension.
- Close your eyes to combat fatigue.
- Breathe deeply. Inhale and blow it out completely three times.
- Lie down if you can and let your muscles release the tension. RELAX.
- Become aware of your body, of your breathing.
- Think of something else instead.
- Repeat.

chances are it's not. As Michael Neill, author of *Supercoach*, states in his book, "Once we give our attention to any given thought, it becomes more and more real to us over time and has more power over our lives."[27]

According to Debbie Ford in *The Dark Side of the Light Chasers*[28]

All your so-called faults, all the things which you don't like about yourself are your greatest assets. They are simply over-amplified.

The volume has been turned up a bit too much, that's all. Just turn down the volume a little. Soon, you—and everyone else—will see your weaknesses as your strengths, your "negatives" as "positives." They will become wonderful tools, ready to work for you rather than against you. All you have to do is learn to call on these personality traits in amounts that are appropriate to the moment.

Recycling through the 4 R's before Responding:

Recognizing, Reflecting, Reframing, Responding

RECOGNIZING
- What am I now thinking?
- What am I now feeling emotionally? Am I feeling highly stimulated by my reframing or decision?
- What is my physiological state as I consider carrying out this decision?

REFLECTING
- What mental biases might be affecting my decision?
- What information about the situation have I not considered?
- Who might be affected by this decision and how?
- What possible consequences of this decision have I not considered?

REFRAMING
- Based on my reflecting, how realistic is my new frame?
- Is my reframing excessively optimistic or pessimistic?
- The ideal reframing is realistically optimistic.

RESPONDING
- Is my plan for responding based on careful reflection?
- Is my plan for responding based on a realistically positive reframing?
- Am I willing to defer a response until I am satisfied my choice is smart, responsible, and aligned with my values?

—FROM THE LENNICK ABERMAN GROUP, INC.

PRESS PAUSE

Press pause by creating a quiet, comfy, relaxed space; pour yourself a favorite beverage and make a to-do list—do a brain dump and write everything down. Read what's written—what feelings come up? Ask what's missing in taking care of yourself and your environment. What are you doing that someone else could do? Can you delegate some of these tasks? Are you overstepping your bounds and being overly helpful to an adult child or an alcoholic or addict, which slides right into codependency and enabling? (Watch for my next book called *It's Time*, focused on recovery from codependency, divorce, and an unfulfilling life. Also keep reading, as codependency and people pleasing are discussed further in this chapter.) I wonder what's on your list that you can take care of and feel better about having done.

> "There is no reason to have a plan B because it distracts you from plan A." **—WILL SMITH**

Think of this concept: "I do this so I can do that." For me, it was yoga. I was very active with my yoga practice until I purchased a condo, renovated it, and sold it over the course of a year. Eventually, after my move, I realized I was resisting starting up again for various reasons, mainly because living in a new area made it necessary for me to step outside my comfort zone. I was also resisting getting into a structured routine. The first step was awareness.

Sometimes we don't know what to do, but our bodies do. Feel like a run? Run. Yoga? Get your mat out. Know you want to paint that room? Paint. Trust the color selection and go with what feels right for you. I trusted my gut even when my builder suggested a more neutral paint color palette for resale purposes, and when my condo sold at the first open house, the buyer thought the colors were perfect for her. Plus, I was able to enjoy them while I lived there.

Is there something you just can't get off the to-do list? Insert it into this example sentence on the first blank, and put something you enjoy in the second blank: I do this _____ so I can do _____.

You may need to change up a bit to make sense:

I practice yoga so I can be flexible, toned, and relaxed.

You know when something is right or "not it, not it, not it!" Your feelings will tell you. You may not have a solution right away, so begin by identifying what it is you *do not* want, right along with "If I did not have to do this, what would I want to do instead?" There's nothing like sitting by your fireplace, listening to music, sipping hot cocoa, and watching someone else move the snow. Maybe you would rather ski, snowmobile, or ice-skate. Or go sledding, throw a snowball, and build a snowman, anything but pick up the shovel. For those who love to get the exercise of moving snow off the car, sidewalks, and driveway—those who find it invigorating—then by all means do it. If it's no longer fun, stop and find someone else to do it. Maybe it means bartering with someone. It could be that someone in your household would do the task, perhaps a teen who would love more time driving your car or getting dinner and movie tickets for doing the job so you don't have to.

I realized I didn't want to mow the grass anymore or take care of a yard; I didn't even want the big house. I wanted a condo where I could pull into the heated underground garage and take an elevator to my home.

"Eliminate what drains you and don't worry about what's going to replace it."

—BOB PROCTOR[29]

STAYING IN THE PRESENT

Another concept is staying in the present moment. Many people going through a situation are not present; their thinking is back in the past or way out into the future of what-ifs. If you struggle with this, I recommend reading *The Precious Present* by Spencer Johnson.

When I was going through divorce, my mind would move back and forth; rarely was I present. This is called vacillating. I had a close friend get upset with me because I would repeat stories. My mind was back in a story, not in our conversation. She would request that I get present or she would not continue our visit. She was telling me my behavior was "not it." I appreciated her feedback since I was *soooo* into my stuff I didn't realize how I was showing up. I was in a constant state of vacillation between should I/shouldn't I get divorced. My pastor finally warned me: "You are giving him mixed messages; this is not fair. Decide and move on, one way or the other." He was saying my behavior was "not it!"

> "Every emotion you experience is a direct response to a thought, not to the world around you. The more clearly you see that your emotions are always reactions to your thoughts, not to the world, the easier it gets to simply feel them and let them go. And the gift of that insight is that you stop needing to change the world in order to change the way you feel."
>
> —**MICHAEL NEILL**, *SUPERCOACH*[30]

One tool I learned to get present was to focus on what I am doing right now.

- I am washing dishes, washing the blue bowl with warm silky water and lots of bubbles. I blow at the bubbles and watch them scatter.
- I am folding towels, fresh and warm from the dryer.
- I am stacking wood. I see a chipmunk. I am stacking straight and even; it looks organized and prepared for winter unlike the pile thrown into a heap from the splitter.

Whenever my mind wanders, I focus on what I am doing physically to get mentally present again.

Periodically, I check in with myself by asking, "What is it I need right now?" Am I doing what I want to do? If not, what would I like to do instead? If I am not able to do it at this moment, can I do it later in the day? If not, I add it to my dream list, my vision board, and wait for it to manifest.

**What you put your attention to grows,
even if you have no idea how;
you do not have to know how,
just know that it will.**

- I am dreaming of an office with a window and add it to my vision board while I sit in my cubicle.

- I am looking out my office window at a gorgeous day and want to be on the beach, so I plan it right after work.

- I dream of combining travel and work. It may not be something I can do today, but if I stay aware of the desire, opportunities will present themselves—maybe first to gain the skills I need to travel for work before the travel happens.

PROCRASTINATION AND FEAR

Procrastination postpones decisions, and every time I think about it and put it off, I expend energy, which causes fatigue and allows negative energy to seep in. Think "to-do" list...

FEAR may also be a block in obtaining our dreams. I have seen various ways of looking at fear:

- False Evidence Appearing Real

- Forgetting Everything's All Right

- Face Everything And Recover

- What we fear appears... the law of attraction

- The terror barrier hits when we are right on the edge of success; when fear consumes us, we tend to go back to safety.

- Feeling Energetic And Recharged (turning fear into a positive, instead of a negative)

"'Procrastinate on purpose' is another way to look at it: what if your procrastination simply showed you the way to living your dream and reaching your true goals? Figure out why you are procrastinating."

—TALANE MIEDANER, *COACH YOURSELF TO SUCCESS* [31]

Action cures fear, according to *The Magic of Thinking Big.*[32]

Indecision and postponement, on the other hand, fertilize fear. When we face tough problems, we stay mired in the mud until we take action. Hope is a start. But hope needs action to win victories. Do what's right and keep your confidence. That's thinking yourself to success.

Also, I like what Marianne Williamson has to say about fear in her book, *A Return to Love*:

Our deepest fear is not that we are inadequate. Our deepest fear is that we are powerful beyond measure. It is our light, not our darkness, that most frightens us. We ask ourselves, 'Who am I to be brilliant, gorgeous, talented, fabulous?' Actually, who are you *not* to be? You are a child of God. Your playing small doesn't serve the world. There's nothing enlightened about shrinking so that other people won't feel insecure around you. We are all meant to shine, as children do. We were born to make manifest the glory of God that is within us. It's not just in some of us; it's in everyone. And as we let our own light shine, we unconsciously give other people permission to do the same. As we're liberated from our own fear, our presence automatically liberates others.[33]

For years I carried around a postcard with a quote from well-known Christian author C.S. Lewis; when it got ratty, I rewrote it. It said:

Remember, tho' we struggle against things because we are afraid of them it is often the other way round—we get afraid because we struggle. Are you struggling? Resisting? Peace, child, peace. Relax. Let go. Underneath are the everlasting arms. Let go, do you trust me so little?

Other notes I have used for inspiration in times of fear include the following:

- Trust in God with all your heart, with all your soul.

- PUSH—Pray Until Something Happens.

- God, guide me to make the right decision and give me the fortitude to cling to it against all pressures and persuasions.

"Go through the proper motions each day and you'll soon begin to feel the corresponding emotions," shares David J. Schwartz, in *The Magic of Thinking Big*. "We can change our attitudes by changing our physical actions. Managed motions can change emotions. Confident action produces confident thinking. So, to think confidently, act confidently. Act the way you want to feel."[34]

AVOIDING BECOMING TOO MUCH OF A PEOPLE PLEASER

There have been many times in my life when it has not been okay to be me, so I have bent over backwards to people please. That behavior is "not it"—not it anymore! When I feel myself going into people-pleasing mode (saying yes when I want to say no), I say to myself: "STOP." I say "not it"; I am okay just as I am and I reevaluate my behavior. I look at the motives behind my behavior—what is driving me to people please? Is it guilt someone is trying to jam down my throat? What is this guilt costing me?

Just because someone tosses the guilt ball to me does not mean I "have to" catch it. Just say no. No more jumping and running. I am setting boundaries—I decide!

In *Become a Better You* by Joel Osteen, he addresses this topic:

> Examine how you spend your time and check your motives as to why you do what you do. Is it out of guilt? Is it because somebody is manipulating or controlling you? If so, make some changes. If you don't take control of your life, others will, and they may take you places you don't want to go.
>
> If people have controlled you for a long time, they're not going to like your putting your foot down. Always do what you must in love, be kind and respectful, but stand firm and make a decision that you will live in freedom... After God, you are your first priority.[35]

In the book *Something More: Excavating Your Authentic Self*, Sarah Ban Breathnach writes of survival by surrender, sharing a story about author Rebecca Harding as an example.[36]

Rebecca received an offer to write her novel as a monthly serial in a new magazine hoping to cash in on her name and following. In order to please her husband, a young attorney, and to supply the income required to support the lifestyle he wanted, Rebecca agreed. Even though she was smart enough to know the magazine was taking advantage of her, the offer was too great to pass up. The result: an unrecognizable version of her book, virtually rewritten by her editors as a romance novel. "Mutilated" is what she called it.

Though in her soul she had set out to write something profound, she was unable to swim against the tide of her circumstances. "A great hope fell, you heard no noise, the ruin was within" was all Rebecca would say about her failure. Rebecca buried her authentic self with denial and surrendered to her husband's choice for her life, a choice that meant the death of her dream, but one that made his dreams come true. She no longer believed in or acted upon the possibility of high achievement for herself. It was the price for children, home, love. There was no one to whom she could speak of the pain and loss she felt while her husband became prominent.

Even though self-loathing had set in, she did convey to her readers that they were not alone in their struggle to survive. Rebecca had hoped to change the world. It is heartbreaking that she did not realize that she had done so, not as the social reformer she'd expected to be, but as a source of comfort and compassion for thousands of nameless women who found their own voices by reading her words.

If I want to be free, I've got to be me—
be 100 percent true to who you are.

- To let go does not mean to stop caring; it means I can't do it for someone else.

- To let go is not to cut myself off; it's the realization I can't control another.

- To let go is not to enable, but to allow learning from natural consequences.

- To let go is to admit powerlessness, which means the outcome is not in my hands.

- To let go is not to try to change or blame another; it's to make the most of myself.

- To let go is not to care for, but to care about.

- To let go is not to fix, but to be supportive.

- To let go is not to judge, but to allow another to be a human being.

- To let go is not to be in the middle arranging all the outcome, but to allow others to affect their own destinies.

- To let go is not to be protective; it's to permit another to face reality.

- To let go is not to deny, but to accept.

- To let go is not to nag, scold, or argue, but instead to search out my own shortcomings and to correct them.

- To let go is not to adjust to everything to my desires, but to take each day as it comes and to cherish myself in it.

- To let go is not to criticize and regulate anybody, but to try to become what I dream I can be.

- To let go is not to regret the past, but to grow and to live for the future.

- To let go is to fear less and to love more.

—Unknown

We get programmed to be a good girl or a good boy or do a good job, to work hard and to people please. We get stuck in ruts and don't even realize it. Our families may see it, but we don't. Our friends may see it, and yet we don't. Someone may even say something to us and we are in denial, so it doesn't wake us up. If we do wake up to find we are on a wrong path, we can look back later and see how programmed we were. Think about the Johari window, a model that describes different kinds of knowledge related to individual growth and the development of relationship with others.

Johari Window

1. Arena: information known to both us and others.

2. Blind Spot: information that others know about us but we don't know about ourselves.

3. Façade: information we know about ourselves but choose not to reveal to most others.

4. Unknown: information that neither we nor others know about us.

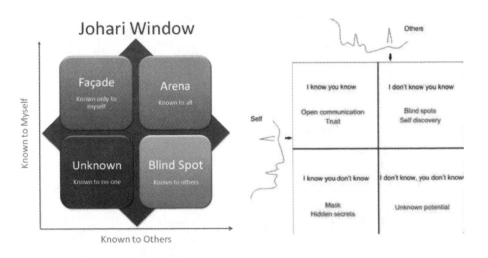

The Johari Window

In 1955, Joseph Luft and Harrington Ingham created a self-help exercise called the Johari window to help people better understand their relationships with themselves and other people.

To do the exercise, a person is given a list of fifty-six adjectives, and chooses a few that best describe his or her personality. Then the person's peers pick a few words from the same list to describe him or her. The adjectives are then placed onto a grid with four sections.

Irish author and philosopher Charles Handy explains this concept as a house with four rooms. Room 1 is the part of ourselves that everyone sees. Room 2 is the aspects others see that we don't. Room 3 is the unconscious or subconscious part of us, seen by neither others nor ourselves. Room 4 is our private space that only we know; others don't.[37]

In alphabetical order, here are the fifty-six Johari adjectives:

- Able
- Accepting
- Adaptable
- Bold
- Brave
- Calm
- Caring
- Cheerful
- Clever
- Complex
- Confident
- Dependable
- Dignified
- Energetic
- Extroverted
- Friendly
- Giving
- Happy
- Helpful
- Idealistic
- Independent
- Ingenious
- Intelligent
- Introverted

- Kind
- Knowledgeable
- Logical
- Loving
- Mature
- Modest
- Nervous
- Observant
- Organized
- Patient
- Powerful

- Proud
- Quiet
- Reflective
- Relaxed
- Religious
- Responsive
- Searching
- Self-assertive
- Self-conscious
- Sensible
- Sentimental

- Shy
- Silly
- Smart
- Spontaneous
- Sympathetic
- Tense
- Trustworthy
- Warm
- Wise
- Witty

AVOIDING NEGATIVITY AND WORRY

Negativity carries forward so don't complain. Not only is it unattractive, but it perpetuates more negativity. Let's say I go to a restaurant and get horrible service, a bad meal, or the wrong food—maybe all three at one visit. If I must complain, I just complain to the manager of the restaurant. Then I let it go and remember the great visit I had with my parents as they shared stories of their recent trip, while being grateful they are able to continue travel.

Don't let people dump their crap in your lap—even if they say it's because they're worried about you. What they're really doing is handing you their fear and negativity in a package with a bow called love. "I worry about you because I love you," they might say. This is one package with return to sender written all over it; see it for what it is—a sign of an unhealthy relationship. Set a boundary. When someone is in "worry mode," they are in fear; they are sitting in their own toxic stew. This is not healthy. Don't take a jar of this stew home in a supposed care package. Yuck! Toxic stew will fill you up with its negativity and sidetrack you from the life you want—it pulls you down. You don't need it. It is not your problem; it is theirs. See it. Open your eyes to it.

What if you recognize that *you* are worrying? Stop. It is fear disguised as worry. God doesn't want you to worry about anything. Believe there is something better on the way. Life changes; you can worry, or look at the opportunities coming with the change and how you can be in a better circumstance. When we worry about someone else, it is not love. It is fear. Share encouragement instead of worry with someone you love instead. Oftentimes, worry is just a story we are telling ourselves. I hear that a loved one is traveling and the roads are potentially bad. I can tell myself a story about this and my story can get worse, including all possible bad outcomes. I am getting myself all stirred up for nothing because I am believing my story. When that happens, recognize it, stop it, pray for their safety, and let it go, believing he or she will be just fine.

> "Worry is often the non-acceptance of situations you can do nothing about."
>
> —DR. HENRY CLOUD IN HIS BOOK *9 THINGS YOU SIMPLY MUST DO TO SUCCEED IN LOVE AND LIFE*[38]

Here's a tool to use when you identify negativity within yourself, such as worry and fear:

Visualize yourself holding a ball of light. Put all the negativity you have into this ball. Push the ball out into space. Turn around 180 degrees and visualize the ball exploding. It's all gone! Yeah! Feel better!

Your positive balls of energy will become larger than your negative balls of energy as you work on removing and staying away from negativity.

When healing from physical and emotional pain, I focus on what I can do, not what I can't. When I injured my back, the doctors gave me restrictions; I initially focused on what I could not do. I felt sorry for myself and became a victim, for a while. Once I began focusing on what I *could* do, I got stronger and better. Don't get me wrong, I still have chronic pain; I have just learned to live with it.

Emotionally, when doors close in our lives, stop looking at the closed doors; look for the open doors.

"Use negative energy like jet fuel to launch into the next right thing for you," Price Pritchett writes in his book, *You 2: A High Velocity Formula for Multiplying Your Personal Effectiveness in Quantum Leaps.*[39]

When I realize I'm in a place I don't want to be, I press pause on the crazies and see what I can do immediately to feel better. Maybe I do something to symbolize the pause, like taking a physical break from my work, sitting with a blank tablet and a cup of tea, and beginning a brain dump. I start hot penning—setting a timer for twenty or thirty minutes and simply writing. I do not let the pen lift from the page; I write anything, even junk. It does not have to make sense. As I do this, some very deep meaningful things can pop up that give amazing insight. (I learned the hot penning technique at a Beginning Experience weekend to work through the loss of a marriage.)

Just drawing a line in the sand will help me feel better. Even if I still have things coming at me that I don't like, I use what I don't like to identify what my preferences are as I move forward. I think about what I want, and when what I *don't want* creeps in, I shift it to identify more of what I *do want* to bring me clarity on my next move.

For example, I was working in an investment department in a bank. My desk was just off the lobby and I had hated being a receptionist at another time in my work life. So every time someone stopped by my desk to ask a question that did not pertain to my department and interrupt my work, I was irritated. I used this situation to clarify my preference of working in the backdrop, setting up systems. My next position was in another investment firm, setting up and documenting the systems for a new division. Once the project was complete, I was ready to move onto officially adding consulting to my coaching business Systems For Change.

RESISTANCE TO CHANGE AND DENIAL

When we notice something is bothering us, we are feeling the emotional charge; what's bothering us is "not it." This means a change is needed.

Having a tough week? There's a lot of growth when you are in resistance. Resistance allows you to define when you are about to have a breakthrough.

I may identify a boundary I want to set: someone has crossed the line one too many times and I've had it. Well, first of all, I allowed it. I press pause before I yell at that person or, worse yet, take it out on an innocent bystander—like the cat or my tantrum-throwing two-year-old. I press pause and go to a quiet spot. Yes, I take a time out by taking in three deep breaths and decide what I believe I want to change, and if appropriate, I communicate that right away. By setting the boundary to clear up the situation as quickly as possible, I keep the monkey off my back.

While attending PSI Seminars I learned that when we are in/out/back/forth, we are not in alignment and we make up stories as to why. Confront what is driving you. Is it effective or not? You are creating what you have. Resistance will come up; you decide how long you stay in it. What do you need to call up to bring forth what it is you want?

When we compare, we are not content.

With surrender and acceptance comes release from pain—the pain is in the resistance.

> **Most of my pain comes not from the truth but from resisting the truth.**

Here's an interesting acronym for denial (which Debbie Ford shares in her book *The Dark Side of the Light Chasers*): "Don't Even Notice I'm Lying."[40]

DEALING WITH RESENTMENT, ANGER, AND SUFFERING

Resentments are about not getting your way. We get angry when we don't get our way—resentful for what we didn't get yesterday, and fearful for what we won't get in the future, as I learned in PSI Seminars.

In Al-Anon I learned, if a resolution is highly charged with anger, resentment, or bitterness, it would be wise to hold back until the hysteria has subsided and I have taken time to consider all the factors calmly. I will remember that a decision I make in a time of crisis might not be the one I would make when the crisis is past. I will not rashly take a step that I may afterward regret.

As Melody Beattie writes in *Make Miracles in Forty Days*, grudges can prevent us from moving forward:

> Bitterness is the biggest barrier that exists to joy and getting what we want from life. While grudges can hurt the person or people we resent, our grudges hurt us the most. Sometimes we're unable or unwilling to release resentments. But when the grudge finally lifts, we may feel like we've been released from prison. Consciously releasing resentments caused us to move forward in areas we previously were stuck.[41]

Arriving early to attend an Easter service at Redeemer Lutheran Church in
Rochester, Minnesota, I thumbed through
books in the library and jotted down this
paragraph without saving the name of the
book: "When we hang on to resentment,
we create an interior concentration camp.
We sit behind bars of anger and bitterness.
Because we say they don't deserve forgiveness. Though they may not deserve forgive-

> "Ah ha! A man is half
> whipped the minute he
> begins to feel sorry for
> himself, or spin an alibi
> with which he would ex-
> plain away his defects."
> —**NAPOLEON HILL,**
> *THE LAW OF SUCCESS*[45]

ness, we do not deserve the consequences that come with a lack of
forgiveness. It's bad enough to hurt the first time and inexcusable to
find yourself imprisoned in the concentration camp for something
you did not deserve. Forgiveness doesn't grant approval, forgiveness
sets you free!"

"Only by believing an untrue thought is it possible to move from
peace into emotions like sadness and anger," writes Byron Katie in
A Thousand Names for Joy. She says:

> As you inquire into your own thoughts, you discover how attach-
> ment to a belief or story causes suffering. The mind's natural
> condition is peace. Then a thought enters, you believe it, and
> the peace seems to disappear. You notice the feeling of stress in
> the moment, and the feeling lets you know that you're opposing
> what is by believing the thought; it tells you that you're at war with
> reality. When you question the thought behind the feeling and
> realize that it isn't true, you become present outside your story.
>
> When you're shut down and frightened, the world seems
> hostile; when you love what is, everything in the world becomes
> beloved... It's just you, crazed and miserable, or you, delighted
> and at peace. Everything happens for you, not to you... Suffering
> can only teach suffering.[42]

Katie also sees criticism as an immense gift for those who are interested in self-realization:

> For those who aren't, welcome to hell, welcome to being at war with your partner, your neighbors, your children, your boss. When you open your arms to criticism, you are your own direct path to freedom, because you can't change us or what we think about you. After you have done inquiry for a while, you can listen to any criticism without defense or justification, openly, delightedly. It's the end to trying to control what can't ever be controlled: other people's perception.[43]

Judith Orloff shares in her book *Positive Energy*:

> I know well how tempting it is to shut down around unbearable people or events. The danger is that defending yourself becomes habitual. Armor turns into a straitjacket, restricting spontaneity and love. You don't want to risk this. Here's an option: instead of armoring, try centering yourself so negativity can't weaken you. Cultivate a solid internal core; nothing external can usurp your power.[44]

Try the meditation shown in the homework at the end of the chapter when you want to center yourself.

LOOKING PAST REGRETS AND APPRECIATING LIFE AS IS

In his book *Missing Out: In Praise of the Unlived Life*, Adam Phillips says much of our "so-called mental life" is spent fantasizing about what we don't have but wish we did. We are haunted by thoughts of what might have been, whether romantically or in our career choices. In our unlived lives we are always more satisfied, far less frustrated versions of ourselves. Phillips argues against indulging in such wistful thinking, not dwelling on supposed missed opportunities, which might have ultimately disappointed us anyway.[47] The myth of our potential can make our lives a perpetual falling short, a continual and continuing loss.

This is what happens when we are looking at the closed door instead of appreciating what we have. We cannot change the past; we can accept what is, and dream of what is to come. Looking at those regrets

The Helper, the Holy Spirit whom The Father will send in my name [Jesus], He will teach you all things and bring to your remembrance all things that I said to you. Peace I leave with you. My peace I give to you.[46]

—JOHN 14:26

can, however, give us clues to what we want our life to become. Maybe the job you loved went away; that doesn't mean there isn't one similar to it and better suited for you around the corner. Features you loved in a former home, a particular shade of blue in the bedroom, a large kitchen island, a convection oven, or that crystal chandelier—these are things you can have again in a future home if you so choose.

Author Napoleon Hill, in his book *Think and Grow Rich,* writes about those who move beyond disappointment and past regrets and then succeed in this way:

> All who succeed in life get off to a bad start, and pass through many heartbreaking struggles before they "arrive." The turning point in the lives of those who succeed usually comes at the moment of some crisis, through which they are introduced to their "other selves."
>
> There is a difference between wishing for a thing and being ready to receive it. No one is ready for a thing, until he believes he can acquire it. Open-mindedness is essential for belief. Closed minds do not inspire faith, courage, and belief.[48]

Dr. Henry Cloud, in his book *9 Things You Simply Must Do to Succeed in Love and Life*, writes:

> A wish is something you desire and want to come true. You can want it with all of your being. The desire for it can be very, very strong. But it is totally subjective and comes totally from you. It is one sided and has no basis in reality. Hope, on the other hand, is not as subjective. It has objective reasons to believe that good things are going to happen.[49]

Ralph Waldo Emerson said, "The whole course of things goes to teach us faith. We need only obey. There is guidance for each of us, and by lowly listening; we shall hear the right word."[50]

Are you listening? God is whispering —can you hear him?

When we fall into the "if only" trap—if only I had more money, if only I was at my perfect weight—the delusion does not last long.[51] When the fantasy is gone and reality is our worst nightmare, we find out that we are who we are.

Limitations—weaknesses put us behind. Focus on the future.

When making new choices, we want to second-guess ourselves. We may tell people our decisions, and feel their opposition. Then we really start to second-guess our decisions even though we know they are perfect for us. We do not need to base our decisions on getting others' approval.

Don't stay stuck in your story—you only perpetuate your pain. If others offer you discounting compliments, say "not it." Wake up! Feel alive—stop sleepwalking through life; stop the autopilot. Be aware of what you're doing and why you're doing it.

The Al-Anon book *Paths to Recovery* offers this advice:

> Act with firmness and kindness without anger, haste, recklessness, or control. The building blocks for respect and trust are courtesy, consideration, and following through on commitments. Work on not taking comments and actions or lack of actions personally. It is a reflection on that person and their sickness and self-esteem. This lesson helps me not to hold a grudge and not to punish the child. We are not the authority on the right way of doing things and need to be loving and supportive of others even when our feelings and methods differ.[52]

You can't love others unless you love yourself—taking care of you is loving you.

Here are some other final thoughts to consider as you get ready to pursue your dream:

- God wants us to have, to be in ECSTACY (heaven), not AGONY (hell), as I was reminded in a sermon by Pastor Jim Heining of Redeemer Lutheran Church, in Rochester, Minnesota. God wants us to have the desires of our hearts instead of being in a painful situation.

- If Satan can't make us bad, he makes us busy. Satan throws a stumbling block to trip us—we can't stand in our strength when the block is in our way. But God says, "Step up on that stumbling block! It's all going somewhere!"

- When you SLIP, Serenity Lost Its Priority, as I learned in Al-Anon.

- Be okay with what is—change your thoughts about it and change your life.

Now that we have identified and addressed unmet needs, unhealthy behaviors, and unhealthy situations, and moved past them, we can get back into dream building and focus on the lives we are dreaming of. The chapters that follow feature examples of what has worked for me and for others. These examples may not be it for you, and you can say "not it" to them. Yet the examples may lead you to look at an area of life you want to change and consider: If not this, then what? And you may discover "Oh, that's it!" That's what I want you to find: what's it for you. Have fun!

Ten Words to Avoid and Thoughts to Rethink

by Lori Bestler, life coach and motivational speaker

Thoughts and words are powerful because they shape our perceptions, affect our behavior, determine our actions, and direct our destinies. Whether the thoughts and words are true or not, they are always true in our subconscious mind when we believe them. Their impact can motivate and encourage, or break our spirits and steal our self-confidence and success.

Regardless of what we believe, many beliefs are lies; lies we've accepted as truth, and when left unchallenged, can rule our perceptions and control our lives. Lies can become the toxic thoughts we think and words we speak, and soon perpetuate a domino effect that can be as destructive as cancer.

Toxic thoughts and words influence the condition of our health, happiness, and state of success more than most people realize. Our acceptance of the thoughts we think, ideas and opinions in our mind, shape our present and future. This is true not only for ourselves, but for those we influence as well.

This fact can prompt us to become more aware of our beliefs, our thinking, and our verbal messages; and when needed, to change our limiting and toxic thoughts and words so that we can begin to get the results we really desire. Here are the top ten words and thoughts to avoid to keep yourself from stinkin' thinkin':

1. Can't

Do you ever say, "I can't stay organized"? This is the biggest success stopper there is. It instantly shuts the door to future possibilities and imprisons your potential from being unleashed into your life. Immediately erase this word from your memory the moment it surfaces into your conscious mind. Eliminate your use of this word, and replace it with what you CAN do, and you will see a significant positive change in your life.

"I can get through all of these paper piles."

"I can take one hour to just see what I can get done."

"I can hire a professional organizer and learn some tips to make organizing easier and keep me focused."

2. But

When used as a conjunction, but negates whatever statement precedes it: "I want to organize my desk, but it will take a lot of hard work." In this contradictory statement, your mind is unclear of what you want and does not focus on your desire to have an organized desk where you can work more efficiently; it only sees the hard work. Get your but out of the way and replace it with and.

"I want to organize my desk and it will take some hard work. It will be worth it!"

3. Should/Shouldn't

Any statement that uses the words should or shouldn't generally promotes guilt, shame, or a feeling of being trapped and forced. Saying, "I should file all those receipts into my folder," makes you feel guilty for not doing that. The worse you feel, the more likely you'll procrastinate on it. Replace these words with choose.

"I choose to go to file my receipts, or I choose to file my receipts when I can allocate one hour in the morning, when I'm more alert."

Saying "I should" is like saying "I have to." Instead say, "I get to." The truth is that anything we should do is a good thing, or why else would we do it? Yet the words should or shouldn't are expressions disciplinarians use, so they feel bad subliminally. Envision the good in the choice, and then you really want to and can say:

"I get to file those receipts today and it will feel so awesome knowing where to find what I need easily."

You will elicit much more energy into your decision to take action as well.

4. Maybe

This word indicates indecision, doubt, or uncertainty as to a course of action. For example, "Maybe I'll clean my closet..." Again, the mind is not sure what you want. It does not respond.

For those of us interested in personal growth, maybe can be used very sparingly. Use I will do it or I will not instead. Make up your mind and confidently move forward, adapting to the changes and altering the action plan as needed in the process. The mere sound of positive words sends the message to our minds that we are confident, and positively influences our actions and well-being.

5. Soon, Later, Someday

These are indefinite time references. They are also non-committal. They can be replaced with a definite time and date. Your mind does not know what to do when, and there is no way to determine when anything will get done. Imagine what could happen to your goals if you use these words frequently. You will not hit the bulls-eye if it is not in plain view.

6. Never, Always

These words are absolute, and once stated, nothing else moves. The use of never or always often suggests a closed mind, which seriously hinders self-growth and relationships. "I never get what I want done. I always procrastinate and feel insecure." Your mind hears that and says, "Okay, if that's what you want, I'll keep doing it."

The words never or always could be better replaced with I wonder or What if... Then you are opening your mind to options, giving yourself permission to hold your belief unless new information heeds your attention to think differently.

"I wonder what would happen if I took Friday morning to file my papers?"

"What if I could get that done in two hours? That would make me feel so much better!"

7. Won't

The word won't implies an unwillingness, reluctance, or closed-mindedness and, like the absolute terms never and always, is quite harmful because it prejudges. This word closes the door to seeing people and situations in a different light and reaching your goals. "I won't get my papers filed in two hours!": this statement creates insecurity. "I won't let distractions stop me.": this statement focuses on distractions and might draw them to you. Using the word will is better.

8. If

This is a small word that carries large expectations and uncertainties; when used often, it paralyzes and prompts inaction, always waiting, gnawing away at your confidence. Instead, decide what is best right now for achieving greater success.

"If this happens, this is what I will do. I will adjust the situation from there."

9. Try/I'll Try

Whenever these words are used, effort is greatly reduced, commitment is lacking, and action is half hearted. Replace I'll try with I will or forget it.

10. Impossible

Just like many other generalizations we hold on to, these perceptions significantly reduce our potential, hinder our experiences, and stunt our personal growth. One must see all goals through the lens of possibilities, thinking "It is possible." The problem lies most often not in the impossibility of the goal, but in the commitment and focused action of the achiever. Libraries are full of books that tell stories of ordinary people doing extraordinary things. Believe and achieve! [53]

—Lori Bestler is also a life coach, who the author met al Lakes Area Women in Business events

HOMEWORK

1. Practice saying, "I am so happy and grateful now that…"
    Examples:

    I am so happy and grateful now that I am a world traveler.

    I am so happy and grateful now that I have order in my home and office.

    I am so happy and grateful now that I have a regular exercise schedule.

    I am so happy and grateful now that I allow myself adequate sleep.

    Fill in the blank with whatever you are happy and grateful about, EVEN IF you don't have it yet.

2. When you are in a quandary about what to do, think of fifty ways to get into your dream career or home, or fifty ways to get out of debt. Just start writing, and come up with any and every idea until you have fifty. If you can only come up with a dozen, dig deeper. You may be able to think of a lot more ideas. Once you are done with your brain dump, say "not it" to the obvious, giving them no more thought; go the next round with what is left. For example: the cheapskate in me says "not it"—this option is too costly. The lazy bum in me says this one's "not it" because it's too much work. Cross them off for whatever reason.

3. Visualize this: you are surrounded by negative energy, but it doesn't get to you. This meditation is an everyday survival tool. Try it out when you're rattled by a demanding boss

or a needy friend. During the heat of the situation, focus on your breathing and planting your roots deeply, safe and secure. Being firmly grounded protects you from getting flattened by negativity. Sit in a relaxed position, eyes closed if possible; focus on your breath to center yourself. With each breath, extend your awareness downward, right into the ground. Picture your breath flowing downward through strata, bedrock, minerals, and soil. Mentally plant a root from your body into the earth's core. Anchored by the rhythm of your breath and rootedness, you become cocooned from the chaos. This exercise was shared in Judith Orloff's *Positive Energy*.[54]

4. Ask yourself what you're tolerating. Put everything down, from the sticky screen door to the computer backup you're planning to get to, the boundary needed with a sibling, or the closet that is so bursting, you don't even want to open the door. You name it, whatever it is, write it down. Once you have your list, tuck it away unless you need to pull it out to add to it. Whenever you do pull it out, cross off all resolved tolerations. It's amazing: when we identify issues, write them down, and tuck them away, it's like putting them in our "God box" and asking him to take care of them. When the item is resolved, you may not even realize it until you review your list.

5. Identify which of the ten words to avoid (see page 74) you are using and make a conscious effort to replace them with better alternatives. Notice the changes in your life when you do.

Making Your Dreams a Reality

Now that you've cleared negativity from your life, you're ready for the fun of making your dreams become a reality.

One of the first steps you can do to make your dreams come true is to become a people watcher—see how others rise and fall in health, wealth, and relationships. From this, you can identify which activities will work and which will not, and tweak as you go. For example, while working in the field of investments, I experienced jealousy and envy of others, feeling a lack of what I had and wanted (the wealth they had). Then I learned that others having what I wanted was evidence that it was possible for me to have it as well. So I became happy for them, knowing that when I saw achievement in others, it increased my belief in the possibility of achieving myself.

I was a little apprehensive about trying the zip line for the first time, until I saw someone else go; then I knew I could do it. This often happens when we do something or even contemplate doing something for the first time. When we see someone else doing what we want, there's no need to be envious of them; they are showing us it's possible. Have gratitude for their gift of possibility. Ever realize making alfredo sauce is really easy after watching someone whip up a batch on a cooking show?

By watching others, we see shining examples of "not it" without having to experience the personal consequences. It's hard to watch someone else struggle, and we see it every day somewhere in our lives. Witnessing others' struggles and consequences allows us to say "not it" and learn without experiencing the consequences ourselves. *Or* we identify "this is it," and watch a mentor go step by step to where we want to be.

Something may not make sense to you yet, but will make perfect sense to someone who has experienced it and has the "aha's." Be happy that it doesn't make sense. Don't try to analyze; just move on and say "not it." I am happy for you if you have not had a challenging experience as others have had. Take what resonates with you; take what you like and leave the rest, as I learned in Al-Anon. The message you did not get was not meant for you.

A tool I learned in coaches' training is to do a screen of the mind—play a movie in your head for a situation in your life. Visualize a positive outcome to a challenging situation. Visualize your dream coming true. What details do you see? Are there clues that say, "Do this. Here's the answer, or action to take"?

In his book *9 Things You Simply Must Do to Succeed in Love and Life*, Dr. Henry Cloud has a whole chapter called "Play the Movie," another version of what I learned. I highly recommend this book for your reference.

Overwhelmed? If you are not getting to the task or goal, do you need to break it down into smaller, more manageable pieces and take each piece at a time?

When we make our dreams a reality, we often learn new things. Look at the quadrant below, which is similar to the Johari Window, The "Four Stages for Learning Any New Skill", the theory was developed at the Gordon Training International by its employee

Noel Burch in the 1970s. The Four Stages of Learning provides a model for learning. It suggests that individuals are initially unaware of how little they know, or unconscious of their incompetence. As they recognize their incompetence, they consciously acquire a skill, then consciously use it. Eventually, the skill can be utilized without it being consciously thought through: the individual is said to have then acquired unconscious competence. Several elements, including helping someone 'know what they don't know' or recognize a blind spot, can be compared to some elements of a Johari window, although Johari deals with self-awareness, while the four stages of competence deals with learning stages.[55]

Gordon Training International

Unconscious Incompetence	**Conscious Incompetence**
Unconscious Competence	**Conscious Competence**

Unconscious incompetence:
Don't know what you don't know

Conscious incompetence:
Know you don't know

Conscious competence:
Know what to do and have to think about it—takes effort

Unconscious competence:
Automatic—doing without thinking

"When in college I used to imagine... home, family, visitors, living alone in city... Through the years fragments of these dreams actually came true... dreams sometimes need revision."

—FRANCES MAYES,
BELLA TUSCANY [56]

Remember when you were little? Your parents put on your shoes and tied them. You did not know that you didn't know how to tie shoelaces. *You were unconsciously incompetent.*

When you got a little bit older and recognized that they were tying your shoes, you knew you did not know how to tie them. *You were consciously incompetent.*

Then came the day when it was time to learn—maybe you were starting kindergarten, maybe you were younger. Nonetheless, you were learning to tie your shoelaces and as you did you had to think about it. It took effort for you to tie your shoes. *You were consciously competent.*

After a while, you were busy going to school, maybe catching the bus; you were running and playing with friends and you tied those shoes automatically without even thinking about it, and you do still. *You are unconsciously competent.*

Just take the first step and the rest will follow—you will get what you need as you need it, no sooner.

Remember that everything is already in God's hands and decision making is a self-correcting process. Wisdom is something I sense in my gut. If I change something and still don't feel right, I go through the process again until God's will becomes clear. I learned this in Al-Anon.

It came to me in puzzle pieces.

I realize what I have now is exactly what I wanted at another point in my life—actually a culmination of things I wanted at various points.

After looking back at your dream sheets, do some dreams need revision? Are some not fully formulated yet? Sometimes when you get just what you are asking for, it's not right. By considering many possibilities, all the things you wanted appear jumbled and not how you wanted them at all. That's when you say, "I would like this, and this or this" or "Any of the above are better than what I have now." Because of your scattered focus, your reality becomes a bit of all of the possibilities all jumbled together, leaving you unhappy with what you get. Instead of considering so many possibilities, as in the broad to narrow concept, just say "not it!" Focus on what you really want with as much clarity as possible and watch it unfold.

Scattered focus equals scattered results. Instead, have a chief aim or goal. When a project on your to-do list seems too large and too overwhelming, break it down and do the next step.

"Do the Next Thing"—by an unknown author—has been my favorite poem for twenty-plus years. My favorite Christian writer, Elisabeth Elliot, used this in her materials:

Do the Next Thing

From an old English parsonage, down by the sea, there came in the twilight a message to me. Its quaint Saxon legend, deeply engraven, hath, as it seems to me, teaching from Heaven. And on through the hours the quiet words ring, like a low inspiration—

"DO THE NEXT THING."

Many a questioning, many a fear, many a doubt, hath its quieting here. Moment by moment, let down from Heaven; time, opportunity, guidance are given. Fear not tomorrows, child of the King. Trust them with Jesus,

"DO THE NEXT THING."

Do it immediately; do it with prayer. Do it reliantly, casting all care. Do it with reverence, tracing his hand, who placed it before thee with earnest command. Stayed on omnipotence safe 'neath his wing, leave all resulting,

"DO THE NEXT THING."

Looking to Jesus, ever serener, (working or suffering) be thy demeanor. In his dear presence, the rest of his calm, the light of his countenance be thy psalm. Strong in his faithfulness, praise and sing. Then, as he beckons thee,

"DO THE NEXT THING."
— AUTHOR UNKNOWN[57]

TOOL

When contemplating a goal, list the worst thing that could happen in one column and the best thing that could happen in another column. Or why you can't do something on one side and how you can on the other side.

 TOOL

Ask yourself, "Where do I want to be in my life? One year from now? Five years from now? What is my ultimate life vision?" Start writing.

When something is not quite what you want, if you would be settling, say "not it." When you are taking good on the way to great, like the size ten on the way to a size six example in Chapter 2, just take it for short while.

Ask yourself, if you could do anything you wanted, what would you do? What does it look like? Feel like? Write it down. Start. Now.

Here are some more tips and tools you may choose to adopt into your life as you stop and think about how you are living:

- Break through your fear by going out and doing it anyway.

- Don't put a time frame on things.

- Lighten up and let the universe provide for you—it's better than you imagined.

Instill new beliefs, such as:

- Everything always works out for me.

- Things may appear negative, but they will work out fine in the end.
- Life is a pleasure.
- All is well.
- This will work out to my benefit.
- Life is effortless—easy.

As we make our dreams into reality, we experience change. Looking at the six stages of change is a good way to see where you are in the change process.

The Six Stages of Change
(from the book *Changing for Good*)[58]

Precontemplation:
People at this stage usually have no intention of changing their behavior, and typically deny having a problem, although others around them can see the problem quite clearly.

Contemplation:
People in this group acknowledge they have a problem and begin to think seriously about solving it.

Preparation:
Most people in the preparation stage are planning to take action in the next month, making the final adjustments before they begin to change their behavior.

Action:
This is the stage in which people most overtly modify their behavior. They make the move for which they have been preparing.

Maintenance:

During maintenance, a person must work to consolidate the gains attained during action and struggle to prevent relapses. Change never ends with action.

Termination:

This phase is where the former behavior is eliminated to the point of no longer being a problem, with no threat of return.

When you are clear about what it is that you want, and know in your heart it's right for you, move quickly. For example: you meet the love of your life, or you find your dream house and buy it, or make a career change. On the outside it might appear that you are flying by the seat of your pants when, really, you are doing the next right thing for you—what you have been waiting to do. You see it and make the move. You may be questioned by your well-meaning family and friends. Just because they react—and they will—doesn't mean you have to second-guess your choices or cancel your plans. Just know in advance that they will need your assurance and you may not get their support.

You already have a support system of trusted others who have been safe to share with and supporting you all along. The safety net you put together in advance is here for you now—they have been waiting for you to jump, for the ball to drop; you've all been preparing, so don't lose momentum. The time is now, no regrets—live the dream and embrace each magical moment.

"Do whatever makes your inner light brighter," Judith Orloff writes in *Positive Energy*.[59] Treat yourself with love, and everyone else too. Find people who support you and your spirit and trust your gut-centered decisions to guide you.

Let an idea evolve—Systems For Change was an idea and this book started as an idea. Focus on an idea and it will grow. Watch it evolve, take shape.

PRESS PAUSE

I gave myself space to press pause and start dreaming by creating a double-duty zone where I could be alone to work on dream building. Once I had my space set up, I would go to my zone and pull out my stuff, quickly and easily, at any free moment I could find. I say double-duty zone because once I was done, it went back to the space it had been before. For you, it could be the living room, dining room, bedroom, office, sunroom, whatever. Wherever it is, it becomes a haven to journal, work on vision boards, study your Bible, or do twelve-step work—whatever brings you back to yourself and out of survival mode. When you are living just to survive, you cannot thrive, grow, or move forward.

Your sacred space needs to be quiet, comfortable, and private— a space to rest, read, and write. It needs to have adequate lighting, space to store supplies for your vision board, and a place to store the vision board to keep it private. It may have a table, a writing desk, a sofa or bed, a recliner, a daybed. I slide my vision board under the sofa; my scissors, pens, Post-it tabs, sticky notes, markers, paper, journal, and Bible all go into a small secretary in a sitting area of a great room that has windows overlooking a beautiful woods.

Give your gifts a setting to flourish, regardless of what others may think of your pursuits. As an artist, my mother has purposely created a space in her home as well as devoted time to her passion which honors her gift by sharing her paintings with people from around the world. This is also

Do not those who plot evil go astray? But those who plan what is good find love and faithfulness.

- Proverbs 14:22[60]

her release. Delving into her passion centers her, gives her life balance, and reenergizes her. When her life gets busy, she knows she needs to press pause and get back to her center by painting. What a great mentor she has been in showing those around her that pursuing her passion is not only doable, even in challenging times, but essential to her well-being. Thank you, Mom, for sharing the beauty of having a hobby!

Believe in your plan. Once you believe your plan is good for everyone concerned—not just for yourself—set your sails and steer a straight course, as I learned in Al-Anon.

In the next chapters, as you step into the various areas in life, you will find more tips, tools, and ideas, as well as examples, that I have uncovered to show "not it" by experience or by watching others. Skip around, take what resonates, and say "not it" to the rest. When we realize that to *have different* we *want to be different*, change can happen.

Remember we can't receive with a closed fist.

HOMEWORK

1. Decide: make a decision on one of your dreams. Pick a date to begin working on it very soon. Tell someone trustworthy and supportive about your dream. Eventually tell everyone you know.

2. When contemplating a goal, list the worst thing that could happen in one column and the best thing that could happen in another.

3. When contemplating a goal, list why you can't do it in one column and how you can in another column.

4. Ask yourself, "Where do I want to be in my life? One year from now? Five years from now? What is my ultimate life vision?" Start writing.

5. Ask yourself, if you could do anything you wanted, what would you do?

6. What does what you want look like? Feel like? Write it down. Start. Now.

Your Nutrition

Many of us have the dream of feeling better about ourselves, inside and out. One of the first steps in this area, in a physical sense, is to improve what you are eating and how much. Making sure you get healthy foods in the right amounts and losing a few pounds along the way will give you the energy you need to keep working on your other dreams.

When I lost more than fifty pounds several years ago, I knew I could not do another diet or weight loss plan, because once I lost the weight and stopped the plan it would come back—a definite "not it" for me. I decided on a lifestyle change that included a healthy eating plan. Do I stick to it 100 percent of the time? No. At first I did, until I lost the weight, and now in maintenance, I don't because I feel deprived and antisocial when I do. I am on my plan 80 to 90 percent of the time. That works for me.

I also knew the healthy lifestyle I was adopting included being very active (more on fitness in the next chapter). It was time to get out of the recliner and get moving! After witnessing others lose weight by only dieting, seeing their skin drooping and sagging, I said not it and knew it was necessary for me to combine the diet and exercise to tone as I reduced my size. Maybe your weight is not an issue, but you just want to feel your best and have a strong, healthy body and immune system. By having a nutrient-rich, fiber-full diet, you will have more energy than you can even imagine. When you begin eating a healthy diet and fully hydrating with spring water, removing chemicals from your environment, you will feel light with more energy; feeling sluggish will be a thing of the past. You will begin getting compliments and hearing how much younger you look—all wins for being healthy, whether you want to lose weight or not. Let a healthy lifestyle be your goal.

In changing my habits, I began saying, "No, not it" to things I knew were not on my "yes list." I worked to eliminate mindless eating. I learned to enjoy what I ate by slowing down, and savoring it. I also learned to sit down for a meal, actually dine. I realized I often snacked while standing up, again part of that mindless eating. I also learned that by brushing my teeth after a meal, I stayed away from food again until my next mealtime.

My Daily Beverage and Food Plan

FRUIT: 1 to 3 servings per day

PROTEIN: Three 3-ounce servings per day, plus 1 to 2 ounces of nuts

VEGGIES: Minimum of 5 servings a day, 1/2 cup cooked or 1 cup raw

Whole grains/legumes: 3 to 5 servings, nothing white

DAIRY: 1 to 3 servings

FATS: 3 to 5 maximum servings of olive oil or butter

SUGAR: 1 to 2 servings raw sugar, dark brown cane sugar, pure maple syrup or honey

DARK CHOCOLATE: Okay

WATER: Minimum of eight 8-ounce glasses

COFFEE/TEA: Unlimited; watch caffeine

Limit processed foods, chemicals, and preservatives that cause inflammation along with other issues.

I knew that, to make my plan work, I wanted to make and plan meals ahead of time, avoiding driving through the danger zones of fast food to feed my family with a quick, unhealthy meal.

To formulate my healthy eating plan, I studied nutrition to see what would work for me for my optimum health. I created a list with the number of servings I needed from the different food groups for my age, weight, and height. This included a consult with my doctor.

My next step was documenting everything I put into my mouth. Once I reached the limit of servings in an area, I stopped

> ⚠ **TIP**
>
> Document your servings daily in your personal planner, which I will share with you in an upcoming chapter, "Your Personal Image." I track mine by using the first letter of each category and a make hash mark each time I have a serving in that category.
>
> Example:
> **WATER** = W /////// for eight servings
> **FRUIT** = F /// for three servings
> **PROTEIN** = P /// for three servings
> **VEGETABLE** = V ///// for five servings
> **WHOLE GRAINS/LEGUMES** = G /// for three servings
> **DAIRY** = D / for one serving
> **FATS** = F /// for three servings
> **SUGAR** = S // for two servings

and filled up with the others. For example, if I had my carbs, dairy, and fruit in by dinner, I made sure I got the remaining protein and veggies in. I did include a small bit of wine and dark chocolate in my plan because it gave me some antioxidants and, more importantly, pleasure, keeping me from rebelling. If I did eat something not on my plan, I made sure I still had my minimum servings in by the end of the day. Also, I found a recipe "yes" list helpful.

I focused on the abundance of great food I wanted to eat instead of what I no longer "could have," or, put another way, what I no longer "wanted." I was actually eating a larger quantity of food while I lost the weight. Because much of it was high in fiber, I felt full. My healthy eating plan centered on beans, greens, lean proteins, whole fresh fruits and vegetables, and whole grains. (High-fiber diets protect against obesity and heart disease by cutting insulin levels. The recommended amount for your daily fiber intake is twenty-one to thirty-five grams.)

I looked at foods in the nutrient-rich categories, focused on the foods I liked, and made recipes and meals from them. I found some great recipes and created new favorites, which made saying good-bye to the old favorites easy. I revised some old-favorite recipes by making easy ingredient swaps. (I will show you how to do this later in the chapter.)

I knew I had to make a change, and looked at the alternatives my doctor and I discussed. I was on the borderline of needing blood pressure medication, with a family history of diabetes and heart disease. I was well on my path to all of the above unless I made some radical changes. And because I am "allergic to needles," I never wanted to give myself a shot or test my blood—what a motivator!

I also wanted to have the energy to do everything I wanted in life—the quality of my remaining time here on earth is important to me.

And not to be overlooked, I felt it was my responsibility to be attractive to the man in my life, and I wanted to be a mentor to younger women and a great example of living a healthy lifestyle. I wanted to give back to all the wonderful mentors I had, too.

Are you a great mentor to those who are watching you?

HOW TO EAT HEALTHY

If your body feels unhealthy and you just don't have the energy to live the way you want, you need to eat good food, as close to as nature intended. This includes fresh organic produce, eggs, and dairy, all of which are not genetically modified; grains such as brown rice, barley, and old-fashioned or steel-cut oatmeal (again, not genetically modified—many grains, especially corn, are); and nothing with growth hormones or antibiotics.

⚠ MORE HEALTHY EATING TIPS

- Drink at least half your weight in ounces of water per day.

- Eat at least 20 percent of your diet in raw green veggies per day.

- Take a high-potency vitamin/mineral supplement daily.

- Limit fast food to three times per week or less.

- Eat clean protein like cold-water fish or white-meat chicken at least three times per week.

- Eliminate consumption of pop/soda; start by limiting to three times per week or less.

Stock up for bad weather and busy times with soup, crackers, bottled water, and organic dark chocolate cocoa. Have a stash of your favorites for when you are sick. When my sons were living at home, I had a flu stash, just in case anyone got sick. It included chicken soup, soda crackers, and lemon-lime soda.

Stay away from artificial sweeteners, high-fructose corn syrup, MSG, processed foods, and fast-food restaurant meals—all will make you feel depressed and stop neurotransmitters (chemicals that help transmit messages from the brain to the body). The aforementioned foods have toxins that block focus and neurotransmitters' vibrations. Toxins caused by metal fillings, Candida, past-bad food ingredients, chlorine, and other chemicals in our water supply also block neurotransmitters.

You also may want to switch to buying meat from animals that have been grass-fed (this meat is lower in fat, has higher levels of omega-3s, has reduced exposure to E. coli, and supports farmers who raise animals in ecologically friendly ways.)

Another thing to consider as you modify your eating habits is reducing your sodium intake. You might not even be aware of how much sodium you are consuming. A single teaspoon of table salt, which is a combination of sodium and chloride, has 2,325 milligrams (mg) of sodium (the daily recommended amount is 2,300 mg a day; 1,500 if you are fifty-one or older, or if you are African American, have high blood pressure, diabetes, or chronic kidney disease). And it's not just table salt you have to worry about. Many processed and prepared foods contain sodium.

Here are some tips on cutting back on sodium (these come from the staff at the Mayo Clinic):

- **Eat more fresh foods.** Most fresh fruits and vegetables are naturally low in sodium. Also, fresh meat is lower in sodium than are luncheon meat, bacon, hot dogs, sausage, and ham. Buy fresh or frozen poultry, or meat that hasn't been injected with a sodium-containing solution.

- **Opt for low-sodium products.** If you do buy processed foods, choose those that are labeled "low sodium." Better yet, buy plain whole-grain rice and pasta that doesn't have added seasonings.

- **Remove salt from recipes whenever possible.**

- **Limit use of sodium-laden condiments.** Soy sauce, salad dressings, sauces, dips, ketchup, mustard, and relish all contain sodium, as well as other harmful ingredients.

- **Use herbs, spices, and other flavorings to season foods.**

- **Use salt substitutes wisely.** Some salt substitutes or light salts contain a mixture of table salt and other compounds.

To achieve that familiar salty taste, you may use too much of the substitute—and get too much sodium.

Know that taste alone will not tell you what foods are high in sodium. Does a bagel taste salty? Well, it has about six hundred milligrams of sodium, and a slice of whole-wheat bread has one hundred milligrams. Read the labels on the foods you buy, so you can choose options that are lower in sodium, and watch out for foods that include sodium-containing compounds, such as:

- Monosodium glutamate (MSG)
- Baking soda (also called sodium bicarbonate)
- Baking powder
- Disodium phosphate
- Sodium alginate
- Sodium citrate
- Sodium nitrite

Be aware that if a packaged food is labeled as having less sodium, that doesn't mean it's your best option. For example, a can of chicken noodle soup that claims to have 25 percent less sodium still has a whopping 524 milligrams in one cup. It's only lower in salt compared with regular chicken noodle soup (790 milligrams of sodium in a cup).

Your taste for salt is acquired, so you can learn to enjoy less. Decrease your use of salt gradually, and your taste buds will adjust. Start by using no more than one-fourth of a teaspoon daily—at the table and in cooking. Decreasing your salt intake will also prevent your body from retaining water, as one salt molecule holds four water molecules.

To improve your overall eating plan, track your daily food intake by writing down everything you put into your mouth every day. This is the start of the homework for this chapter. Begin with your existing diet, tracking for a week while you create your new food plan. It sounds like a lot of work, but it isn't really; it's just a matter of keeping a small notepad with you, like in a pocket or lunch bag at work, or in your kitchen at home. A perfect tool is the planner described in the "Your Personal Image" chapter. So you would track your day like this:

Breakfast: Brown rice with cinnamon and raw sugar, coffee

Midmorning snack: mixed nuts

Lunch: 2 cups salad greens with veggie soup and whole-grain crackers

Afternoon snack: Pumpkin pudding (this is a favorite recipe I will include in later in this chapter) and herbal tea

Dinner: Roast beef sandwich on whole-grain bread, steamed asparagus, and homemade sweet potato fries (See recipe section on how to make them.)

The next step of your homework will be to determine your "yes" food ingredients list. If something's not on the list, due to not being on your plan, don't eat it.

Many clients I have coached have found it hard to keep fresh food on hand. They end up throwing out a lot of food and get very frustrated with the money they have wasted. Remember: most fresh food only lasts from one to five days (strawberries lasting one day and carrots lasting five). I use a three- to five-day rule on the contents of my refrigerator unless it is dated differently. Watch for expiration dates on food containers and buy only what you want for the next couple of days. Any longer than that and plans change, causing our menus to change. Also remember that some containers say to discard the food five to ten days after opening; this means the expiration date may be a long way out, and once you open it you start counting the number of days. One way to track this is to keep a marker and write a new expiration date on the cover or container; you can even put a sticker on it. I like to keep blank labels in my kitchen and label my containers of homemade food with a use-by date or the date it was created, staying consistent with one date or the other.

Cooking is also education; it raises your awareness of what you're feeding your body and sharpens your taste buds, which can help you develop the sort of relationship with food that inhibits overeating. Change the way you think, and the way you eat will follow. Change the way you eat, and the pounds will take care of themselves. Conversely, let a diet book or plan dictate the how, what, where, and when you eat, and you will learn nothing and only postpone the inevitable relapse.

As Mireille Guiliano says in *French Women for All Seasons: A Year of Secrets, Recipes, & Pleasure,* healthy eating is about embracing the seasons and seasonality, and making eating and savoring life a more intense experience.[61] It's learning the way to find pleasure in all things—living life to its fullest. Healthy eating is a non-diet with a holistic approach of rediscovering the pleasures of eating and cooking. It is more of an investment in time than plugging numbers into a calorie chart. Results do come in direct proportion to application. The more you think about change, the more you wind up changing; the more you change, the better your whole life becomes. Good habits can help us endure stress and, if properly instilled, they can be maintained under the most adverse circumstances.

Always have a variety of options on hand and offer them, even to picky eaters. If you didn't get to try a wide variety of fruits and vegetables as child, now is the time to try them. Or try those foods you didn't like back then—remember those Brussels sprouts?

⚠ EVEN MORE HEALTHY EATING TIPS

Here are some more nutritional tips I learned from dietician Zonya Foco at a Go Red for Women workshop:

- At a sit-down dinner, take one bite of dessert first. If good, pass on the roll; if not, take the roll if you like it.

- Reduce your calorie intake by 120 calories a day. (120 calories x 7 days x 52 weeks = 43,680 calories per year. With 3,500 calories in a pound, that equates to 12 pounds per year = one size)

- To get blood pressure down, eat fruit and drink water every four hours.

- Replace oil with fruit in recipes—use applesauce, bananas, and pineapple.

- When grocery-shopping, purchase foods based on the number of servings needed, based on the number of people in the household.

- Learn how to prepare new foods. Get instructions on how to open a pomegranate, peel an avocado, or cook an artichoke.

- Regular soda has thirty-one teaspoons of sugar in it. Would you let your children put thirty-one teaspoons of sugar on their cereal? Think about it!

- Diet soda is full of artificial sweeteners. Phosphoric acid doubles the chances of type 2 diabetes, depletes calcium, and is bad for bones. Limit diet soda to one serving a day and switch to water or tea instead.

- When cooking dinner, use a pretty glass tray with sliced veggies set out to munch on instead of crackers or chips.

Portion control is key. Portion sizes:

- Carbs: Hockey puck

- • Proteins: Bar of soap
- • Fruits/Veggies: As much as you want,
    five to nine servings recommended
- • Use more spices for flavor in cooking.

Things will taste different now, if you prepare them correctly. Play the game of "not it" by trying new things. Don't limit yourself.

Think about your senses—does it look good; is it presented well? How does it smell? Can you hear the sizzle? Does it sound crisp? How does it feel: creamy, cold? How does it taste: sweet, salty, sour?

How about the environment? The sounds and view? Eliminate bothersome noise and increase soothing sounds when you are eating. Turn off the TV and replace it with your favorite music. Eliminate clutter, including old decor; have a pleasant view to enhance your dining experience. You will enjoy your meal more, feel less stressed, and actually eat less, feeling more satisfied.

Did you know when you feel cruddy, you self-medicate and crave simple carbs—pasta, bagels, fudge? This increases your stress level. Instead, eat low-glycemic foods—the lower the glycemic index, the less the food affects blood sugar and insulin levels. Instead of emotional eating, work through your emotions. Remember whole, fresh, healthy foods—think beans, greens, and proteins. For example, a French baguette's glycemic index value is ninety-five or high, but wheat bread's is fifty-three or medium; pumpernickel bread's is forty-one, which is low.

MEAL PLANNING AND SHOPPING

The trouble I see most often for people trying to eat healthy is a lack of planning ahead. Instead of having a menu in mind before going to the store, whatever looks good is tossed into the cart and then brought into the kitchen. Then life happens and where did the time go? You did not get to all the fresh stuff as planned, and look how much ended up in the garbage, causing you to wonder why you spent the money on it, and why try again—it's just a waste of money. I used to think like that, and do I get it right 100 percent of the time when I shop now? No, of course not; but I do try to salvage what I can when life changes. Using the freezer is a great help. More tips on that to follow.

Sometimes when we entertain, like during the holidays, we are afraid of not having enough. So thinking we will run out, we overbuy ingredients, saying that we will have planned leftovers, just in case. Not only are we overspending, but now we also have an overabundance of high-calorie holiday food in the freezer to use up just in time for our January diets. Solution: instead buy a few healthy dishes to be warmed up quickly in case the rest is running low, like a can of baked beans or frozen veggies, such as peas or corn.

Planning ahead by creating a weekly menu takes a small amount of time and effort, but it pays off. You can coordinate this activity with looking at your weekly calendar at the beginning of the week. The best place to start is to shop your kitchen. What is in the freezer, refrigerator, and pantry that has to get used up? Start there. Next, pull the grocery ad and see what's on special. Then create your menu, grocery list, and shop. Add coupons if you like.

If you want strawberries for a meal on Thursday and you are shopping on Sunday, don't even buy them. Purchase them that Wednesday or Thursday, or get the frozen variety depending on the recipe and time of year. You may also want to freeze your own leftover produce, to keep it from going bad. Some vegetables you can easily freeze include the following:

- Onions and peppers: dice and freeze, and use in countless dishes—just sauté when you are ready to use them.

- Green beans, broccoli, or asparagus: blanche—putting in boiling water for a short amount of time—before freezing.

- Mushrooms: sauté before freezing.

- Spinach: to wilt spinach to freeze it, put a small bit of olive oil in a skillet on medium/low heat, place spinach in skillet, and stir as the leaves "wilt," or soften, and reduce in size. Freezing at this point makes the spinach easy to use in pasta or a dip later on.

- Tomatoes: freeze whole and use in chili or tomato sauce—run the frozen tomato under hot water to peel the skin and toss the frozen tomato into the chili pot or goulash or spaghetti sauce with the other ingredients.

Another tip I learned from Zonya Foco: after buying a bunch of fresh veggies, wash and cut them up right away, preparing a veggie tray in the fridge everyone can munch on. Include extra veggies to use in your meals. Planning for both creates quicker meals and fast healthy snacks with just a little prep time. When you see there's a few veggies left and know you won't get to them, freeze them, make a soup with them, or plan a weekly stir fry night when you know you will want to use them up.

Your best practice is always to plan ahead. Use what you have on hand first, buy what is on special, and post your menu

> **⚠ TIP**
>
> To get ideas about more vegetables that can be frozen, just look in the freezer section at the store. If you can buy it frozen, you can freeze it on your own with the proper preparation.

so your family knows. As life happens, adjust. Salvage before spoilage; act instead of react.

As part of your meal planning, make a weekly meal menu format. For example, on Sunday have a Big Meal Night—cook big and have planned leftovers for the week. The rest of the week could look like this

- Monday: Pasta Night

- Tuesday: Mexican Night

- Wednesday: Breakfast for Dinner

- Thursday: SSS = Soup/Salad/Sandwich

- Friday: Fish

- Saturday: Paper Plate Night (with fun food like pizza or burgers)

Some of these can remain constant like SSS on Thursdays, and some can change. Do what works for you. The key is to select good recipes, decide on healthy ingredients, and have fun with it (and let your companions or family join in). See the sample menu below.

THIS WEEK'S MENU

SUNDAY	Chicken, mashed potatoes, mixed vegetables, whole-wheat dinner roll and butter, salad greens
MONDAY	Spaghetti, salad greens, garlic toast
TUESDAY	Beef enchiladas, salad greens
WEDNESDAY	Blueberry pancakes, sausage, fresh fruit cups
THURSDAY	Tomato soup, grilled cheese, salad
FRIDAY	Grilled salmon, asparagus, and squash
SATURDAY	Turkey burger on whole-grain bun with sweet potato fries and salad greens

I used to make a weekly calendar, writing down my food plan for the week ahead. I used a small, magnetized calendar; it did not have dates printed on it. I kept it on my refrigerator, which helped me stay on track with what I

> ## ⚠ ROAD TRIP TIP
>
> Keep basic food items in the car, just in case you are caught hungry—stock up on granola bars, packages of trail mix, and, depending on the weather, bottled water and dark chocolate.

wanted to pull out of the freezer a day in advance, or if I needed to stop at the store on the way home from work the next day for fresh ingredients. This also reminded me of things coming up, such as leaving early on Saturday to drive to my son's, and needing to pack something to eat in the car rather than stopping for an expensive unhealthy meal on the way.

Use the Systems For Change weekly planner shown in the "Your Personal Image" chapter as a way to menu-plan, using the project example, Keeping in Your Kitchen.

EASY INGREDIENT SWAPS AND RECIPE CONVERSIONS

Once you get your favorite recipes selected for your weekly menu, you may need to substitute in healthier ingredients, especially in old family favorites. For easy ingredient swaps and recipe conversions, I found the following helpful:

- I keep nothing white in my cupboard—no white rice, pasta, flour, sugar (okay, I take that back, I still have sea salt, baking soda, and baking powder...)

- Fats: I only use butter and olive oil.

- Fruits and veggies: I only have fresh or plain frozen.

- Crackers and cereals: I stock mostly organic whole-grain ones, without added preservatives.

Family Menu Planning Project

Objective: To plan nutritious meals for yourself and your family, using what you have and with a minimum of cost and time.

1. Identify what you have; do a food inventory. What is in your cupboards, refrigerator, and freezer? What has to get eaten? What sits in the refrigerator after only one use until it spoils? What do you want to buy in a smaller quantity or use in another recipe? Can you freeze it so as not to waste it?

2. Identify what you usually buy, get from "take out," and order at a restaurant. What do you like to eat? Is it something you can make at home?

3. Split up your favorites into a spring/summer menu and fall/winter menu. Switch with the weather and holidays.

4. Identify recipes you use on a regular basis. What is it about these recipes? Why do you make these regularly? Are they easy to make? Family favorites? Are they using items you can easily pull out of your pantry and throw together? Identify and file—you now have your point of beginning.

5. What recipes can you double, freezing one for a future meal? Lasagna? Enchiladas? Tuna noodle hot dish?

6. What about freezing smaller servings of healthy homemade dishes to easily heat in the oven? This can be your own version of convenience food without the sodium and preservatives.

7. For each day of the week, have a consistent plan: breakfast for supper, soup night or SSS (soup/salad/sandwich), steak night, burger night, pizza night, pasta night, and so on...

Saving Money Eating Healthy

Many people feel that cost is a hurdle when considering eating healthier. Here are some tips on how to save money and eat better too:

- Make your own stock, such as chicken or vegetable, for pennies on the dollar.

- Calculate the cost per pound and find the savings in buying whole watermelon, cantaloupe, or pineapple instead of precut versions. This same principle goes for buying a head of romaine lettuce versus pre-chopped romaine lettuce.

- Buy blocks of cheese you shred instead of pre-shredded cheese. Any time there is processing involved, there is more expense and usually more artificial and preservative ingredients that can interfere with good health.

- Skip the premade mixes and sauces and make your own. Not only does this save you money, but it's healthier because you choose the ingredients.

- Dairy: It was tricky for me because of some allergies. I swap out sour cream with Greek yogurt, and use organic milk or almond or soy milk instead of regular milk.

Because I identified an ingredient "yes" list, it's easy to look at a recipe and swap:

- Recipe calls for white flour; use whole wheat.

- Recipe calls for white sugar; use dark brown cane sugar.

- Recipe calls for an unhealthy oil; use olive oil. In addition, use butter instead of shortening or margarine.

- Recipe calls for cream sauce; I make my own sauce using organic half and half or whipping cream.

- Also, make your own sauces instead using of jars of sauce filled with preservatives.

When converting a recipe, I take a favorite old recipe (like the banana bread recipe I revised and share with you at the end of the chapter) and substitute better options for the white flour, shortening, and white sugar. I swapped these for whole-wheat flour, butter, and brown cane sugar (watch when you are buying brown sugar, as some brands are white sugar with molasses added). Also, I decreased the amount of sugar in a recipe.

Test recipes, and with a little trial and error, you will develop healthier new favorites. One I laugh about is using garbanzo-bean flour in pizza crust. It was dry and did not hold up. I am sure garbanzo-bean flour is great for some things, but that was "not it."

This measurement conversion table is great when you want to increase or decrease the size of a recipe. When my boys were growing up, I usually doubled or quadrupled a recipe; later as an empty nester, I find myself halving recipes, although I still keep a stash in the freezer—my version of fast food.

Measurement Conversion Table

Cup	Fluid Ounce	Tablespoon	Teaspoon	Milliliter
1 C	8 oz	16 tbsp	48 tsp	237 ml
3/4 C	6 oz	12 tbsp	36 tsp	177 ml
2/3 C	5 oz	11 tbsp	32 tsp	158 ml
1/2 C	4 oz	8 tbsp	24 tsp	118 ml
1/3 C	3 oz	5 tbsp	16 tsp	79 ml
1/4 C	2 oz	4 tbsp	12 tsp	59 ml
1/8 C	1 oz	2 tbsp	6 tsp	30 ml
1/16 C	0.5 oz	1 tbsp	3 tsp	15 ml

⚙ TOOL: RECIPE SORT

- Gather loose recipes from magazines, newspapers, old cookbooks, and the Internet.

  TIP: When I work with clients, I find that many have a large collection of cookbooks and don't use them. If they do use them, it's one or two recipes from each book. Take those recipes out and pass the book along to someone else, reviewing it quickly first to make sure there aren't recipes that fit the new plan you may want to try. Gradually get rid of those extra recipe books. Rome wasn't built in a day. It's a process; have fun with it. Experiment, and play with it. As you will find in the "Your Home" chapter, I promote eliminating excess and spending less on expensive real estate.

- Sort loose recipes into envelopes (recycle those large ones you get in the mail).
- Then sort into folders. I like folders with side pockets and a center with fasteners to add a page protector for small, loose recipes that are clipped out. I file the printed ones in the left pocket and magazine tear-outs in the right pocket.

With the initial sort, I grab a stack and very quickly arrange by the above categories. Later I will take each file out and determine what recipes exactly I want to try and toss the rest. You may want to block off time to do this, or it will sit there unfinished.

If questioning what category you can file a recipe under—for example, a magazine article may have a week's worth of recipes related to a theme or menu—find the recipe or recipe type you pulled the article for and file there. If you pulled for breakfast ideas, do not file in the beverage file even though there may be beverage recipes within the article. This makes it easier to search later.

When you have a few moments while you are waiting for the repairman or company to come, take out one folder and sort through it for a few moments. Cut out the recipes you want to keep and discard the rest. After determining the recipes you want to try, it is time to decide when you want to try them. Is this a seasonal recipe? Do you want a cookbook just for holiday meals and treats? Is this specific to summer grilling? Maybe you want a binder just for grilling. Scanning into a computer file counts too. Some of us are high-tech, some of us are low-tech; you decide what works for you.

Once you try a recipe and decide you love it, file it with your permanent recipes in the appropriate category or section.

If you can't decide when to use the recipes, and a season does not seem clear to you, then either toss them or file them back in the folder. Do not spend precious time in analysis

THE IMPORTANCE OF HYDRATION

No matter what you eat, make sure you are doing what you can to be properly hydrated throughout the day. I closed my insurance office a few years ago and had a lease on the spring water cooler, which I could not bring with me. I let my son and his roommate use it and he said to me later they had not been drinking much water beforehand because the taste of the city water was awful. So they were drinking soda much of the time instead. Once they started drinking the cold spring water, they noticed how much better they were feeling. Try it; see what a difference this can make to you.

Consider a water cooler with a five-gallon bottle as an alternative to buying smaller "to-go" water bottles. It is not only healthier than soda, but it is less expensive—hmmm, more healthy and financially fit, a win/win. Do tests before you say "not it"; see how you feel when you are getting enough. Do not substitute other liquids for water even if they contain water. This will help flush your body of toxins. Your skin, hair, and nails will be happy, and you will have fewer headaches and more energy. You will be less constipated, especially if you combine with a high-fiber diet, which will keep your colon happy and help you lose weight.

Also consider cutting out your caffeinated drinks, or at least reducing them, as this will help keep you hydrated. I had an unexpected thing happen recently. My whole adult life, I would make a daily pot of coffee; I had to have it. Whenever I would visit with family and friends, coffee was involved—especially in the morning. At work in the morning, it was one of the first things I would grab. It helped me to focus. I loved my coffee. This past February, when I would have my coffee, it just did not taste right. So I started to naturally decrease the amount I was drinking. By the time it was summer, I decided this might be a perfect time to get off the caffeine. After a month of regular cold-pressed coffee (because I love cold coffee drinks in the summer), I switched to half-caf for a month, and by fall, I was drinking decaf. I was tired of coffee driving my behavior. Before, I could not do anything without my coffee; it was a chore and a challenge when traveling, especially camping, because I had to have my coffee. It conflicted especially with my exercise schedule. It got to the point that when I dumped the coffee grounds, I felt like a smoker dumping my ashtray. (Yes, former smoker here, over twenty-five years smoke free!) Now that I am off caffeine, my actions are not driven by the addiction. I am free. I still order a coffee when out with friends, or when visiting my family, as long as it's decaf. Now it's a treat and not a ball and chain. Yeah!

CONSTIPATION ISSUES

Staying well hydrated also can help you avoid constipation. But constipation can be the result of getting too little exercise or not enough fiber, too. Surprisingly, bad breath can be an indication that you may be constipated. When toxic waste remains in your body, gasses rise up to the mouth, giving a person putrid odors there. Although constipation may not seem like a very serious thing, it honestly can be. The physical ailments that constipation can lead to are no laughing matter. If you can't make a bowel movement, you can start feeling angry or aggravated, experience weight gain, have body odor and skin eruptions, develop hemorrhoids, and experience headaches.

Constipation also can cause some very serious medical troubles. Bacteria in our feces may start to multiply in our intestinal tracts, and dangerous fungus can grow. Health writer Kanika Khara notes that this may lead to a whole host of problems throughout the body—gallbladder problems,

> **⚠ TIP**
>
> To avoid constipation, eat brown rice weekly to support your colon.

varicose veins, heart disorders, arthritis, hernias, appendicitis, and, in extreme cases, bowel cancer.[62] Constipation also weakens your immune system, reducing your body's ability to fight illness.

A great natural way to avoid becoming constipated is to eat the correct amounts of insoluble fiber. Insoluble fiber cannot be absorbed by our bodies; however, it helps us to get rid of waste. It reduces the amount of toxins that are left in our intestinal tracts.

Some food options to increase your insoluble fiber are wheat bran; white, black, kidney, and pinto beans; oat bran; coconut flakes; wheat germ; avocado; dried peas; raspberries; brown rice; almonds; lentils; sunflower seeds; raisins; and blueberries.

Also, drink the recommended amounts of water every day as mentioned earlier. Water helps flush waste from your system.

If necessary, laxatives can be utilized to aid in the removal of waste from your system. If constipation worsens or you experience any other effects, you need to see your doctor immediately.

Causes of Constipation

Insufficient intake of dietary fibers

Inadequate consumption of water

Intake of different drugs like antacids, antidepressants, etc.

Medical conditions like an underactive thyroid, spastic colon, gut disorders, etc.

Slow bowel movements due to pregnancy

Physical or emotional stress

Symptoms of Constipation

Difficulty in evacuating the bowel

Infrequent and painful bowel movements

Passing hard and dry stool

Abdominal pain and cramps

Excessive gas and bloating

Change in bowel habits

Distended abdomen

Nausea and headaches

Loss of appetite

Foul breath and bad mouth taste

"Gardens, floral scents, and memories… Scents operate like music and poetry, stirring up wordless feelings that rush through the body not as cognitive thoughts but as a surge of lymphatic tide."

—**FRANCES MAYES IN** *BELLA TUSCANY* [63]

Boosting Your Lymphatic System

Ever think that feelings rush on a surge of tide within the body? Ever wonder about your lymphatic system? As I have gone through coaching, I have heard about feelings getting stuck in our bodies, causing physical and emotional pain. Is it our lymphatic system that moves them along? I have no idea really, but I know several people who have claimed that by getting the stuck feelings unstuck, they remove pain from the body. I have no claims to this and know some people see this as "woo-woo" stuff. I am not going to go there, but thinking about your lymphatic system and how to nutritionally support it is warranted.

The lymphatic system supports the immune system. To support this system that supports you, you can consume polyunsaturated fatty acids, which can be found in nuts, seeds, fish, and whole grains. Polyunsaturated fatty acids also can be found in vitamin D from dairy, tofu, and leafy greens; vitamin A from sweet potatoes, kale, pumpkin, carrots, and fish oil; and selenium, found in meats, fish, and grain.

Increasing your potassium can also boost your lymphatic system. Plus, potassium slows excretion of calcium, which helps you avoid bone loss. A minimum daily intake of 4,700 milligrams is recommended for adults. The richest sources of potassium can be found in vegetables and fruits, as well as various other cheeses. See the list below for your choices.

Look at labels and research online to see what the potassium content is for these various options—funny thing is that I thought I could only get potassium from bananas and kiwi! The list that follows does not contain all the options available, just a sampling. It is a source for many other vitamins and necessary nutrients, which is why I promote a diet rich in whole, fresh, healthy foods.

Potassium-Rich Foods

Beans	Oranges	Chickpeas
Grains	Tangerines	Lentils
Sweet potato	Kiwis	Navy beans
Carrots	Mango	Black beans
Spinach	Apricots	Lima beans
Red pepper	Watermelon	Kidney beans
Broccoli	Raspberries	Split peas
White potato	Grapefruit	Tofu
Winter squash	Blackberries	Quinoa
Snow peas	Honeydew	Whole wheat
Romaine lettuce	Peaches	Buckwheat
Asparagus	Pineapple	Bulgur
Green peppers	Blueberries	Barley
Green peas	Cherries	Wild rice
Avocado	Nectarines	Brown rice
Parsnips	Pomegranates	Oats
Rutabaga	Bananas	Couscous
Cabbage	Plums	Yogurt
Artichoke	Prunes	Milk
Mushroom	Apples	Cottage cheese
Corn	Pears	Mozzarella cheese
Papaya	Grapes	
Cantaloupe	Soybeans	
Strawberries	Pinto beans	

VITAMINS AND SUPPLEMENTS

Vitamins and supplements are another important part of living a healthy lifestyle. Below is a list of the major vitamins our bodies need, and how they help our bodies.

Vitamin A: Important for normal vision, the immune system, and reproduction. Vitamin A also helps the heart, lungs, kidneys, and other organs work properly. It can be found in poultry, fish, and dairy products (preformed vitamin A), and in fruits, vegetables, and other plant-based products (provitamin A). Foods with vitamin A include salmon, broccoli, carrots, squash, cantaloupe, apricots, mangos, and dairy products.

Vitamin B: The body needs vitamin B6 for more than one hundred enzyme reactions involved in metabolism. Vitamin B6 is found naturally in many foods, including the poultry, fish, and organ meats, as well as potatoes and other starchy vegetables.

Vitamin B12 is a nutrient that helps keep nerve and blood cells healthy and helps make DNA, the genetic material in all cells. Vitamin B12 also helps prevent megaloblastic anemia, a type of anemia called that makes people tired and weak. Nerve problems, such as numbness and tingling in the hands and feet, can also occur. Other symptoms of vitamin B12 deficiency include problems with balance, depression, confusion, dementia, poor memory, and soreness of the mouth or tongue. You can get recommended amounts of vitamin B12 by eating a variety of foods, including the following: beef liver and other meats, clams, fish, poultry, eggs, milk, and other dairy products.

Vitamin C: In the body, it acts as an antioxidant, helping to protect cells from damage caused by free radicals. Free radicals are compounds that form when our bodies convert the food we eat into energy. People are also exposed to free radicals in the environment from cigarette smoke, air pollution, and the sun's ultraviolet light. The body also needs vitamin C to make collagen, a protein required to help wounds heal. In addition, vitamin C improves the absorption of iron from plant-based foods and helps the immune system work properly.

Fruits and vegetables are the best sources of vitamin C. You can get recommended amounts of vitamin C by eating a variety of foods, including the following: citrus fruits (such as oranges and grapefruit) and their juices, as well as red and green peppers, kiwifruit, broccoli, strawberries, cantaloupe, baked potatoes, and tomatoes. To find out if vitamin C has been added to a food product, check the product's label. A food's vitamin C content may be reduced by prolonged storage and by cooking. Steaming may lessen cooking losses. Fortunately, many of the best food sources of vitamin C, such as fruits and vegetables, are usually eaten raw.

Vitamin D: Vitamin D is needed for health and maintaining strong bones. It does this by helping the body absorb calcium (one of bone's main building blocks) from food and supplements. People who get too little vitamin D may develop soft, thin, and brittle bones, a condition known as rickets in children and osteomalacia in adults.

Vitamin D is important to the body in many other ways as well. Muscles need it to move, nerves need it to carry messages between the brain and body parts, and the immune system needs vitamin D to fight off invading bacteria and viruses. Together with calcium, vitamin D also helps protect older adults from osteoporosis. The body makes vitamin D when skin is directly exposed to the sun, and most people meet at least some of their vitamin D needs this way.

Very few foods naturally have vitamin D. Fatty fish such as salmon, tuna, and mackerel are among the best sources. Beef liver, cheese, and egg yolks provide small amounts. Mushrooms also provide some vitamin D.

Vitamin E: Vitamin E supports the liver, immune system, and DNA repair. It can be found in almonds, olive oil, and spinach.

Other nutrients our bodies need include conjugated linoleic acid (CLA) and gamma linolenic acid (GLA). CLA is an antioxidant with cancer-fighting properties which lowers cholesterol. CLA is also known for its body weight management properties, which include reducing body fat and increasing lean muscle mass. It is an essential fatty acid found in meat and dairy products; the best source is from grass-fed beef. GLA may be useful in treating rheumatoid arthritis, allergies, attention deficit hyperactivity disorder (ADHD), and breast cancer. Both are most often consumed in supplement form.

And finally, the chemical magnesium has much therapeutic value. According to *The Magnesium Miracle* by Carolyn Dean, magnesium can be used to help treat the following:

1. Anxiety and panic attacks (helps keep adrenal stress hormones under control)

2. Asthma

3. Blood clots

4. Bowel disease (Magnesium deficiency can cause constipation and other bowel problems.)

5. Cystitis

6. Depression (Serotonin, which elevates mood, is dependent on magnesium.)

7. Detoxification (Magnesium is crucial in removing toxic substances and heavy metals such as aluminum and lead from the body.)

8. Diabetes (Without magnesium, glucose and insulin can build up in the blood, causing various types of tissue damage.)

9. Fatigue (Magnesium-deficient patients commonly experience fatigue because several enzyme systems are not functioning well.)

10. Heart disease

11. Hypertension (With insufficient magnesium, blood vessels may go into spasm and cholesterol may rise, both which lead to blood pressure problems.)

12. Hypoglycemia

13. Insomnia (Sleep-regulating melatonin production is disturbed without sufficient magnesium.)

14. Kidney disease

15. Migraines

16. Musculoskeletal conditions (Fibrositis, fibromyalgia, muscle spasms, eye twitches, cramps, and chronic neck and back pain may be caused by magnesium deficiencies.)

17. Nerve problems

18. Obstetrical and gynecological problems (Magnesium helps prevent premenstrual syndrome and dysmenorrheal—cramping pain during menses. It is also is important in the treatment of infertility and alleviates premature contractions, preeclampsia, and eclampsia in pregnancy.)

19. Osteoporosis (Use of calcium with vitamin D to enhance calcium absorption without a balancing amount of magnesium causes further magnesium deficiency, leading to bone loss.)

20. Raynaud's syndrome (Magnesium helps relax the spastic blood vessels that cause pain and numbness of fingers.)

21. Tooth decay (Magnesium deficiency causes an unhealthy balance of phosphorus and calcium in saliva, which damages teeth.)[64]

The recommended daily allowance of magnesium is just over 300 milligrams for women and 400 milligrams for men as a general rule.

Magnesium Content of Common Foods

(Based on 3 1/2-ounce serving)

Food	Milligrams of Magnesium
Kelp	760
Wheat bran	490
Wheat germ	336
Almonds	270
Cashews	267
Molasses	258
Buckwheat	229
Peanuts	162
Wheat grain	160
Pecans	142
English walnuts	131
Rye	115
Tofu	111

Brown rice	90
Figs, dried	71
Apricots	62
Dates	58
Shrimp	51
Avocado	45
Cheddar cheese	45
Beans, cooked	37
Raisins	35
Green peas, fresh	35
Potato with skin	34
Crab	34
Banana	33
Sweet potato	31
Beets	25
Broccoli	24
Carrot	23
Beef	21
Asparagus	20
Chicken	19

See how easy it is to pull together meals rich in magnesium? Think about a beef-and-bean burrito with avocado and cheddar cheese. That's a total of 148 milligrams of magnesium; add a banana, a hand full of nuts, and a molasses-spice cookie (see "Molasses Crinkles" in the recipe section) and you're probably good for the day.

READY, SET, GO

So enough of the excuses. You now have the tools to get started. The results you seek will show up shortly after you begin, and those initial results will help motivate you further as you continue your healthy lifestyle journey. You know that there's always something that needs to be done; our to-do lists don't get done. Just like dishes and laundry, the minute you complete them, the next batch is building up. Just put a healthy eating system in place and you will get it done on a consistent regular basis. You can do it. Yes, you can! Say, "Yes, I can!" Yeah! Go for it! Don't let anything or anyone stop you. Remember the reasons you are doing this; remind yourself of the alternatives if you do not—can I say needles? Yikes! Or maybe needles don't bother you, and your motivator is looking great at your next class reunion. Whatever your reason, let it motivate you to the life of your dreams.

Have your cake and eat it too! Just not the typical white cake and buttercream frosting. It's all in moderation. I offer a few healthier dessert recipes later in this chapter so you can enjoy desserts at least weekly and more often if you wish. There's also a bit of sugar in the daily food plan I use, and some days I have none and other days I have a bit more and it evens out. We need to cut ourselves some slack and enjoy life without getting carried away; that's how I combated feeling deprived. I am not deprived; I still eat my cake and ice cream. I'm just very selective about what ingredients are in them, and I'm also selective about when and with whom I'm enjoying them.

HOMEWORK

1. Track your food intake before changing your food plan for one week.

2. Determine your yes list—foods you like that fit your new plan.

3. Review your recipes to see what works and what doesn't.

4. Add new recipes to support your plan.

5. Begin changing your diet with your new plans, tracking the number of servings you're eating.

6. Create a weekly menu using the family menu-planning project.

7. Create a shopping list or use the Systems For Change Weekly Planner.

8. Create a recipe binder or file (paper or electronic).

9. Study nutrition.

Lori's Favorite Recipes

Basic Pasta Combinations

Ingredient combination: any whole-grain pasta, sauce, meat, veggies, and cheese (warm or cold)

Example 1: Pasta shells, mushroom sauce, tuna, peas, cheddar cheese = tuna casserole

Example 2: Pasta shells, real mayonnaise, tuna, peas, cheddar cheese = tuna salad

Example 3: Bow tie pasta, Italian dressing, turkey pepperoni, cherry tomatoes, cannellini beans, artichoke hearts, peppers, black olives, mozzarella cheese = Italian pasta

Example 4: Rotini pasta, marinara sauce, browned hamburger, mushrooms, peppers, onions, cheddar and mozzarella cheeses = pasta bake

Example 5: Tator tots instead of pasta to top mixture of browned hamburger, cream of mushroom soup, green beans, and cheddar cheese = tator-tot hot dish

Example 6: Wild rice, brown rice, browned hamburger, cream of mushroom soup, corn, cheddar cheese = Minnesota hot dish

Example 7: Egg noodles, chicken or turkey, cream of chicken soup, broccoli, cheddar cheese = chicken noodle hot dish

Example 8: Egg noodles, leftover steak or roast cut into chunks, cream of mushroom soup, a little milk, plain yogurt, cheddar cheese, green beans = stroganoff hot dish

* Tip: use homemade mushroom sauce (recipe below) instead of canned cream of mushroom soup for these recipes and also for green bean casserole.

Homemade Mushroom Sauce

Melt 3 tablespoons butter in pan, then sauté one small package of sliced fresh mushrooms with a bit of minced garlic, or sprinkle a small amount of garlic powder on the mushrooms. Once browned and softened, sprinkle on 3 tablespoons whole-wheat flour, whisk together, and cook a minute or two. Then pour in a cup of chicken stock and a cup of half and half. Cook until thickened. Then add a bit of fresh ground pepper. The key is, this takes time. Let the mushrooms cook slowly down, and let the sauce simmer slowly while stirring often. This is great to make when you are cooking other things and in the kitchen anyway. Make extra and freeze.

Vegetable Stock

9 cups spring water
4 carrots, coarsely chopped
4 stalks celery, coarsely chopped
2 onions, coarsely chopped
1 leek (white part only) coarsely sliced
3 cloves crushed garlic
Good pinch of sea salt
4 black peppercorns, crushed
Small handful each of parsley, rosemary, and thyme stems
2 bay leaves

Bring all ingredients to a boil over high heat. Skim off any scum that forms on the top. Lower heat and simmer for twenty-five minutes. Strain stock into a bowl, discarding solids. Allow to cool, and refrigerate up to two days or freeze.

Mom's Meatloaf

1 pound grass fed beef hamburger
1 small onion chopped
1 egg
1/2 tsp. sage, or use chopped fresh sage
1 cup old-fashioned oatmeal
1 cup Annie's Organic Ketchup
2 tbsp. yellow mustard
1/3 cup brown cane sugar

Mix hamburger, onion, egg, sage, and oatmeal. Place in loaf pan and top with mixture of ketchup, mustard, and brown sugar. Bake at 350 degrees Fahrenheit for about an hour. Serve with baked or mashed potatoes, carrots, and peas. Thanks, Mom, for this family favorite.

Black Bean Hummus

3 1/2 cups black beans, drained
1 small onion, diced
Half a green pepper, diced
3 cloves garlic, minced
2 tbsp. ground cumin
1 1/2 cup olive oil
2 tbsp. chopped fresh cilantro
1/4 cup vegetable broth

Place olive oil in skillet and set over medium heat. Add onions, peppers, and garlic, and sauté for three minutes, until vegetables are fragrant and starting to brown slightly. Add cumin and stir well. Reduce heat to medium and cook another two minutes. Place beans in food processor and pulse several times. Add vegetable mixture and pulse a few more times. Add vegetable broth in small batches to thin the dip to the desired consistency. Garnish with chopped cilantro. Serve immediately or store in refrigerator for up to ten days. Makes eight 1/2 cup servings with 123 calories per serving.

Beef Enchiladas

1 pound grass-fed beef hamburger
1 15 oz. can fat-free spicy refried beans
Whole-wheat tortillas
1 10 oz. can enchilada sauce
Shredded cheddar cheese
Black olives
Shredded romaine lettuce

Brown the hamburger and add the refried beans, combining together. Fill the tortillas with the mixture, rolling the tortillas up and placing them in a baking dish. Pour the enchilada sauce over the rolled-up tortillas. Top with cheddar cheese and black olives.

Bake at 350 degrees Fahrenheit for thirty minutes. Serve with shredded romaine.

(P.S. I am looking for a great homemade enchilada sauce recipe, readers, if you have one.)

Healthier Fries

1 potato or sweet potato per person
Olive oil

Preheat oven to 425 degrees Fahrenheit. Slice potatoes into strips and place them into a one gallon zippy bag. Pour olive oil into bag, seal, and shake. Herbs and spices can be added at this time; for white potatoes, I use green herbs like dill, oregano, or Italian herb blend with no sodium. For sweet potatoes, I use cinnamon, cloves, and a small bit of raw sugar. Bake until crispy, maybe turning halfway through. Time depends on number of potatoes used, generally thirty minutes.

Calico Beans

1 pound lean grass-fed hamburger
Half an onion
1/2 cup Annie's Organic Ketchup
1/4 pound crisp fried bacon crumbles (use turkey bacon if you have it)
1/2 cup brown cane sugar
2 tbsp. yellow mustard
1 28 oz. can baked beans
1 15 oz. can butter beans, drained & rinsed
1 15 oz. can kidney beans, drained & rinsed

Brown hamburger and onion. Mix in ketchup, bacon crumbles, brown cane sugar, yellow mustard, and all the beans. Put mixture in crockpot. This is a crowd pleaser that can be easily quadrupled and frozen.

Golden Beet and Pomegranate Salad

3 golden beets
1 cup diced red onion
1/4 cup red wine vinegar
1/4 cup chicken or vegetable broth
3 tbsp. triple sec or orange juice
1 tbsp. raw sugar
1/2 tsp. grated orange peel
1 cup pomegranate seeds
1 cup each arugula and butter lettuce leaves
1/4 cup crumbled feta cheese

Roast beets for one hour in your oven at 375 degrees Fahrenheit. Let cool, and then peel and dice into half-inch cubes. In a medium skillet over high heat, bring diced beets, onion, vinegar, broth, juice, sugar, and orange peel to a boil, stirring often until liquid is reduced to 2 table-spoons, about five minutes. Let cool to room temperature. Stir pomegranate seeds into the beet mixture. Serve on top of greens on individual plates and sprinkle with feta cheese.

Broccoli Salad

1 bunch broccoli, chopped
1/2 small red onion
6 strips bacon fried crispy and crumbled (use turkey bacon to save calories)
1 cup whole sunflower seeds
1/2 cup raisins or 1 cup red grapes
1 cup real mayonnaise
1/4 cup raw sugar
2 tbsp vinegar

Mix together first five ingredients in a bowl. Whisk together mayo, sugar, and vinegar. Pour over remaining ingredients, and stir and chill. Tip: I buy bacon at a meat locker which tends to be fresher, and have less fat and more meat. The butcher will slice as thick or thin as you wish.

Scrambled Egg Burritos

Scramble two eggs per person with 1/8 cup spring water. Add a breakfast meat like sausage, bacon, ham, or Canadian bacon that you have left from a previous meal. Add chopped onions and peppers (pull the peppers off the veggies you've already cut up and put on a tray in the refrigerator, if you followed that previous tip), and then whatever cheese you need to use up as desired. Spoon onto tortilla and top with salsa and fresh avocado. Use whatever you have on hand. Mix it up a bit.

Berry Smoothie

Combine 1 cup Greek yogurt, 1 cup mixed frozen fruit like berries and bananas, 1/2 cup organic milk (or almond, rice, or soy milk) in a blender. Add fruit juice to thin out if you want. Blend ingredients and adjust the amount of fruit, yogurt, or juice depending on if you want something to drink with a straw or something to eat with a spoon.

Aunt Carol's Banana Bread (Revised by Lori Rehnelt)

Cream:
1 cup brown cane sugar
2/3 cup butter
2 eggs
1 1/4 cup mashed bananas (3 bananas)
1 tsp vanilla

Add:
2 cups whole-wheat flour
1 tsp. baking soda
1 tsp. sea salt

Mix well.

Add:
2/3 cup sour milk or buttermilk

Mix well. Then pour in two loaf pans or one Bundt pan (use olive oil to grease pans). Bake one hour at 350 degrees Fahrenheit.

Tips:
To sour milk, add 1 tsp. vinegar or lemon juice to milk.
Use ripe bananas, and if previously frozen, thaw for a couple of hours before baking.

Ground flax seeds or wheat germ work well as additions to this recipe.

Fruit Crisp

Cream 1 cup brown sugar, 1 cup whole-wheat flour, and 1/4 pound softened butter. Mix in a cup of old-fashioned oatmeal and optional 2 tablespoons wheat germ or flax seeds. Line bottom and sides of an 8x8 pan with mixture, fill with fruit: apples, blueberries, peaches, or rhubarb. Sprinkle 1/4 cup of raw sugar and 1 teaspoon cinnamon over apples or 1/4 cup raw sugar over other fruit. Cover fruit with remaining crumble mixture. Bake at 350 degrees Fahrenheit for about forty-five minutes.

Pumpkin Pudding

2 eggs
3/4 cup raw sugar or brown cane sugar
2 cups pumpkin puree
1 tsp. ground cinnamon
1 tbsp. molasses
1/2 tsp. ground ginger
1/4 tsp/ ground cloves
1 1/2 cups evaporated milk (I have successfully used organic milk, almond milk, rice milk, and soy milk too.)

Coat baking dish or eight small single serving dishes with olive oil. Mix eggs and sugar. Add spices and pumpkin, mix. Then add milk and mix. Pour into baking dish(es). Bake at 425 degrees Fahrenheit for ten minutes and 350 degrees Fahrenheit for thirty-five to forty minutes. Serve warm or refrigerate. Top with fresh whipped topping. Just like pumpkin pie without the crust.

Banana Vanilla Ice Cream

Blend 1 frozen banana and 1 teaspoon vanilla per person in a food processor until smooth. Freeze like ice cream. Top with fruit like dark sweet cherries, nuts, and dark chocolate sauce.

Molasses Crinkles

(Molasses has a high magnesium content and this recipe uses whole wheat for fiber—both good ingredients for your immune system. These cookies are a treat for a healthier type of dessert or as swap for bread.)

1 cup packed brown cane sugar
3/4 cup butter
1/4 cup molasses
1 egg
2 tbsp. milk (almond)
2 1/4 cups whole-wheat flour
2 tsp. baking soda
1 tsp. ground cinnamon
1 tsp. ground ginger
1/2 tsp. ground gloves
1/4 tsp. sea salt
Small bowl of raw sugar to roll cookies in before baking

Mix brown sugar, butter, molasses, egg, and milk. Sprinkle in baking soda, cinnamon, ginger, cloves, and salt, and mix in with wet ingredients. Gradually add flour, and mix. Cover and refrigerate one hour.

Heat oven to 375 degrees Fahrenheit. Shape dough into round 1-inch balls. Dip tops in raw sugar and place sugared side up, about 3 inches apart on cookie sheet. Bake just until set, ten to twelve minutes. Immediately remove from cookie sheet. Makes about four dozen cookies.

Date Cake

Mix:

1 cup dates
1 tsp. baking soda
1 1/2 cups boiling water

And set aside to cool.

Cream together:

1 1/4 cup brown cane sugar
1/2 cup butter
2 eggs
2 cups whole-wheat flour
3/4 tsp. soda
1/4 tsp. salt
And add to date mixture. Pour into 2 round cake pans.

Mix:

1/2 cup brown sugar or raw sugar
1 cup dark chocolate chips
1/2 cup chopped nuts

Sprinkle this on top of batter as frosting. Bake at 350 degrees Fahrenheit for thirty to forty minutes until a toothpick comes clean.

More menu ideas:

- Add 1 cup cooked broccoli to scrambled egg and cheese.

- Add chopped dried apricots and almonds to oatmeal.

- Make a breakfast burrito with scrambled eggs, 1/2 cup black beans, and salsa on a whole-wheat tortilla.

- Make a California turkey club by spreading 2 tablespoons mashed avocado on two slices of whole-wheat toast. Top with three slices of turkey, bacon, lettuce, and tomato.

- Make a Southwest rollup by spreading 3/4 cup warm refried beans on a whole-wheat tortilla. Add salsa, cheese, greens, onion, and black olives.

- Make a BBQ chicken wrap with cooked chicken, barbecue sauce, and slaw mix (broccoli or coleslaw) on a whole-wheat tortilla.

- Make a chicken salad with grapes and pistachios. Use chopped chicken, small amount of real mayonnaise, French or ranch dressing, pistachios, and red grapes over greens.

- Make a spaghetti shrimp toss with 3 ounces cooked whole-grain spaghetti pasta, 3 ounces precooked shrimp (thawed), and 1 cup frozen stir-fry veggies. Saute Shrimp & veggies with 1 tablespoon sesame oil and 1 tablespoon soy sauce, toss with pasta.

- Make a black bean taco salad with 3/4 cup black beans, half an avocado chopped, 3 cups greens, 1 cup salsa, and tortilla chips.

- Make BBQ salmon with 4 ounces salmon filet, covered with 2 tablespoons barbecue sauce. Broil eight to ten minutes and serve with 1 cup green beans and 2 table-spoons slivered almonds and a small baked potato.

- Roast beets and sweet potatoes. Chill and slice on salads. Yum.

Your Health and Fitness

Living a healthy lifestyle is more than just eating healthy—it also includes exercising daily. And for me, exercise is best when combining fun with the great outdoors. My goal is to: stay healthy, keep away from the doctor's office except for routine checkups, have a good quality of life, feel good, have a toned and attractive body, and do everything I want to pain free. Having a plan with a purpose keeps me on track, blending what I want to do with the why I do it. It's the "I do this so I can do that" concept (see Chapter 3).

Before I got out of the recliner and got moving, I was in victim mode, often watching TV with a heating pad. I had injured my back in a bad fall, and had restrictions on what I could do and how I did it. Combined with working full time and raising a family, I gained weight (which caused emotional pain). After ten years of gaining weight, I could not stand it anymore. I was tired and did not have energy like I had before. When I took my kids to their activities, I would sit in my van with a book and wait. The weight gain continued. I felt more tired and ate more, because I wanted more energy. I would get a sugar high and crash. Not a happy situation.

STARTING SMALL

One day, I decided to get out of the van because the kids would not be done with their activity for thirty minutes. I arrived amazingly early, and I walked while waiting for them. I loved it. I felt better. I took one small step to a healthier me, starting with one little decision. This did not lead to big change. Not yet anyway...

Notice the word *healthy* starts with the word *heal*.

At first I was gentle with myself, a concept I learned when introduced to Nia, a fun dance class. After years of living with the chronic pain of an old injury, the thought of being gentle with myself was a relief. I started small, first getting off the recliner and looking around at the home I was living in. What could I change here? I got busy, just deep cleaning and organizing. The next step was painting and yard work. Are these part of a big exercise program? No. I just had to get moving. Sweat is sweat; any activity you do that causes you to sweat equals calorie burn, including deep-cleaning your house.

Then I began walking down the driveway, up and back, totaling about two miles per day. I did whatever I could do to work up a sweat. I also did my best to reduce stress to help feel better and lose weight. Even though my sons were active in the military by this time, and serving in the Iraq War, I was able to take the focus off of where they were and what they were doing and put it on the only thing I had control over: me.

Next was getting involved in yoga and Nia classes, and finally joining a gym, buying a bike, and enjoying the trails. I have in the years since added cross-country skiing, downhill skiing, ice skating, inline skating, running, hiking, tennis, and golf to my list of favored activities. And I just ran my first 5K this fall—in my fifties!

To get some exercise into your life, just start where you are. Maybe it's lifting your arms over your head, making arm circles, and

All about Nia

So what is Nia, the type of class that I began taking as part of my commitment to an active lifestyle? Nia is a sensory-based movement practice that draws from martial arts, dance arts, and healing arts. It empowers people of all shapes and sizes by connecting the body, mind, emotions, and spirit. Classes are taken barefoot, and soul-stirring music is used as the background. Every class offers a unique combination of fifty-two moves that correspond with the main areas of the body: base, core, and upper extremities. Inexperienced beginners and highly fit athletes alike can do Nia, choosing to set their intensity levels as they see fit.

One of the most important aspects of a Nia workout is choosing pleasure over pain. It's about joyful sensations and listening to the wisdom of your body, which allows you to create a strong environment for good health. Consider that a person's positive or negative attitude can make a difference in weight loss and fitness. Saying, "Yes!" to things that feel good creates a dynamic that makes life joyful. On the other hand, a lack of enthusiasm about your goal for an active, healthy lifestyle leads to missed workouts and emotional eating, and only makes you feel worse.

Discover Nia by checking out this website: www. nianow.com

walking and doing gentle stretches. Listen to your medical professionals, and listen to your body. Get strong, feel better, and don't let discouragement set in. Adopt an attitude of "not it"; discouragement is not allowed. Remember to be gentle, and tweak as you go.

Make exercise happen. Physical activity, whether it is cleaning, painting, or walking, burns calories. Just get moving.

As we age, it is even more important to stay strong and active so we can continue to do the things we love. Continue to play tennis, golf, ride your bike, ski, and skate, or walk, run, hike, or fish. Do whatever it is for you and stay in shape. Imagine something in your life that you love. How would your life be if you could not do it again, ever? Is there something you must do? No matter what?

Stay healthy and in shape not only for your health and wealth, but also to stay attractive to your special someone. Don't allow a sedentary lifestyle to set in. You do not deserve the consequences. I can hear the resistance you have coming up: "I can't because..." "Are you kidding me—when?" "I work full time, have kids. I have to clean the house and cook dinner; I have this and that and the other thing that keeps me from it. And darn it, I'm tired; I just want mindless TV." "I work hard. I deserve some down time." "I want to stick my nose in my book." Even short workouts, like walking for twenty minutes, count. Do what you can do. Maybe you'll have another ten minutes later in the day. Do what you can when you can. It all counts. You deserve to feel good, and you deserve to be healthy as much as you deserve the down time.

When you stay active and eat properly, you aren't fatigued. Instead you become energized! Make yourself a priority.

CHARTING WEIGHT LOSS AND YOUR MEASUREMENTS

Charting my weight loss progress by measuring my body and graphing my weight was an easy way for me to get a visual on how many pounds I was losing. I found a pattern of three pounds off, plateau, three pounds off, plateau. So I would focus on the next three pounds and not the fifty-plus pounds I was working toward. Focusing on the baby steps made this process more doable.

After a couple of weeks, I noticed what my pattern looked like. I measured my body weekly, selecting the same day of the week and blocking off twenty minutes in my calendar. I found a time when no one but me was home; I had privacy.

I would measure the same side consistently, starting with my ankles, lower calf, upper calf, knee, lower thigh, upper thigh, lower hips, upper hips, around the tops of my thighs with legs together. I measured my thigh area with my legs together because it was the widest part of me. Next I measured my waist, breast, and upper arm. It was fun to compare week to week and see the progress.

If you don't want to graph and measure, notice how your clothes are fitting. Baggy jeans = weight loss.

It takes six weeks to get in shape and only two weeks to get out of shape. Do something daily. Use it or lose it.

I found many exercises in books and magazines, and I put the exercise pages together into a three-ring binder; then I could easily pull together a new routine, which gave me variety and prevented boredom. Create your own boot camp at home or join a gym with a personal trainer. Find the moves that work for you, whether they are lunges, squats, yoga poses, or leg lifts, and do those. Eliminate the ones you won't do either because you have restrictions or you don't like them for whatever reason. Say "not it" and find better

⚙ TOOL: WEIGHT LOSS PROGRESS CHART

To chart your progress, on graph paper, put dates across the top column and weights on the side column, starting with your high weight on the top. I found weighing myself first thing every morning was easiest for me; you decide when works best for you.

Lbs.	12/2	12/3	12/4	12/5	12/6	12/7	12/8	12/9	12/10
190									
189	X								
188			X	X			X		
187		X			X				
186						X		X	
185									X
184									
183									

ones that do work. Keep your collection clean with only those that work and rotate for variety, just like with your recipes.

I started my binder with the exercises given to me for recovering from my injury and added exercises from magazines when I lost weight and gained strength later on.

If you have an exercise space in your home, post the exercises you currently use on a poster or bulletin board. Create a reward system for yourself; remember the gold stars you got in grade school? Those gold stars are very inexpensive and an easy way to track your progress. If you don't want the stars, use a checkmark system or a personal exercise log. Use the planner described at the end of the "Your Personal Image" chapter. However you want to document your consistency with your exercise routine, plan a reward at the end. Maybe you'll get a new pair of tennis shoes or a massage at the end of a designated time of consistent working out. Maybe you'll buy yourself smaller clothing. Take the time to give yourself the high fives and pats on the back you deserve. When you receive a compliment as people notice your progress, say thank you and truly take it in. Enjoy!

You decide what is right and do it.

Muscle weighs more than fat, so as you are working on weight loss, you may see a pound or two increase in weight as you work your plan. Don't freak out; it will go back down. You are toning, and you will be able to see the difference. Be diligent and you will see the progress. If you see an increase on the scale, but find your clothes are fitting looser, you know you are gaining muscle. It's progress and you're on the right track!

BOOT CAMPS AND EXERCISE PLANS

If you want to hold your own exercise boot camp, start with range of motion and gentle stretches. Next, warm up with walking or jumping on a mini trampoline, something low impact and easy. This is not when you do your more intense cardio moves; this is when you are gentle with yourself.

After warming up, go into floor mat moves. Do some calisthenics. Add in some yoga, Nia, Tai Chi, or whatever it is you enjoy. How about squats? Lunges? Bring out the weights. Then do your cardio routine, and cool down. This type of a workout is great if you have an hour or two to devote at once. It gets exercise out of the way for the day, and you can shower up. If you must break it down, still do a warm-up and cool-down with the more intense segments. Start and end your day with gentle stretches, like yoga.

There's no reason to guilt yourself to do this or for someone else's approval. Do this so that you can feel your absolute best.

Remember, this is for your health; it is putting your oxygen mask on first, to take care of you, and it is absolutely something you cannot delegate. So make it fun!

Take a dance break. ☺

As I have collected exercises over the years in my binder, in a similar fashion to the recipes I discussed in the last chapter, I have identified some basic exercises that are repeated year after year in various magazines I collect—lunges, standing calf raises, crunches, leg raises, mule kicks, push-ups, shoulder presses.

Not all exercise plans are suitable for everyone. Discontinue if your exercises cause pain.

I've found adding pictures of how I want to look while exercising and the results I seek to attain to my binder and vision boards is fun and motivating. I have a picture of a woman in a leotard with a little girl in a ballet tutu working together in a dance studio with the words on "Burn It Off!" When I saw it, I thought, "That's the kind of grandma I want to be." I also have pictures of women running, on bikes, in yoga poses, lifting weights. I use whatever inspires me, whatever says, "This is what I want, this is the new me!" As your exercise routine develops, update your photos. Once you gain strength and lose weight, your goals will change and things you never thought you would be able to do, such as certain yoga poses, may be possible.

> **⚠ TIP**
>
> If you have a condition that prevents you from following a fitness plan, follow your doctor's recommendations and do what you can.

Personal Exercise Log (Minutes)

Exercise description	M	Tue	W	Thu	F	S	S	Weekly total
Weights	15 min		15 min		15 min			45min
Cardio	30 min	45 min	30 min	60 min	20 min	30 min	30 min	245 min
Floor mat	20 min	20 min	10 min	20 min	10 min	10 min		90 min
Range of motion	10 min	10 min	20 min	10 min	10 min	10 min	20 min	90 min
Yoga		60 min		60 min			60 min	180min
Total	75 min	135 min	75 min	150 min	55 min	50 min	110 min	650min

The above shows three days of weights; a daily walk, run, or bike ride; morning and evening stretches; and three yoga classes. To some people, this is nothing and to others, it may look overwhelming. If you currently do nothing, do what you can, starting with the minimums as your goal. Once you reach the minimums, keep working up and do what is right for you. If this log looks too complicated, just say "not it" and move on. Track your progress, or not—*you decide*.

You can use this type of tracking in the planner I will share with you in the next chapter, "Your Personal Image."

Create a "moving" ritual: take a walk after dinner with someone special or alone if you want alone time. Plan a date night at the club and create a fun, healthy dinner afterwards. Go to your weekly yoga class. You name it; get into a routine where you not only move, but also meet up with friends and have fun.

Again, think about where you are and where you want to be. As a coach, I help people look at where they are, see where they want to be, encourage them, support them with tools, and for those who hire me, I work with them on being accountable. You may have a friend you can buddy up with, so you can be accountable to each other.

I got into a routine of walking before work and in the evening. Life happens, and there were times I wasn't able to go, either due to weather, a meeting, or a life event coming up. If I missed a walk here and there, I was not concerned because of my routine. To this day, I plan some sort of exercise daily, and if I miss a day: not a big deal. When I decided on my initial walking plan, I had a goal of doing it three times per week. So let's say I had it set for Monday, Wednesday, and Friday, and I missed Monday, hit Wednesday, missed Friday, hit Monday, and missed Wednesday—you get the picture. The bigger the gap between my workout days, the more likely I would be to stop the routine and say, "This is not working for me."

Have a plan for an off day. Maybe you can't get out and walk, but you have a mini-tramp inside to bounce on. Maybe you can't get to a yoga class, but can pull your own mat out and pop in a DVD to follow along with. I have a couple of yoga moves I incorporate into my day, every day, which help with my balance. Backup plans for off days help you to stay on track. I live away from family, so visiting means long car rides. I incorporate walk breaks when I can. It may only be walking around a parking lot when I stop for gas, or I may locate a trail on a frequently traveled route to walk. Some rest areas have short trails. Living in Minnesota, I found having a way to work out within my home helped when I was snowed in,

⚠ MORE EXERCISE AND HEALTH TIPS

- (Gathered from dietician Zonya Foco's presentation at a Go Red For Women workshop)
- Do seventy jumping jacks daily, consistently. It makes a difference.
- Do not wait for time to exercise.
- If you watch TV, bring your arms up and down for at least thirty seconds on every commercial break.
- There's no need for a stair machine. Use your stairs, and climb up and down, up and down, up and down.
- Become more active every day.

or it was icy and I didn't want to set foot outdoors in below-zero temperatures.

Whenever my family and I travel, we incorporate fitness into our day, walking a new city, kayaking, bringing our bikes or skates, and searching for hiking or biking trails. Swimming at the hotel pool and working out at the hotel gym are other ways to stay active while away from home. Plan ahead and pack for your journey. Encourage your traveling companions to join you and make sure there are bubbles of time in your travel schedule to accommodate this. While traveling in France, my dear friend and traveling companion Carol and I walked all over, which helped combat the calories in those delicious chocolate croissants.

GETTING ON THE RUNNING TRACK

Are you a runner? No? I wasn't always, and I'm still not much more than a beginner. I run enough to be healthy, to get my cardio goals met as an alternate to walking and biking. I used to say, "Don't make me run," and back in high school I used to walk the track instead of running it. Not that I was overweight—I weighed just 115. But I was defiant with a "you can't make me" attitude. When I began running in my forties, I was on a walk and had an urge to run. My thighs wanted to run, so I did. In just a bit of time, I got winded, but it felt physically good. I spoke with my sister who actually runs marathons and she encouraged me. As I researched, I found that what I was beginning to do on my own—walk/run/walk/run—was normal and even a way recommended for beginners. Of course, what my body intuitively wanted to do was right on track with the recommendations. Remember we may not know what to do, but our bodies do, and so it was in this case.

The recommendations I learned for beginners were to start slow, mix it up, and get used to hills and all types of surfaces. Don't

⚠ THE BENEFITS OF EXERCISE

So what specific benefits do certain exercises have anyway? Read on:

- Aerobic exercise: increases overall stamina, reduces stress, burns fat

- Core-strengthening exercise: increases range of motion, improves posture, amps up athletic performance, reduces back pain, creates a more stable center of gravity by improving balance and stability, helps with incontinence

- Yoga: increases flexibility, improves breathing, strengthens your core and balance, provides for meditation and relaxation. (Yoga is critical to keeping joints flexible and pain free, which is great for those who have arthritis. Doing certain poses in proper sequence and attention to alignment are important to experience this benefit. Seek out a yoga professional for sequence tips if you are curious. It's best to have someone in your area you know and trust.)

- Tai Chi: increases flexibility, relieves stress, and helps develop concentration. Tai Chi also eases problems of poor circulation, high blood pressure, and back pain, and it improves breathing.

---

overdo it. If you do too much too soon (not just for running, but all types of exercise), you can become injured or get burnt out. Try 10 percent more per week to get to where you want to be. If you ran 90 minutes this week, try for 100 minutes next week; if you ran 120 minutes, run 132 the next. If you get to 150 minutes, go 165 the next. Amazingly. I just ran my first 5K with my granddaughter. We plan to do more; it was fun!

BUILDING STRENGTH AND ENDURANCE

If your body has a weak spot, I challenge you to research how to strengthen that area to improve your life. Yoga is a great way to build strength and endurance. It also helps to properly align your body, which helps it work much more efficiently. Your internal organs are less cramped and circulation is smoother. You are allowed to breathe deeper, digest food better, and move with greater ease and comfort.

Having a hard time sitting at your desk all day? Your spine shortens throughout the day. Try this yoga pose: sit on your chair with your feet on the floor, hip-width apart. Put the heels of your hands on the tops of your thighs as close to your hips as possible and push down, with your shoulders rising to your ears. Remember to breathe and hold until you feel relief.

Also consider the benefits of meditation—not only can it relax you, but it can build up your mind and body. Meditation allows you to get into the present moment. When you are present, you sit effortlessly and comfortably. You sense your breathing.

There are two types of muscles: mover muscles and stability muscles. Your bigger muscles are mover muscles and do a bigger share of the work. When mover muscles are used for stability, they cannot be used to move. When you are present, you move better through the awareness of how you are moving, recognizing the difference between body knowledge and knowing in your mind.

Think of a string attached to the top of your head when you are sitting or standing and feel yourself slouch; just imagine pulling that string way up and let your body follow to align your posture so you are sitting and standing straight and tall.

BEYOND PHYSICAL FITNESS TO PHYSICAL HEALTH

Being physically fit (or at least on the road to an active lifestyle) isn't the only area to address to improve your physical well-being. Other health factors are also important to consider. Do you have insomnia? Always seem to be getting sick? Even improving your posture can make you feel better.

One of the best ways to become healthier is to stop smoking. I can't believe how many people still smoke even with the awareness to all the health hazards and financial costs. If you get nothing else from this book, stop smoking. I smoked when I was in my late teens/early twenties and stopped when I grossed myself out with the taste and smell of cigarettes. It took about six weeks of weaning myself off and that was it. I realize I quit when I was young and it may not be that easy for you. Make it your mission to quit. Find a method. If one doesn't work, say "not it" and find another. You will feel infinitely better very soon. If you don't smoke, congratulations. Don't smoke, but know someone who does? Set boundaries with them, so you are not inhaling secondhand smoke.

Eliminating stress is one of the biggest health tips I can give you, second to stopping smoking, which you already heard plenty enough about earlier. If you're the type of person who has each day filled with activities, responsibilities, and piles and piles of

> ## ⚠ TIP
>
> Doing yoga and meditation can improve your posture. Poor posture and a misaligned spine can lead to a number of medical conditions, including lower back pain and sciatica. Poor skeletal alignment places stress on adjoining muscles, which then affects other body parts including the back. Conscientious body positioning while sitting and standing can help to prevent spinal misalignment, while exercises designed to strengthen the muscles surrounding the spine help to keep the back erect.

things on the to-do list, with lots of checkmarks ticking off completed tasks, you are probably stressed out and running on adrenaline, as if you have superhuman energy. Living like that is akin to a having caffeine high or a drug high. And just like using those stimulants, running on adrenaline can be addictive and dangerous to your health, as Suzanne Somers shares in her book *Ageless*.[66]

> "Strong, pure, and happy thoughts build up the body in vigor and grace. If you would perfect your body, guard your mind. If you would renew your body, beautify your mind."
>
> —**FROM** *AS A WOMAN THINKETH* [65]

Symptoms of shot adrenals, or "adrenal exhaustion," include fatigue, heart palpitations, recurrent infections, achiness, and low blood sugar. When your adrenals are shot, you have no energy; you feel a racing inside that makes sleep impossible, further blowing your adrenals.[67] This lack of rest exacerbates the situation; things get worse and worse and insomnia sets in. What do you do when you are exhausted? You drink coffee, a stimulant that gives a false sense of energy. Then, you don't sleep soundly for days, weeks, and months, which can lead to depression.

Burned out adrenals also can lead to chronic high cortisol and ultimately a heart attack or stroke. The body can't handle this kind of stress. It's not easy to make the choice to change your life for health's sake, but what choice do you have?

To change your life, to get back to the calm baseline, Somers writes, it is important to reprioritize your daily schedule and make time for sleep.[68] Practice yoga three times or more per week to help you relax. Remember that relaxation time is just as important as being busy was. Stop staying up late; instead be in bed by nine and asleep by ten o'clock. It takes retraining. Readjust your social schedule so you are not out too many nights in a row.

Getting out in the fresh air and sunshine daily is another great prescription for health, along with a little outdoor activity. Get outside at least a little while every day. Walk if you can. Breathe fresh oxygen. Oxygenate your body. Exposure to sunshine produces vitamin D, which you require daily.

An ounce of prevention is worth a pound of cure (well, according to Benjamin Franklin) and so it is when we use sunscreen. Sunshine is essential, but even sunshine burns when you get too much. So remember the sunscreen; even in the winter, the sun can burn you.

One of the simplest ways to avoid illness is to practice proper hand-washing. I've worked in enough hospitals and nursing homes over the years to know that proper-hand washing is a key to stopping the spread of germs, a key to health. Yet I see women all over the world who rinse their fingertips under a bit of cold water, which does not kill germs. Are they afraid of getting dry hands by doing too much hand-washing? You can combat dry hands by using gloves when washing dishes and applying a really great hand lotion often. Hand sanitizers are great in a pinch, yet they do not replace proper hand-washing. Use hot water and lots of soap. Scrub your palms, the backs of both hands, and in between your fingers for several minutes. This will improve your health and the health of those around you. We can all do our part.

In dealing with insomnia, what you do first thing in the morning and before bedtime makes a big difference in how you sleep. Try to wind down at least two hours before bedtime (no news, no paying bills, no TV). Instead write your to-do list for the next day. Or meditate or do some deep breathing exercises. You can also take a hot bath to relax you. Remember not to eat treats before you go to bed, and start your day off right: eat a healthy breakfast and do aerobics early in the day to really wake up.

Remember the benefits of hydration and fiber from the nutrition chapter.

And on the topic of proper posture, posture expert Janice Novak says sitting up straight and walking with proper posture can greatly reduce neck and back pain. For proper posture, your ear, shoulder, hip, and ankle need to be a straight line, in alignment, Novak says in her video *Posture, Get It Straight.*[69] Proper posture also takes off years from your appearance as you regain lost height and take an inch or two off the midsection by unrounding your shoulders. So thinking of appearances, let's jump to the next chapter, "Your Personal Image."

HOMEWORK

1. Are you willing to take yourself on physically? In what way? Describe.

2. Are you happy with your health? What steps can you take to improve?

3. Describe what you physically love to do. Why aren't you doing it?

4. What part of this chapter gave you an emotional charge? What did you decide to do about it?

5. Do you have health concerns? Is there family history that concerns you (heart disease, diabetes, cancer)? What steps are you taking to prevent diseases? What steps would you like to take to prevent them? What else can you do?

Your Personal Image

As much as we don't want to judge a book by its cover, we often do, especially in the area of someone's appearance. Ratty clothes, disheveled hair, unclean fingernails, and stinky breath give off the wrong impression, that's for sure. But sometimes, we're stuck in a rut, with the same haircut or makeup or baggy clothes (I'm talking to you, moms). Or we decide we have too many clothes, much of them the wrong size and we need to purge. Or maybe we want a change on the outside to reflect who we have become on the inside, as we have grown personally. As we journey to a fresh start, we realize our old looks are just "not it" anymore. It's then time for a personal image makeover.

BUILDING YOUR WARDROBE

Have you ever looked into your closet, bursting with clothes, and said to yourself, "I have nothing to wear"? Usually this happens when you're in a hurry to get somewhere and you didn't have time to plan ahead to decide what to wear. What you would like to wear, of course, is in the laundry or has a tear, a stain, or doesn't fit. Whatever the reason, you do not have a plan B and are frantically looking for something, anything, to wear, as quickly as possible. One way to avoid this situation in the future is by having a wardrobe session.

This is something fun to do with a close, trusted friend on a seasonal basis. I have done it for over twenty years in the spring and fall. Now working as a life coach, I have combined my coaching with a wardrobe session for clients. Creating a wardrobe you feel amazing in, that fits and flatters, that identifies and eliminates the "not its"—a win-win!

Just as many other processes I've developed have come out of necessity, this one is no different. You can say I had a champagne taste on a college budget. When I was a little girl, my family would get bags and boxes of hand-me-down clothes and have fun creating outfits from the various sources. This practice continued as I was a young mom and a college student. I would go to garage sales, thrift stores, and clearance racks, along with collecting clothing castoffs from friends and family. I learned to sew and mend, taking great care of my clothing and altering things to fit even better. If you do not have a knack for sewing, hire someone to do the mending and alterations so your clothes look and feel great and fit you perfectly.

Before your Wardrobe Day, think about filling your closet with multifunctional clothing. For example, I bought a summer dress in the Bahamas that I can dress up or down. One day, I wore it to my parents' for a summer morning coffee, attended a graduation open house and a bridal shower, then went off to the swimming pool (I hiked up the skirt while wading in the baby pool with a toddler), and finally to the grocery store before going home. I wore the same dress all day and it was appropriate all day, for all my occasions (of course, I wasn't doing professional work that day). To add multifunctional clothing to your closet, think about how layers and accessories could be added to certain pieces so that skirt, dress, or shirt can be worn for more than one purpose. Professional clothing can be multifunctional too. A great pair of black or tan pants, a matching jacket, a nice neutral-color button-down shirt—these can be mixed and matched and accessorized for lots of options.

Before really digging in to see what you have, what you want to toss, and what you want to add, do a preview shop day. But here's my challenge:

Do a preview shop day without spending money.

Bring bottles of water, put a small cooler in your car, and bring snack bars and your own lunch to enjoy in the food court or a nearby park. Carry your water, snack, and notebook in a reusable bag. Carrying a bag gives you the feeling of already purchasing, which makes you less apt to buy something just because you are shopping.

Today, you are shopping for ideas.

Stay hydrated and fed. This will prevent you from spending money to cover an unmet need. You will keep up your energy level as well, because you are satisfied.

Leave your credit cards at home; instead bring a notepad, pen, and camera. Write down or take photos of whatever strikes you to capture the style of this season, yet make sure it fits your personal style. Jot down where you find items you love, what brands they are, and what sizes they are.

Make sure to venture into some new stores, ones you haven't tried before. You never know; you may find something great. You may even find a new favorite, saying "not it" to the others. Even if you go for ideas in a high-end store, you do not need to do all your shopping there. Maybe you start your actual shopping day at a garage sale or a thrift store and move on to Target if you cannot find what you want for cheap, before moving on to the mall. But also remember to avoid buying clothes just because they are inexpensive.

⚠ WARDROBE DAY TIPS

- On your preview day, pick up free catalogs to give you current fashion ideas once you are home.

- On your shopping day, shop end-of-season sales if you can, with a list of what you want to add or replace for the next season.

- After your Wardrobe Day and shopping trip, create a wish list of clothing items you still want and share it with family and friends for gift ideas.

Cheap in price usually equals cheap in quality. Do not sacrifice quality. I recommend good used stores for high quality. When you buy new, the item will become used in a short time anyway.

The only, and I mean only, time you get to break the no-spending rule on your preview day is if you find the perfect piece (I mean perfect!) and it's on sale and it may not be in stock when you return. Buy it with the option to return it if it does not work. Be disciplined in this: do make sure to return it if it isn't right. Otherwise, save your money for the real shopping trip after your wardrobe day, when you've compiled a list of what you really want. Today's *preview trip* is to see what colors and styles are "in" this season. Consider what you have at home that already works during your day for inspiration.

I challenge you to find a friend and team up for revamping both your wardrobes from start to finish, starting with your inspiration shopping trip, having a wardrobe day at each home, and a final shopping trip to treasure-hunt for what is on your list.

Keep each other accountable and in check.

It's an adventure, a project—have fun! Replace recreational spending with a plan and a purpose.

There are books and consultants that can help you with what colors and styles might work for you. Check out Jill Krieger Swanson's book *Simply Beautiful: Inside and Out.* You can borrow books from a friend or the library if you are on a budget. Having no money is not an excuse. It can be fun to share the info with a friend before a wardrobe day.

Keep a folder with tips and current trends from magazines and catalogs that you collect, and have a coffee day with your closet friend to compare notes. You can also do this during your preview day so that when you're going through your closets later, you can identify easily what still works or new combinations of your clothing to create an up-to-date look.

Then, after your day of inspiration, hit your closets. Figure out what fits, what doesn't, what you want to get rid of, what needs mending or altering, and what's too out-of-fashion or ragged to keep.

Before your wardrobe day, go through your accessories. All broken pieces go away, including jewelry, worn-out scarves, and worn-out shoes and socks. This is also a good time to make sure you have great foundations—don't neglect this area. It can make or break your look, and you feel better when you have nice-looking foundational pieces that fit you perfectly. Yes, boys and girls, I am talking about your undies and bras, and even socks. You don't want panty lines to wreck your look. Having your undies in a bunch can cause you to act ugly (see Chapter 2) in a hurry. When your actual wardrobe day arrives, you will have the "yes" accessory pieces to include in this season's wardrobe.

Don't forget your purses.

How many of us have multiple purses and bags for every occasion? Some are more functional than others, with pockets for everything. If you can have one basic, everyday, classic purse that holds essentials, whatever those are for you, you will be less likely to lose things by switching purses or, worse yet, showing up without an essential like your wallet because you were interrupted while switching. I recently made a trip several hours away and that's exactly what happened—I got there and I had no wallet because I had

⚠ **PURSE TIPS**

Clean your purse out every day. There's nothing worse than watching a woman dig through her purse to find something and either not find it or find something embarrassing that pops out instead. Also, keep in mind that when you are out in public, you are vulnerable to theft. On top of that, heavy purses pull on your shoulders and can cause pain.

switched purses. Thankfully, my bank had a branch in the city I traveled to and I was able to take out cash, even without my ID, by remembering the answers to my security questions. If I wouldn't have remembered them, I would have been in a tough spot.

Just like showing up with old beat-up shoes, an old beat-up purse or bag can tarnish an otherwise great image, so be mindful of that as you go through your closet. Look at the condition of your shoes (and polish them if needed), the bottoms of your purses, and inspect any accessories.

When it's time to do your actual Wardrobe Day, when you go through your entire closet, realize that you generally have favorites that you live in, your BFFs. Think of the old 80/20 rule: 80 percent of your clothing sits in your closet and 20 percent, you wear. So let's just keep the 20 percent you wear in your daily closet, removing the 80 percent to another closet, or to donate or toss.

Think of the luxury of space you'd have then. How nice would it be to have your entire current season's wardrobe that fits and matches in your closet? It would be easy to grab and there would be room to hang items without getting wrinkles. No more cramming things together. No more re-ironing shirts that got smushed.

When you're going through your clothes on Wardrobe Day, make sure your core pieces are high quality. Pick up clearance or used classic pieces when you can. Core wardrobe is where to invest your clothing dollars. A few seasonal trendy pieces can be picked up inexpensively, as they will go away the next season; this keeps you

How to Do a Wardrobe Day

Objective: Take the best of what you have to build a wardrobe around, while eliminating clutter and removing everything that's a "not it," to end up with fit and flattering clothes in a closet that looks like a personal boutique.

- Before you begin, gather your tools:

  o Bags and boxes to discard and donate unwanted items

  o Notepad and pen to create a shopping list

  o New, matching hangers

  o Cleaning supplies

  o A friend—ideally swap wardrobe days

  o Treats and favorite beverages

    ▪ Plan a quick, easy lunch ahead of time with table set for a fast break to get back to the task quickly. Use paper plates to reduce dishes.

  o Scissors

  o Wastebasket

- Bring in all clothing, footwear, and accessories from everywhere.

  o If this is a two-person closet, separate wardrobes into two rooms to work on separately.

- Empty all closets, dressers, boxes, and bags.

- Sort into categories on the bed: workout wear, business dress, casual, intimates.

- Clean out the closets and dressers before putting anything back in them.

167

o Vacuum and dust.

(Note: All of the above can all be done before your friend arrives to help on the wardrobe.)

• Find another space to store anything not wardrobe related; move items not related to your wardrobe to another room to be sorted through later, never to return to your "personal boutique." These could be:

o Hidden gift items

o Toys that have been taken away or put into storage

o Extra household goods and supplies

• Start sorting all clothing by using the OHIO method: Only Handle It Once—one category at a time.

• Ask, "Is it in season?" for each item.

o If no, then put it in a pile for that season and only work with the current season. Next season's clothing will be dealt with and stored separately.

▪ The exception: You know in this moment it has to go because it doesn't fit, you don't like it, or it is in bad condition.

o If yes, it's in season. Ask next, "Does it fit? Is it in good condition? Stained? Torn?"

▪ If it doesn't fit or is torn or stained, put the item in the discard or mending piles.

• Then ask for remaining items: "When was the last time I wore it?"

o Don't wear it? Why not?

▪ Is it your style?

▪ Have you already replaced it with new favorites?

▪ Do you love it and have nothing to wear it with?

- Want to shop for something to go with it?

  - Shop your closet first to see if there's anything to pair it up with.

  - Designate an area for these orphans that you decide to keep after you have finished your sort.

- Do you not like it, or it doesn't fit or flatter you?

  - If you feel frumpy or dumpy in it, IT'S GOTTA GO. It's "not it"—GOT IT?

  - It doesn't matter who gave it to you.

  - It doesn't matter how much you paid for it! If it's not it, it's not it! Got it? Good!

o Ask, "Is this really me? Does it make me feel amazing?"

  - If you don't feel great when you wear it, it's "not it."

o What is your energy level when you examine the item?

  - Clothing that fits and makes you feel fabulous raises your energy level.

Select a basic core wardrobe out of your current wardrobe consisting of easy-to-maintain, classic, elegant items, such as:

- 1–2 great pairs of jeans that fit you perfectly

- 1 crisp white no-iron blouse

- Black slacks

- Black dress shoes

- Great running shoes and clothing for whatever type of fitness you're into

- Warm boots, coat, and gloves

- 1–2 great suits (if your career or social calendar requires)

- Ladies: 1 black dress and skirt

- Seasonal accessories in the latest colors

- Basic shirts, dresses, slacks, skirts, and shorts

Less is more (keeping a few great trendy pieces and some fun costume jewelry is a low-cost way to boost your options).

Creating outfits out of what you have left in your closet is the most overlooked part of the day. Schedule a second session just to compile the outfits before you go shopping. It is the key to maintaining a great wardrobe. Otherwise, you have just weeded out the obviously bad items and not really created a wardrobe that works for you.

Finish Wardrobe Day by only putting back into your closet what you love and fits you perfectly. Arrange by color in categories: work wardrobe, athletic wear, casual clothes.

Take all discards to the car to drop off at a consignment store, to sell, or give to a charity, family, or friends. Do this at your earliest opportunity so you are not going back to the discards to recontemplate.

Put the mending pile by the sewing machine and put away the cleaning supplies. (Remember to block off time to do the mending in your planner.) Take a look at the finished project and pat yourself on the back. Well done! You will enjoy the results for months.

Then store your "to-buy" list in a place where you'll be able to find it quickly when you're ready to go shopping.

up-to-date on a budget. You do not need tons of clothes. Think of the "less is more" concept, using simple, elegant, clean, classic, and easy-to-maintain looks. Or think of this concept: build on what you have (or start where you are). Think of building a basic wardrobe with inexpensive seasonal items added to it.

We can cut a beautiful figure, as Frances Mayes says in her book *Bella Tuscany*, by dressing and grooming well without a mountain of clothing.

I know there are those of you who say "not it" to this concept of being in style; you are just not into fashion. That's fine. Move along to another section of the book that speaks to you. But if you've felt overwhelmed by clothes shopping, doing a Wardrobe Day (and subsequent shopping trip) is a way to deal with that. It's a method you can at least consider. Sometimes saying you're "just not into fashion" is a cop-out—you actually have a belief you cannot afford a wardrobe, or what you do in life does not require a polished look, which really reflects your lack of confidence. It shows you do not care. When your behavior shows you do not care, remember that actions speak louder than words. The relationships around us are hurt because we are telling others we do not care or lack confidence in ourselves. I think of people I coach who are passed up for promotions or are divorced. One thing we discover as we work together in coaching is that they stopped caring about what they looked like.

> "We see but we don't see—the gorgeous man in the Armani suit taking his espresso in the bar, glancing at La Republica. In Italy, there's a concept of la bella figura, cutting a beautiful figure. The gorgeous man in Armani might live in a depressing back room of a store. At least he can dress well and go out in the piazza in a cloud of devine cologne."
>
> —FRANCES MAYES, *BELLA TUSCANY* [70]

GETTING RID OF WHAT YOU NEED TO

One issue that trips people up when going through their wardrobe, especially when it comes to what to keep or get rid of, is their emotional attachment to clothes. In Sarah Ban Breathnach's book *Romancing the Ordinary: A Year of Simple Splendor*, she shares a story about a woman who bought an expensive black lace cocktail dress for a special date with a guy. When the relationship turned out to be "not it," the dress was always a reminder. Yet she convinced herself each time she cleaned out her closet not to get rid of it. To her, it cost too much money to give away. Still, she could not get over her feelings of frustration, disappointment, and anger around the dress so she could wear it again. Finally she did give it away, passing it on to a friend who looked good in it and made it her "lucky in love" outfit.

"It's easy for us to get rid of clothes we've physically outgrown," Ban Breathnach writes. "But severing the emotional threads that bind us, whether they're silk, wool, or gossamer, requires unconditional commitment to our future happiness and sometimes that desire takes longer than we think it should to make its way down to soul level."[72]

> "The real waste in clothing comes not in the buying, but in not using it."
>
> —**SARAH BAN BREATHNACH,** *ROMANCING THE ORDINARY: A YEAR OF SIMPLE SPLENDOR*[71]

Sometimes people have a hard time whittling down their wardrobe to only the basics, with a few fun add-ons. What if they get rid of something they later want again? I advised my client Rachel, who had an overabundance of clothing, to pick just one or two of the eight pairs of black slacks she had, or three of her twelve white blouses. To make that easier for her, I told her not to get rid of the rest of her clothes, but put them in an extra/off-season area so she could have her everyday current closet and shop the extras closet if she decided she wanted something one morning. This is a great strategy when you have a lot of items, many of which you're ambivalent on whether to keep or not. See how it feels with the luxury of a closet full of space, where all your clothes fit, you have something you can wear with every piece, and all the pieces are in season. Play with combinations to find a seasonal wardrobe you feel great in.

On your next seasonal Wardrobe Day, you can go through the clothes you decided to stash away because you weren't sure about giving them away. Have you worn them since storing them there? Do you really need them? Feel the power of giving them away if you haven't worn them in the last few months. Just give them away. Get a tax deduction. Another option is to sell them at a resale store. I did this for a while when I was losing weight and I took the money I made to cover the cost of my next size-smaller clothing. That was fun!

⚠ TIP

If you're buying new hangers for your closet and you don't live alone, buy a different color for any other family members living with you. That way when laundry day comes and you need to hang up clothes, you can grab extras from every closet and know quickly what clothes can go on what hanger, also making it easier to quickly put away the clothes. Donate the old hangers when you donate your clothing so you aren't tempted to use them again.

THINK ABOUT A CLOSET MAKEOVER

While doing your Wardrobe Day, think about your closet itself. Does it need to be painted? Need new components so it's better organized? Contemplate these changes. Do you need more shelving? Baskets? A mirror, dresser, or chair to create a dressing room if you have the space? Buy matching clothes hangers, even if they are the cheap plastic ones. Using matching hangers is a fast way to create a boutique look.

Maybe you won't make all the changes to your closet this season, but you can plan to do more next season so you have space that really serves you best.

GROOMING

Another way to look your best is to focus on grooming. In fact, consider spending less on your clothing and more on grooming. Make sure your hair and nails are done impeccably. Is your makeup up to date? You can have all the clothes in the world and still make a terrible impression because of improper grooming. When you get compliments on your hair, makeup, skin, or nails, you know you're doing well.

If you think you're due for an update in the hairstyle department (or it's been more than a few years since you changed your hairstyle), go through current catalogs and magazines and look for a hairstyle that might suit you. You can also think about a makeup update this way. Have fun contemplating your current look while letting go of how you looked in the past. Have you ever seen someone who wears the same hairstyle and makeup they wore in high school?

Also take time to learn how to work with your hair. If it is frizzy, do you need a special product to tame it? Are you sick of fighting the way your hair is naturally, by trying to force it into a style suited for a different hair type? My hair was baby-fine and straight growing up, and as it became gray, the texture became curly and frizzy. I read in a magazine that shifting hormone levels for women decrease the diameters of our hair by strand and increase frizziness.[73] Accept your new texture and change your styling routine to match it. I spent a lot of time blowing my hair dry and flat ironing it, but it took a lot of effort and did not stay. So I learned to let it air dry with a conditioning product meant to tame it down into soft curls. I get more compliments with this, and since I color, the gray is gone.

Some of you might be ready to go gray. One of my clients decided, after coloring for years, that she could not continue keeping up with her roots. Mary had been using a temporary color as she thought about going gray, so her roots that had the temp color were quite long. She stopped coloring and gradually let the temporary color get washed out, pulled her hair back one summer under a baseball cap, and by fall cut it short. Next she grew the short cut out to the length she wanted and had the style she envisioned. What a transformation.

Remember: when you stop getting compliments, it's time for a change.

Don't forget to create a spa day for yourself on a regular basis. Maybe you have date night on Saturday night, so you plan your spa time a day or two beforehand, or as you get ready for your date. Scheduling a spa day at an actual spa is a wonderful treat, although the cost can really add up over time. If money is no object, and you don't mind running out to have your services done by others, then by all means do it.

> **⚠ TIP**
>
> Wear glasses? One of the things I notice often is dirty glasses. Take time to clean them. Not only will you see better, you will look better—another win-win.

However, if you are on a tighter budget or prefer privacy and it makes more sense to do your spa day at home, then make it special and fun. A hair color at the spa can be well over one hundred dollars, but a box of color is under ten dollars. I do both; I go to the salon for special occasions and do the home spa treatments in between. I do this with my hair color, manicures, and pedicures. I have a professional handle brow waxes and haircuts for me.

When my sons were younger, I purchased a buzzer and gave my boys haircuts to save money. You can pick up a small personal trimmer for about ten dollars, and all those little unwanted hairs can be zipped off. As we age, we get hair in places we don't want and this is a great option to handle them in the privacy of your home and keep expenses in check. I'm surprised by how many people don't know about these. The point is to take care of yourself so you feel terrific about how you look without spending a fortune.

For you guys out there, find a great barber and visit him frequently. It is well worth the money. Or buy a buzzer and trim your hair at home with the help of a family member or friend. Shavers and personal trimmers are a must for you guys; use them daily. A great moisturizing lotion is very important to keep your skin looking great—use SPF 15 when outdoors. How about an SPF lip balm to go with it? Chapped lips are not cute. Also guys, think about your pearly whites. Keep them white with whitening strips or have them whitened at the dental office. Most of the tips for wardrobe sorting apply to you as well. You may not carry a purse, but you may have a backpack for your laptop, or gym bags. When your closet is in order, it will take less time to get ready, and if you neatly hang clothing, you will not need to iron as much. And finally, put your best foot forward by making sure your shoes are clean, polished, and in great shape.

When it comes to skin care and makeup for you ladies, keep it simple. I have seen both extremes, those who do nothing and are comfortable with it and those who look like clowns because they have so much makeup on.

⚠ SPA DAY TIPS

If you're going to do your own personal spa day at home, make it fun by using special towels, bath salts, music, and candles. When it comes to do your manicure, consider using a basic clear nail polish. I've found that works best for me, as I can get extremely busy while I consult businesses and get to the gym. Clear polish doesn't show if there's a chip or it starts to wear off as much. Also, make sure to use good quality hand cream to further improve the condition of your hands.

⚠ SPA DAY TIPS

I am a lipstick girl and have many tubes going at once. What I've found is that the lipstick has about 1/4 inch inside the tube that can be scooped out and used with a lip brush. I found a couple ceramic boxes with hinged lids to keep in my bathroom, one for pinks, one for berry colors, and one for brown-toned lip color. The colors do not have to be all the same, just from the same color family. When I add the remnants of a tube, I mix the colors together. This saves me money when I use them up at home. I've also found pillboxes at the drug store, and instead of pills, I put in leftover lipstick and carry this and the lip brush with me in my purse and travel and gym bags.

I've been a Mary Kay beauty consultant for over twelve years and a glamour girl since my teens, and I've found that making sure my skin is clean and moisturized with basic makeup that matches my skin tone keeps me looking my best and helps me stay on a budget. You can spend a fortune if you want to, but most of us don't. Working as a skin care and glamour consultant, I saw many large collections filled with buying mistakes that took up way too much valuable real estate and were costly. When I sort through a collection with a client, most of it has been kept so long it isn't any good anymore, anyway.

Find a couple of shades of neutral lip color to wear with anything and a few great basic eye colors, a good mascara, foundation, and eyebrow pencil. Then you're set. This doesn't have to cost a fortune. Have a basic daytime look and an evening look for special occasions. Many women I have consulted wear one look, look the same always, and when the special event arrives, they don't look all that special. They look the same old, same old. Avoid that. Again, remember to have fun!

Some women get carried away thinking that looking good will compensate for other areas they're lacking in—experience for work, for example. It's better to spend more on training and let your natural confidence exude without being overly made up. If you find you are wearing makeup thinking it will cover up something inside, think again. It may only make it more obvious. Another thing I see is women with a makeup look suited for someone much younger—this actually makes them look older.

For those of you who are a bit older, don't neglect moisturizing your neck and hands. These areas show your true age faster than others.

Also remember that no matter what your age is, wearing a smile is one of your greatest assets.

Organizing Your Personal Care Items

Your stash of personal care items can get unruly if you don't organize it. Take an hour and pull all of your personal care stuff from your bathroom, gym bag, travel bag, and anywhere else you have items stored. Make sure you have everything you want, ready to dash out the door at a moment's notice, with everything clean and organized. If you believe you're too busy to do this periodically, press pause and see where you want to slow down. It doesn't have to take a lot of time, especially once it's under control. Just stay on top of it—like housework, which we'll get to in the next chapter.

Create a shopping list of items you need. What are you low on or out of? Go through each category: shower supplies—do you have the soaps and shampoos you love? Conditioner? A shaver? A towel for your gym bag if your gym does not supply them? Antiperspirant? What about a nail clipper, tweezers, and Q-tips? Create a travel or gym set of toiletries and personal care supplies so you can have them ready at a moment's notice. You never know when you may need to quickly run out the door to meet someone at the gym or want to take a spur of the moment trip for fun or have to zip out the door for an emergency.

When putting together your gym or travel set of toiletries, use small sample bottles and refill them to take up less space.

Also take this time to get rid of stuff you don't want, that is too old, or you just don't use anymore. If you don't like it, get rid of it! How often do we hang onto stuff we do not like because we paid good money for it or have not replaced it with something we really like? For example, while traveling I ran out of hair conditioner and picked up something convenient. It got me through the trip, although I realized I did not like the smell of it. After the trip, I kept refilling my travel bottle with this conditioner just to use it up, and each time I used that bad-smelling conditioner, it would irritate me and my energy diminished. Negative emotions can grow if not checked. By getting rid of this conditioner, I got rid of the opportunity for a negative emotion to arise in me. I got rid of the potential trickledown effect—when negative emotions build they can cause us to act ugly. A negative downward spiral can start just that easily or quickly. Of course, there are bigger things in our lives we tolerate, which may be considered harder to dispose of. Start noticing what's in your life that you really don't like and how great you feel when it goes away, freeing up energy and allowing positive emotions to grow. Start small. Just start noticing.

KEEPING YOUR TEETH CLEAN

Yes, your smile is one of the most special things you can share with others, so why not keep your teeth as white as you can and your breath as fresh as you can? A side benefit of removing the plaque is that you protect your teeth and heart. Commit to scheduling an appointment twice a year with your dentist to have your teeth professionally cleaned.

Then, of course, brush often and floss daily. These are simple consistent practices that have so many benefits. According to the American Dental Association's website, taking good care of your teeth and gums isn't just about preventing cavities or bad breath. "The mouth is a window into the health of the body. It can show if you are not eating foods that are best for you or signal that you may be at risk for a disease. Diseases that affect the entire body may first be noticed because of mouth sores or other oral problems."[74]

Also, studies have shown that periodontal (gum) disease may be connected with diabetes and cardiovascular disease (heart disease and stroke).

By taking good care of your teeth, you will not only avoid these problems, but feel better about yourself; caring for your body is telling yourself that you are important and worth caring for.

THE IMPORTANCE OF TAKING CARE OF YOURSELF

Over the years I have worked with many people who do not take care of themselves. They put others first and neglect themselves— they don't take the time to think about what they wear, what they look like, even sometimes whether they have showered or brushed their teeth. They aren't able to bring their best selves forward. Often I see them in "victim" mode, where they opt not to better their circumstances, blaming others, having a "not their fault" attitude, sometimes gaining something from others because of their self-pity. Some of these people (often women) never learned to take care of themselves in the first place. They either do not grow up with good role models, or they end up burnt out from caring for their children or their own parents.

Often trying to do it all, they end up at the end of their ropes. If you find yourself there, press pause; draw a line in the sand, and say, "Enough." Take a physical break when you recognize a need for a change. Grab a pen and paper with a beverage of your choice, and find a quiet spot where you can be uninterrupted and ask yourself what you want right now. What do you want to see change? What can you do about this situation now? Start writing. Once you have an initial brain dump, take a deep breath and blow it out hard. Do it again. Take in two more breaths and blow them out really hard and say, "Ahhhhhh."

Take any initial action you can to feel better. Next time you have a moment, go deeper and ask, "What would I want in my life if time and money were not a consideration?" Maybe you want someone to take the kids for an hour so you can sleep, or someone to scrub the bathrooms for you weekly. Whatever it is, write it down. Maybe you just want to be outside more, or home more, or on the beach more. What you identify might be very doable, very soon.

In the meantime, think simple luxuries—ways to bring everyday elegance into your life.

Money doesn't have to be an issue. Maybe bartering is an answer. "I'll clean your bathrooms if you watch my kids," you might say to a friend. What are you willing to do? Once you start and your needs are being met, what you want on your list will change.

Take time to write down what makes you feel good—everything you can think of. Keep this list in a place where you can find it when you are feeling bad, and do something on the list to feel better; do something as soon as you recognize you are not feeling the way you want to.

It could be a bubble bath, time in the sauna, swimming, yoga, Nia, walks, a pedicure or manicure, having your hair styled, having a clean house or clean car, running, riding your bike, traveling, studying French, listening to music, drinking wine, dining at a really nice place, eating healthy food, being on top of your finances, making your bed, visiting friends, being on the beach, sailing, boating, shopping, reading, having a cup of tea, decorating—there are lots of options.

By feeling good on the inside, you are more likely to put the effort into looking good on the outside, whether that be how you dress, style your hair, or take care of your body.

TIME MANAGEMENT

Believe it or not, time management has something to do with your personal image—it affects how you show up in life. When you are on top of your projects and calendars, you exude confidence, and your stress level is down. When you show up with what you need all pulled together, you are attractive. When you scramble to pull yourself together at the last minute, looking disheveled, running late because you're zipping into the store on the way to the party to buy the card and gift, you show up frazzled. Want that? "Not it." Or what about showing up at work with two different shoes on, maybe the same style, but in two different colors, a black and a brown, because you were dashing out the door? I can think of countless ways of showing up unprepared. And those are "not it." When you are running on adrenaline, it shows. You may not realize it, but this affects your personal image in a big way.

To manage your time better, be disciplined about using a calendar, writing down everything you want to do on a certain day. When something new needs to be added to your calendar, write it down right away. Otherwise, notes about upcoming events or things you want to accomplish go floating in and out of your notice by being tucked here and there, sometimes found much later and too late to do anything about.

For an easy, inexpensive time management system, on a spiral notebook or a clipboard with scrap paper (recycled from the mail), draw the grid below with room for tasks to get done during the week listed underneath:

September 19 to 25

M 19	T 20	W 21	TH 22
Work			
Errands—p.m.	Bake cookies	Work	
Return the buying mistake	Work		
Banking	Bible study, 6:30 –8:30		
Gym			

F 23	SAT 24	SUN 25
Food prep for picnic	Early a.m. drive	Church
Pack for weekend	Picnic with family	Brunch with family
	Fishing	Outdoor activity
		Prep for next week

Leave space for a list of overall weekly tasks, which could look like this:

- Magazine sort—take discards to gym.

- Check new gym class schedule and add to fall calendar.

- Check on status of _____.

- Follow up on _____.

If you do not wish to create your own planner, the above can be purchased on my website, www.systemsforchange.net. If you are more high-tech, use your computer, smartphone, or tablet to track your daily calendar.

When deciding what can be on your schedule, think about what your priorities are. Let's say they are faith, family, friends, fitness, and finance. How will you live by these priorities?

- Invite your friends to attend church?

- Make time as a family to do photo projects together, have a family game or movie night, or go on a hike together?

- Go to the gym with family and friends?

- Set up a budget and then take the time to keep track of your spending?

Add your priorities to your calendar.

Also establish great daily habits. Stay on top of your finances daily by looking at your accounts online. Do your gym workout before work, using the gym in your office building if there is one. Bring a lunch to work to save money and pack items with healthy ingredients so you are eating better. Make your bed every morning and wash dishes at each meal to keep your home at its best, which helps you feel your best.

Add your great habits to your calendar.

Again, these are suggestions, tools, tips, and examples for you to look at how you're living your life. For examples that resonate, say, "I like the idea; this will work for me," or "I want to try it." For those ideas that don't resonate, say "not it" and move on.

More tips on time management will be found in the "Your Home" and "Your Career" chapters.

HOMEWORK

1. Commit to doing a Wardrobe Day with a friend from start to finish.

2. Go through your toiletries to ensure you have everything you want for all your "bags," like your gym and travel bags. Discard all the odds and ends, and create a shopping list for missing items.

3. Treat yourself to a spa day—at home or away and see how much better you feel about yourself and notice how others respond.

4. Are you consistently using a calendar? If not, get one, make one like the one above, or use your smartphone, or computer. Find one you like and will use. Order from my website, www.systemsforchange.net. Next, press pause, get out your pen and favorite beverage, and spend twenty or thirty minutes blocking off time for your priorities. Not sure what that looks like? Take a step back and identify your priorities first and determine the activities to add to the calendar based on your values.

5. If you find yourself at the end of your rope because you've been taking care of everyone else, press pause; draw a line in the sand, and say, "Enough." Take a physical break when you recognize a need for a change. Grab a pen and paper with a beverage of your choice, and find a quiet spot where you can be uninterrupted for a short while and ask yourself what you want right now. What do you want to see change? What can you do about this situation now? Start writing. Take any initial action you can to feel better. Next time you have a moment, go deeper and ask, "What would I want in my life if time and money were not a consideration?" Maybe you want someone to take the kids for an hour so you can sleep, or someone to scrub the bathrooms for you weekly. Whatever it is, write it down. Maybe you just want to be outside more, or home more, or on the beach more. What you identify might be very doable, very soon.

Your Home

"When we clean and order our homes, we are somehow also cleaning and ordering ourselves."[75] That quote from Sarah Ban Breathnach's *Romancing the Ordinary: A Year of Simple Splendor* really sums up how we can approach our homes when we decide what we've been doing is "not it." Keeping an orderly house helps reduce stress, lets us focus on other important matters, and gives us a sense of peace, knowing we have a place that lets us clear our minds and recharge and relax. All of these things help us keep order in our lives outside of our homes too.

Ban Breathnach writes:

> For many years I could not reflect order on the outside of my life because there was no order within. Psychically exhausted and overwhelmed by the emotional and physical energy of trying to hide the unsightly in plain view, I lived reactively rather than reverently. Now whenever I feel stuck or mired in frustrating or distressing situations that I can't seem to change, I take a look at the piles surrounding me, whether its files, newspapers waiting to be read, or cookbooks waiting to be reshelved. Then I start sifting, sorting, throwing out, and putting away.

I find putting my belongings in place helps me to find order within. For just as we can't really think clearly in clutter, when we're messy, we feel unfocused and frustrated. I know myself well enough to realize that life is messy, and there will always be a little mess. But I also know that there is great relief in a tidy sanctuary. Whether it be a room or a relationship, sometimes we need to clean up.[76]

Remember what I suggested in the "Your Personal Image" chapter: if you don't have time to do something, press pause and look at your schedule. Taking care of yourself and your home comes first; these are parts of filling your bucket so your bucket is overflowing to share with others.

Most of us don't think of fixing up our homes as a pleasurable pursuit because we usually approach it as a feat requiring more physical, psychic, creative, and financial resources than would be necessary to scale the most formidable mountain in the world, as Sarah Ban Breathnach shares in *Simple Abundance: A Daybook of Comfort and Joy*.[77] However, if we approach our house as a hobby instead of a chore, maybe we'll find the time to stain the front door, refinish a dresser, varnish the hardwood floor, or create a nook of our own.

Your home can provide you with not only a place to eat and clean up, but also a place to rest your body and mind, a place to connect with others on a deeper level. Yet, the sad truth is that more often than not, people's homes are not that sanctuary. And that can lead to running toward other "shelters," whether that be depression, addictions, workaholism, or perfectionism, as Kathryn Robyn writes in her book, *Spiritual Housecleaning: Healing the Space within by Beautifying the Space around You*.[78]

To avoid all that, I want to share some ways to create a sense of order in your environment, beginning with your home. I'll start by sharing a story about a client, Laura. Laura was embarrassed for anyone to see her home because it was so small and full of stuff, it was bursting at the seams. Many times, items were so buried in the clutter that she bought replacements for them, ultimately adding to the already full space. She had no energy left to deal with it all and really felt stuck. On top of that, her family didn't support her making changes. She had given up because in prior attempts to clean, her work was soon undone by the chaos of her life and her unsupporting family. Why try again? Why? Because she had absolutely had it. She wanted to change something, anything, at the point we met.

She was a single parent of three elementary school-aged children, working full time, juggling all their activities. When we began, we started small and implemented simple solutions to create a more stable home environment. I listened to her and coached her. First, an out-of-the-way space in her basement was set aside for "staging" or sorting while she went room by room. As she cleared rooms, she had that space to gather the odds and ends, to sort for storage and donations. She allowed her children to keep their rooms the way they wanted without her interference while she focused on the rest of the house. She began with the main bathroom and half-bath because they were small and unsanitary. She deep-cleaned them, painting them and putting out fresh towels. Her goal

> ⚠ **TIP**
>
> Create a date night or a family night where everyone pitches in for an hour or two for the weekly chores; plus, have daily chores to stay on top of it. Establishing good habits allows for more fun on the weekends, rather than a mess building into an overwhelming avalanche of work for Saturday and Sunday. If you just can't wrap your mind around this idea, get a housekeeper. Pay the price and don't stress or struggle about it. Having fun with your family is more important than fighting about who has to clean the toilet.

was to maintain those rooms while expanding out to the rest of the house. We began with a daily, then weekly, cleaning schedule (shown on page 191) to do the minimum as she gained control of the mess and began feeling better. Once she began establishing the cleaning list herself, her family saw her changes and responded positively. She was off their backs while she focused on what she could do.

Gradually, she began asking for help from her family with the daily items first, then the weekly. When they were helping, she would show them where the cleaning supplies were and what they could use for their rooms (yes, the power of suggestion), and they actually cleaned their rooms, their own way. Her oldest son did an outstanding job on his from top to bottom and invited her in. When she went to look, she noticed something sticking out from under the bed and learned that he stuffed much of the clutter under it. She complimented him on the nice job and they both laughed with the under-bed storage he created. She did not get mad; she just made light of it and left the room. It wasn't long before he cleaned that up too. Did his room stay clean? No, but it got better. Did the situation with her uncooperative family get better? Over time. They tested the waters to see how far they could push her and she stood firm with her new boundaries. Her problem middle child was a challenge, digging in his heels and keeping his space a disaster, and she realized her youngest daughter had her wrapped around her little finger (Laura had been giving in to her).

It took her about ten months to clear the whole house, and when they get really busy now, she presses pause, takes a break in the action, and doesn't let things get bad like they were before. She has also learned to hold family meetings, assigning tasks without being the authoritarian she was in the past, and sharing with the children how the home could function best for them. The kids often have great ideas for her too, and like being included in creating ways to keep their house in order.

My client Jane's problem was different. She had been spending eight to twelve hours every weekend cleaning her house, making sure things were perfect for her family and in case someone came over. She liked having a clean, orderly, spotless home. But then she started getting tired of spending every weekend cleaning; she realized most other people were out living their lives and having fun on Saturdays and Sundays. She still wanted an orderly home; she just didn't want to spend all of her precious time to get it. Jane and I discussed her perfectionism, and she pressed pause and we discussed her findings. She noticed she wanted help from her family; she wanted them to have fun together on the weekends. After implementing a new cleaning schedule, Jane was happy to find that now she and her family focused more on the fun activities they wanted in their lives; preparing for activities such as meals and family outings and cleaning up afterwards by unpacking the car, doing laundry, or dishes just became part of the drill. "My family is much happier now that I am not acting out the perfectionist," she said in appreciation after implementing the new system. Her family appreciates her more now that she is not wound up so tight regarding how things have to look; she is no longer rigid with them on how she expects them to behave. Jane learned to lighten up and not be so bothered with appearances. Her family has a good time, even when they are cleaning together; they learned how to make it fun! Wins all around.

Here is a sample of the cleaning system I shared with both Laura and Jane (tweaking to their individual needs as was necessary):

Cleaning Schedule

Daily

- Put dirty clothing in hamper; wash when full.

- Straighten up bed.

- Put garbage in the trash can, and recycling in proper containers.

- Put dirty dishes in dishwasher (run when full); wipe sink and counters.

- Fill pet dishes with food and water in the morning and evening.

- Put needed paperwork and bills in home office or entryway desk "in basket." Recycle junk mail.

Weekly

- Do laundry (wash sheets first).

- Wipe down kitchen counters, appliances, and sink with multipurpose cleaner.

- Clean sink, toilet, bathtub, and showers (spritz shower with cleaner first, but scrub down last).

- Make sure you wipe down toilet flush handles and door handles, especially if anyone has been ill.

- Dust furniture and shelves.

- Clean mirrors and glass tops of furniture with glass cleaner.

- Take trash to dumpster.

- Vacuum.

- Wash tile and wood floors.

- Water plants.

- File paperwork and shred anything with personally identifiable information.

- Clean cars inside and out.

Monthly

- Clean out bad food and wipe out refrigerator.

- Deep clean one area per month. Here's a sample of what to do when:

o   January: taxes and paperwork/office area

o   February: family room

o   March: master bedroom, bath, and closet

o   April: stairwells, hallways, and closets

o   May: spring outdoor chores; raking, planting, doing paint projects, organizing your garage

o   June: kitchen

o   July: guestroom and bath

o   August: laundry, entry, and pantry

o   October: fall outdoor chores; prep for winter projects, clean up planters, rake

o   November: dining room

o   December: getting your home ready to celebrate Christmas

Spring/Fall

- Clean windows and patio doors.

- Wash shower curtain in washing machine (gentle cycle/cold water; partly dry and hang back in bathroom immediately) or replace.

- Clean light fixtures.

- Wash walls, fronts and insides of cabinets, doorknobs, light switches, and garbage cans.

- Wash bedspreads and blankets (do this at the Laundromat to make it go faster; take snacks).

- Touch up paint on walls where marked up, especially halls and stairwells.

Holidays

- Redecorate by swapping out seasonal décor.

- Do your deep cleaning day in advance so all you have to do is decorate and have fun!

⚠ CLEANING SCHEDULING TIPS

Break down your weekly cleaning tasks. Some things make sense to do all at one time, but others, such as filing paperwork, can be done before or after you pull out the cleaning supplies. Schedule your monthly deep-clean project in your Systems For Change calendar. By intentionally blocking off the time, you are more likely to do it. Also, when scheduling your monthly project, you may want to break it down to do different parts at different times. Let's say you want to clean the carpets. Do other projects first and schedule that separately. Or you may want to redecorate, whether that means painting walls, replacing window coverings, or furniture. Break down these tasks and schedule in the proper order.

When my friend Deb Lansdowne, an interior designer, and I developed this cleaning schedule in the 1990s, we looked at each room, one at a time; we asked ourselves, "How does this room function? Is this how I'd like it to function? What would I change if I could? Do I need more storage? Is it a multifunctional space that needs more definition? If I do not like it, and don't want to spend time in it, what can I change? Is it a better fit for someone else in the family or another activity?"

When I was a girl, I was taught to have a place for everything. Even though I did not always practice this concept, it was at those times I didn't that I quickly realized how important it was. The times I was in chaos and confusion were when I wanted order; I knew how much easier it was to automatically put something away where it belongs so I could automatically go right to it and FIND it when I wanted it. When you have a place for everything and everything in its place, you preserve your sanity. There is an old saying I remember, probably from one of my grandma's church cookbooks, that goes: "If you take it out, put it back; if you open it, close it." My friend Deb Lansdowne's grandma put it another way: "Why lay it down there when, with a few more steps, you can have it put away?"

When organizing an area, think of SPACE: Sort, Purge, Assign a home, Containerize, Equalize (which means doing what you can to maintain order).

ORGANIZING 101

First, before you start organizing your home, create a staging area to take items for sorting. Then, come up with areas that are available for storage within your home. Think outside the box. Where do you use the item you are looking to store? In the kitchen, store recipes; in the dining room, extra candles; in the guest room closet, desk, or dresser, a special occasion binder with extra greeting cards

=== ⚠ **MORE CLEANING AND ORGANIZING TIPS** ===

- Create a cleaning closet to make retrieving what you need, and seeing if you need to restock supplies, convenient.

- Store all your paper cleaning products on the top, heavy vacuums and buckets on the bottom, and baskets of tools and supplies at eye level and in arm's reach for efficiency.

This way, you can quickly get what you need and actually get your cleaning chores done, rather than searching for what you need.

and small gifts; in your sunroom or near a reading area, what you need for your Bible study or dream-building sessions; and on and on. Organize an out-of-sight, easy-access spot where you use something. Baskets and decorative boxes are storage options to consider. Keep it easy and consistent.

By storing things where you use them, you will be more efficient, saving time and energy on looking for items. I have multiples of the same items, such as pens, notepads, and scissors, in various spots, such as the kitchen, bathroom, office, my purse, and my reading nook, so I have them when I need them.

What about those of you with young children who have toys everywhere? If the kids got everything they wanted from Santa, sort through their old toys. Toss any broken ones, and then designate a spot for the remaining toys (and just for toys), so the kids know where they are to put them back. Do this when the kids are not with you, or you will hear, "No, Mom, not that one. You can't pack away my little special stuffed animal." When the toys are out of sight, they are out of mind. When fewer toys are in play there's less mess when the kids pull them out. Have a bookshelf just for their books. Also take four boxes and put some of the leftover toys and books in there. Each week you can pull out one of these boxes so the kids have something new to play with or read. Rotating these toys and books gives the kids something new to experience, and any toys or books that don't get played with can go in the pile for the next rummage sale or in the donation box. Store items that are not age-appropriate, but

---

⚠ CAR TIP

Your vehicle is part of your home environment too (especially if you spend a lot of time in it each week). So it's important to purchase a vehicle you love to drive that suits your family requirements. Then maintain it properly, and keep it clean and clutter free, just like your home. Then it will last you a good while and you will feel more at peace in your clean, well-running car.

⚠ TIP

To declutter your home, put in place as many organizational systems as you can. For instance, have a routine when you come home that will keep your entryway free of junk and keep the mail you just brought in sorted.

When you walk through your door, drop your keys and mail on an entry desk. Remove your shoes and jacket immediately and put them in the appropriate spots, so you will not be searching for them later. Have a letter opener on your desk and a garbage can nearby. Also store notepads, pens, stamps, envelopes, and coupons in your entry desk. Have an in-box for mail in a desk drawer. This box can be sorted weekly, and bills taken care of, junk mail tossed, and important financial statements or insurance information filed. Another drawer can be used for storing gloves and hats. Also keep this in mind when it comes to the mail—OHIO: Only Handle It Once. Don't get it from the mailbox, set it on the counter, move it to the office, open it, etc.

---

you want to keep, in two boxes—one for items they will use when they're older and one for items they have outgrown but you want to save for other little ones (other toys that are not age-appropriate can be donated or given away).

What about a junk drawer? Do you have one? I've seen many hold tools and odds and ends that do not belong anywhere—keys to who knows what, buttons found, batteries, and on and on. When we are using prime real estate like a kitchen drawer for such things, perhaps we need to consider moving these items to a small box in the utility room as a temporary holding place until they can be put in their rightful place or when we can determine if they belong in the garbage. Tools can be stored in a toolbox in the utility room or garage, wherever you have an out-of-the-way space.

When finished with a project, make sure to pick it up and put it away. Sounds simple; however, there are those of us who bounce from mess to mess. I know many times I've had multiple projects going at the same time, and when I would leave them out with great intentions of getting right back to them, life happened and I ended up with multiple messes instead. Better to put your project away and take it back out each time you need it. You define how you want your space to be; sometimes a home is "lived in," meaning it is basically clean yet life is in process, rather than a perfectionist's place or the other extreme, a mess. Even when you're working on something, make sure to close all doors and drawers as you go. I have gone into many homes as an insurance agent or Mary Kay consultant to find the kitchen cabinet doors are standing open—and what's displayed is usually a mess.

**If you don't have time to do it right,
when will you have time to do it over?**

THINK ABOUT HOW MUCH YOU ARE STORING

I'm all about buying things before you need them, especially when they are on sale, but with a word of warning: think about how much stuff you are storing in your home. There's a difference between getting your next bottle of expensive shampoo on a rare sale and storing boatloads of paper products just to save fifty cents. Think of the storage space in your home as expensive real estate. How much is what you're buying costing in the long run? Is it costing more real estate than it should? I know several people who buy ahead at garage sales and have tubs of clothing for years as their children grow. If you have the space, it's a great concept unless you get carried away (ever watch the show *Hoarders?*). You may not need

IT'S ALL IN THE DETAILS

Staying on top of small details with just a little regular maintenance makes life so much easier. We are bombarded daily with so many little pieces of information, having a place to easily put them makes for a stress-free life. If you find yourself in an avalanche of stuff, press pause, sort it out, get back to feeling on top of things, and move on.

- Create a "how-to" binder, a little instruction book for infrequent processes, such as how to load music from a CD to a computer to an iPod playlist, how to do a mail merge with your computer's word processing software, how to operate the voicemail and call forwarding features on your phone, and how to download photos from your camera or phone onto your computer and file them.

- Create a password notebook for all your electronic passwords, but stash it away in a very secure location (lock it up if you can and do not keep it on your computer.)

- Make a list of all-important items and where they might be found—your birth certificate or passport, important documents, keys, passwords, credit cards.

- Create a home manual binder.

  - o Using page protectors in a three-ring binder, slip in all the manuals for your appliances and electronics.

  - o Store this in your office or an area in the furnace room or basement, anywhere out of the way.

- Create a garden binder to remind yourself what you planted and where in your yard.

- o   Use a three-ring binder with notepaper, page protectors, and sketch pad.

- o   Determine what is planted where and note it on a sketched map or notes.

- o   As you add to your gardens, this is an easy way to keep track of what you love and what is "not it."

- o   Keep a three-ring pencil pouch in the binder to store the plastic plant description stakes that come with the plants when you buy them.

- o   Keep articles you wish to save on garden topics in the page protectors.

- Create a sewing binder with all instruction manuals for your sewing machines and sergers, plus instructions on calculating fabric yardage requirements.

- Create a travel binder to gather information as it comes in for everywhere you may want to visit.

  - o   Use page protectors to hold maps and brochures and notepaper to capture recommendations you receive from people.

  - o   Periodically pull out your information and plan your next adventure. (This is a great date night activity. Planning a trip to Mexico? Bring out the margaritas, chips, and salsa. Going to Italy? Well, then it's pasta night!)

as big a house as you think if you can eliminate clutter and watch the amount of storage you require. Really consider this when you decide to downsize. I like the "use it or lose it" concept. If I have not used something in a year, I *really* consider if I want to keep it. Here's another rule we have in our home: something in, something out. That means when you add something new, you get rid of an older item to make space for it. It's simple, even though I know it's easier said than done. I have spent so much time and money over the years accumulating stuff and getting rid of it. I had an insurance office ten years ago and just now parted with the remaining remnants of that office.

Last summer, I picked up salad bowls at a garage sale that were the perfect size and match for my dishes, but I had think about where they would go once I ran them through the dishwasher. I usually go through my cupboards to clear out things that aren't being used in spring and fall. However, I needed to make room

---

HINTS FROM ONE MESSY PERSON TO ANOTHER*

- Don't get sidetracked looking through old photos and letters when you are organizing your home. Stay on task.

- Don't make too many piles; you'll only have to sort through them again later.

- Don't overstuff a drawer; if something doesn't fit, put it somewhere else.

- Don't put something neat away into something messy. If you have to, refold all the sweaters before you start putting others into the drawer.

- Don't put something in the wrong place just to have it out of sight. You will lose it and then you will lose your mind trying to find it again. So make sure that everything has a place and everything goes in its own place.

- Don't let your mess overflow into someone else's space. Keep it to yourself.

- Don't abandon your work for a cup of coffee or tea. If you take a longer break than five minutes, you might never come back.

- Don't promise yourself you'll do it later. You won't.

- Do sit back and enjoy the view of your room with something wonderful to drink when you're finished, because it's probably not going to look like that for long. Now, take out the box with the old photos and letters. But remember to put it back again (and put your dirty glass back in the kitchen).

*These tips are paraphrased from Sarah Ban Breathnach's book *Romancing the Ordinary: A Year of Simple Splendor.*[79]

for these immediately. So I used the same process as when I do seasonal cleaning, only I limited myself to going through just a small section of storage space to create room for the bowls.

Before I begin to reorganize, I ask myself the following: How much space will it take? What am I no longer using that can be tossed or what am I using infrequently that can be moved to a spot a little farther away? I keep what I use daily close at hand and store the less frequently used items farther away. I use the same approach for my bathroom cabinets, linen closets, cleaning closet, and coat or clothing closets.

> ## ⚠ TIP
>
> I found a new favorite company to order natural products from online; I get a discount every time I order. I buy household cleaners, bath and beauty products, and vitamins and supplements all at the same time, and they're delivered to my door. I'm not only reaching a health goal, eliminating unnecessary chemicals from my environment and my body, but I'm not over-shopping by being tempted by stuff at the store. And I'm saving time by not having to go to store when I need one of these items. This time and money savings is a win-win!

Don't buy it, don't even be tempted, if you don't think you have space for it. Maybe you think you need to buy it because it's on sale and it's something you'll use. But by doing that time after time, you end up with an overabundance at home because you did that the last few times you shopped. Also people really don't save so much money with all this stocking up; buying for "good" deals is a trap. I used to do this, but I realized finally that these things go on sale all the time and why have my cupboards and closets bursting if I can just wait until the item goes on sale again? Having so many items cluttering up your storage area is ineffective and frustrating.

One more thing: don't forget to shop your house before spending more money on items you might need. More tips like this will be shared in the "Your Financial Goals" chapter.

KEEPING YOUR PANTRY, REFRIGERATOR, AND FREEZER ORGANIZED

You can also implement an organizational system for your pantry, refrigerator, and freezer. To do that, start by cleaning your cupboards each season to check for outdated canned and boxed items (look for expiration dates). For food in your refrigerator or freezer, consult in a cookbook or look online to see the recommended time to toss them.

I have a general rule for storing fresh produce or meats (which I shared in the "Your Nutrition" chapter): basically, keep these three to five days before freezing. I go through and toss old spices on a yearly basis, frozen items within one to three months, and canned goods within six months, unless the expiration date says otherwise. Dry goods, such as pasta, flour, sugar, and baking ingredients, can be kept in the cupboard three months, unless dated otherwise. For leftovers, do your best to use them up within five days, depending upon the ingredients. Use the menu plan in the nutrition section to accomplish this, shopping your kitchen first. Then food storage becomes a small issue.

Many of the tips and tricks I've shared so far in this chapter aren't new; I've seen them many times over the years. If they say "not it" and you know of a better way for you to organize your home, great! Do that. If you want to share ideas with me, I'll be happy to receive your feedback and may

"The house gives me an outlet of exertion, this one productive as well as healthful. We are too quick to write off and evade as drudgery activities that keep the blood flowing while giving us a small but satisfying sense of accomplishment. We all need such a sense in this world we've created, where the goals we set ourselves can be so complex."

—MIREILLE GUILIANO, *FRENCH WOMEN FOR ALL SEASONS: A YEAR OF SECRETS, RECIPES, & PLEASURE*[80]

even share it on a Facebook page or my website, or in a newsletter or blog. Contact me at lori@systemsforchange.net if you have something to share.

MAKING YOUR HOME MORE "GREEN"

Over the last few years, more and more people have been going "green" with their homes and cleaning products, and reusing items to reduce the amount of stuff they put in the trash. Taking this approach is better for your health, but also keeps more out of the landfill—another win-win. If you want to make your home more "green" or eco-friendly, consider the following tips:

- Use old toothbrushes for scrubbing grout and tight spots.

- Turn old flannel and cotton shirts into rags for dusting and wet cleaning. (Rewash and reuse again after your cleaning work.)

- Make "picture pockets" by sewing old blankets, towels, or thick fabric the size of the accessory, picture, or painting you want to store into a pocket, the shape of a pillowcase with one end longer than the other to tuck in like a pocket. These are great to store any decorative items in totes or boxes.

- Cut down old sheets and towels to usable size for rags. Serge the edges so they'll hold up to use again and again.

- Make your own cleaners with simple nontoxic ingredients, such as vinegar and baking soda.
    - For an all-purpose cleaner for hardwood floors and woodwork, mix 1/4 cup distilled white vinegar to one gallon warm water. Use a cloth that can be wrung out to damp, and focus on spot-cleaning where you need to.

    - To disinfect and deodorize a toilet bowl,

       sprinkle baking soda in the bowl, let it sit a few minutes, and then pour a small amount of vinegar over that; then scrub and flush.

    o   To make homemade window cleaner, mix three tablespoons white vinegar in one gallon of cool water. Spritz on glass and wipe with newspapers.

- Buy light bulbs that use less energy.

- Use natural cleaning product concentrates that allow you to mix your own.

- Use your dryer less by hanging loads of laundry to dry in your laundry room on a clothes rack or outside on a clothesline. You'll save on electricity and wear and tear on your dryer and your clothing.

- Keep your clothing whites white by soaking them in 1/2 cup dishwasher detergent for thirty minutes and then add normal detergent and run as normal, avoiding more heavy-duty cleaners or bleach.

- Every three months, run one quart vinegar in an empty hot wash cycle in your washing machine to clean out any mold or bacteria and prolong the life of the wash tub.

- Implement a shoes-off-at-the door policy to keep your floors cleaner, saving you time and cleaning product.

- Use non-chlorine bleach when you need to use bleach.

- Use a biodegradable scouring powder, such as Bon Ami.

- Use nontoxic all-purpose cleaners and detergents free of chemicals.

- To prevent mold and mildew from growing in your house (which can cause rashes, headaches, dizziness, nausea, allergic

reactions, and asthma attacks), use a HEPA filter on the vacuum and make sure to use the bathroom fans during every
bath and shower. Think about getting your HVAC ducts
cleaned out if you haven't recently.

- When buying a new appliance, or furnace or air-conditioning
  unit, make sure it's an energy-saving unit.

- When thinking about what home remodeling projects need to
  be done, consider getting energy-efficient windows installed
  or upgrading your home's insulation to save on utility costs
  and cut down on the energy required to keep your home
  comfortable.

⚠ BEDDING TIP

Because sleep is so important to your overall health, put your
money into buying a really good pillow for yourself, invest in a
supportive mattress that you will have for a long time, and buy
some really great sheets. If you are tolerating nubby sheets that
distract from your perfect sleep experience, put them in the rag
bag and reuse them for covering your plants during frosty weather
or the patio furniture you're storing for the winter. Then get out
there and buy a really nice set of sheets; look for a sale and get a
great sleep. I learned a great trick while traveling to Napa Valley,
California. While staying at a hotel, the bed was so "cush," I had
to lift up the covers and sheets to see what kind of a mattress
it was—I discovered there were two pillow-top mattress covers
layered over the basic mattress with really smooth crisp sheets;
I slept like a dream.

DECORATING AND FURNISHING YOUR HOME

Even when it comes to decorating and furnishing your house, there are ways to save money and time. To save money on furnishing your home, spend your dollars on great basics, like a bed, dining set, and sofa. Choose pieces that aren't trendy, but rather classic so they will look good for years in your home. Don't neglect looking at used furniture pieces (auctions and Craigslist often have good options). Have fewer pieces, so you have less clutter and a home that is easy to clean. Think about spending your money on really good appliances rather than the latest kitchen gadgets or gizmos. Remember that a few basic pieces of really good cookware and knives can replace a whole cupboard of needless gizmo junk. Buy basic neutral dishes and quality silverware that will last you a long time.

When thinking of bigger remodeling costs, consider what a decorating update might do. A new paint color on the wall, new light fixtures, and new cabinet hardware might add a fresh look to your home and save money. Then you can add a new sofa or dining table when you have the money for it.

When choosing candles, decorative pillows, and hand, kitchen, and bath towels, look for them in this season's hot colors. If you pick up a few inexpensive accessories like these, you can keep your home looking up to date without spending a lot of money. You can also buy some great pillow forms (the base of

⚠ KITCHEN APPLIANCE TIP

My favorite kitchen appliance is a KitchenAid mixer that my parents surprised me with at Christmas years ago. My youngest son later made a comment about it we will never forget: "Grandpa, that is the best thing that ever happened to our family!" I used it daily by creating homemade meals, and almost twenty years later I still use it, though just weekly as I'm not cooking for two growing boys any longer.

SHOPPING FOR REDECORATING IDEAS AND ITEMS

Remember in the "Your Personal Image" chapter, how I shared how to do a Wardrobe Day with a friend? You can do the same thing with your home. Before you redecorate, sort through home décor magazines to see what look you might try to achieve in one of your rooms. Then, without spending money, shop for more ideas in a preview day at home improvement and decorating stores. See what ideas you can find either on display at these stores or in their various catalogs, etc.

Save your money for the real shopping trip after making your renovation plan, when you have your shopping list in hand.

I challenge you to find a friend and team up for evaluating and redecorating both homes from start to finish, starting with your inspiration shopping trip, having a home day at each home (where you "shop" for what you already have that could work in your new space), and then a final shopping trip to treasure-hunt for what is on your list.

the pillow under the covering, which can be either feather or foam in a variety of sizes) and recover them when you feel the room they're in needs a style update. I found four feather pillow forms in twenty-inch squares on a clearance rack close to twenty years ago and have made up-to-date pillow covers every few years as "in style" colors have changed. The regular price for these forms at that

> **⚠ TIP**
>
> When you have a buying mistake or something no longer fits in your lifestyle, let it go. Sell it, even at a loss if you have to, or give it away. Don't drag it with you because you spent good money on it. Cut your losses and run.

time was twenty dollars each and I got them for five dollars each. The fabric I use to make pillow covers is from the clearance racks too; with me keeping in mind the current trends and colors. I got this tip from my interior designer friend Deb Lansdowne (you can visit her website, debralansdownedesigns.com, to find out more about her services).

Be grateful for all you have—you will know when something new or different is needed.

Were you given a hope chest when you were a teen or young college-bound student to gather what you would need on your life journey? Did you receive a quilt from Grandma? A journal? Many a hope chest has become a place to store special mementos through the years: your babies' christening gowns, old letters received from your son when he was away at college or serving in the military, your

> **⚠ TIP**
>
> As much as coming home to a clean, well-organized, and well-decorated place can relax you, don't forget that there are other ways to establish a sense of calm in your home. One way is to eliminate noise pollution. That means turning off the TV when it isn't being watched. If you really need background noise, turn on some uplifting music instead. You'll be surprised how it affects your mood.

high school class ring and letter jacket, love letters from when you and your spouse were dating, on and on. If you aren't using your old hope chest for treasures, if it has become a dumping spot for odds and ends, maybe it is time to recreate your hope chest. As you are going through your home, find a special place for it again and let it hold your hopes and dreams for the future in your dream space. Or maybe as you sort and clear out the clutter in your home and you run across special treasures, it can hold those mementos and become a memory box.

If you don't have a hope chest, maybe you want to create a space that represents one, or go and buy yourself one. A dresser or a buffet can become a hope chest in a spare room; you can get creative with it. Of course, you may say "not it" to the whole hope chest idea—that's great! Keep playing "not it, not it, not it."

As to how your decorating choices can save time, buy one color of bath towels and one color of kitchen towels, so you can wash and dry them in the same loads and avoid getting dark nubs on light towels and light nubs on darker towels (my mother-in-law shared this tip with me and it works; it couldn't be simpler!)

Simple is in; complex is out.

HOUSE HUNTING

How do you know when it *is* time to move on from your current home? When *do* you really need more (or less) space to accommodate your lifestyle? When the space you are currently residing in is giving you signs of "not it," then it's probably time to go. How about when a young family has a small home bursting at the seams, with too few bedrooms for their growing family? Or when the empty nesters decide their home is too big? Sometimes the signs are obvious, such as when you're relocating for your career, and sometimes subtle, when you slowly realize you want a lifestyle change.

Another example of "not it" comes from a young man I recently spoke with. His roommate had two refrigerators in the house. Unfortunately, because this young man was renting a space from his roommate, the space designated for his food in one of these refrigerators was taken up with beer, which was not his. He had no room for groceries, a definite sign of "not it." He moved.

Once you decide you want to move, think about how many bedrooms and bathrooms you want in your new home. How many garage stalls? Is there a specific square footage that you think will work? Consider how many common spaces you want, and how large you want them to be. Do you need more space to accommodate your hobbies? Storage for sports equipment? A sewing room? How many home offices do you need? Do you love to entertain and cook? What components must your kitchen have? Do you really want a pantry?

Then get specific about what location would work best for you, and what type of home. Does your home need to be in a good school district? Close to mass-transit stations? Are you looking for a single family home, a condo, or a townhome?

Document your wishes and create a binder with pictures out of magazines to visualize your ideal home, or create this on a computer. This is the same process used for visualizing your dream job or dream spouse (more on that in the "Your Relationships" and "Your Career" chapters). Know what it is you want. Start with a map of the area to help you focus and clarify your ideal home location along with your wish or requirements list for the new home.

Here's a sample of what your wish list might look like:

- Quiet, an adult environment without kids running around
- Fireplace
- Balcony or patio
- Office space
- Close proximity to walking/biking trails
- Lake view
- Space to sleep six (one to two bedrooms with space for air mattress)

- Okay if cosmetic updates are needed
- Space for indoor parking for my car and guest parking outdoors
- Storage space for holiday decorative items
- Easy drive to work
- Open floor plan with high ceilings

While you work on your wish list, dream about the new house, and then check with a mortgage lender about how much money you will qualify for when it comes to getting a loan. If you think you might need to do any necessary financial cleanup before trying to secure a loan, get a credit check first. If you need to start clearing up some other debts before buying a house, make a plan to do so (see the "Your Financial Goals" chapter for more tips on this).

When you're financially ready with a pre-approved loan amount, it's time to start looking. Of course, it's easy to become overwhelmed when you get to this stage, trying to find the right house for the right price. I worked with a woman during her house-hunting process, and knowing that she liked to play games for entertainment, I helped her sort through about twenty pages of listings she had printed off the Internet, making the task like a game. She had looked at several of the homes and was on a deadline to find something because she had sold her home and needed to move quickly. We discussed what was on her wish list and the locations she preferred; then we discussed the pros and cons of each home on her printout list. She shared with me what she liked

"How we care for our homes is a subtle but significant expression of not only how we care for our self-esteem, but the contentment of our soul."

—**SARAH BAN BREATHNACH,** *ROMANCING THE ORDINARY: A YEAR OF SIMPLE SPLENDOR*[81]

and what she didn't, such as if it had a great kitchen, but wasn't in the right location. Eventually we worked our way through the stack, putting the "not it" choices in a discard pile and narrowing it down to about four possibilities. She went out to see them and was able to select the one that was right for her. This settled down the stress she was experiencing, and she was able to move forward to the next stage of packing and moving.

After buying your home, keep track of your major upgrades so that when you sell it someday, you can help justify the price you are asking for it. Note when you replace the roof, the furnace, the air-conditioning unit, carpeting, and appliances (also don't forget to keep those home appliance manuals and pass them along to the next owner). And when you decide to sell, talk with your real estate agent about how much these improvements will impact the price of your house.

Keep in mind that, at some point, you may need to move out of your current ideal home to be open to the next phase in life and create a new dream home. You can't receive what life might have next for you if you have a closed fist. For me, that meant selling a condo I had purchased and renovated when I had lived in it just over a year. Why did I decide to leave? Because I had another dream fulfilled—meeting my dream man and deciding to move forward on a life with him. I decided not to look at all the work I had done renovating this condo as a bad thing, but instead felt I served God in renovating the condo. Having the condo is what I did while I was waiting for my dream man to arrive. If I wouldn't have had the experience of owning the condo, my dream man wouldn't have gotten to know the me who created and accomplished the renovation, and see the way I was able to handle my finances in doing it. My girlfriend, an interior designer, said, "People like you are angels to buildings like this," as I worked on the renovation, and when I sold it, the condo neighbors thanked me for making the building more valuable and giving them hope that, by making improvements to their homes, they too could sell their units quickly when the time came. And even the woman who bought it is grateful for my work, as she tells me that her new home is perfect for her.

SELLING YOUR HOME

When you do decide it's time to sell your home, where do you start? First, think about how quickly you want to sell, if there is indeed a deadline you need to meet. Do you have a date to be somewhere else, a closing on your dream home, or are you relocating to a new job in a faraway location? Decide on your ideal timeline and work within it. Don't be concerned if it seems unrealistic at the moment; things will fall into place.

After your timeline to buy a new house is in place, contact a realtor or decide if you're going to do this on your own. This may depend upon your timeline, desires, and abilities. I recommend interviewing three realtors at least, but not too many. You want to feel comfortable not only with the realtor, but also with the company he or she represents, the marketing plan to sell your home, and the fees. You may have to go through a few cases of "not it" when it comes to realtors, but once you find the right one, you'll know. Having a good comfort level with your realtor will reduce your stress through the process. There were times when I just had to listen to my realtor Ralph and trust he was right. He asked me to create a "WOW factor" in my condo—which was going above and beyond what is normally expected to declutter and depersonalize, and ensure everything was clean, coordinated, and in perfect working order—and once I did, he sold it very quickly.

Staging your home is also important, so important that I paid for the services of a real estate stager; Debbie did a fabulous job in making sure the setting was just right. She and I shopped for missing items; the furniture was arranged perfectly; and the accessories on the walls were hung properly.

I also deep-cleaned the whole place before putting it on the market. I enlisted the assistance of friends and family to help me paint the walls and trim, and eliminate excess household items.

I reached my timeline to sell my condo because I listened to my realtor, staged my home well, and had it looking its best. True story: on the first day of a vacation to Mexico, when my realtor was hosting the first and only open house, the second person in the door was my buyer. She walked in and could see herself living there. When I called the realtor from Mexico the day after the open house, Ralph said to me, "Boy, am I happy to hear from you; we have an offer!" So we took care of all the paperwork from the property management company in Mexico. I had a feeling it would go fast. I even kidded to my traveling companion that because we were going on vacation, it would probably happen then, and it did!

Break down the steps you need to take to get your house ready to sell and then block out time in your calendar based on your time-line to sell. Use the Systems For Change project planner. Ask for and enlist help if you need it. Don't be afraid of spending the extra money on whatever the realtor and stager recommend. Think of time as money and how it will cost you if you don't sell right away. How many showings do you really want to prepare for? Make sure everything is in good repair in advance, so you won't have anyone trying to squabble with your price because he or she wants you to "take care of a few things."

Decide while you are cleaning and clearing what you want to take with you and pack. This is a great time to say "not it" to all the excess stuff you have kept over the years. Do you still need to keep the driving permit you had at age fifteen? Do you still need to keep that doodad that you never really liked even though someone special gave it to you years ago? Remember earlier in this chapter when I brought up the amount of stuff we store and how we are spending expensive real estate space on storage? Also don't let past decorating mistakes follow you, or out-of-date styles. Remember the story of emotional attachment in the wardrobe chapter.

Take the time to be ruthless now and it will make your whole staging, maintaining, and moving process so much easier. It is more work in the short run to have less work in the long run.

Only bring what you love as a start or base to your new home, new life, and new look.

Remember that less is more; practice the art of restraint.

I hope you have fun caring for your home. If you don't, say "not it," and hire someone to do some of these tasks and do what you love!

HOMEWORK

1. Press pause with a notebook and walk through your home, jotting down notes about each room and how it functions, or not, and what you would change if you could, if time and money were out of the equation. Once you determine all the changes, look at your list and ask yourself, "What can I do right now to make my home even better?" "What can I do in the next week, month, season, or year?" I recommend doing all the quick, easy, no cost, or low-cost items first and begin to save for the ones that are out of budget. Are there items to sell to cover the cost of what you really want? Are you tolerating a less than comfy bed or mismatched dishes?

2. Implement a cleaning schedule. Start daily and work from there, enlisting your family to help.

3.   Are there projects that have been on your list for a long
     time and you just aren't getting to them? Can you create
     a staging area and sort them out, such as sewing pillows,
     scrapbooking old photos, creating a travel binder, what-
     ever it is? Once identified and sorted, can you designate
     a time to do the first project by blocking off time in the
     next week? And then a weekly time until it is complete?
     If you say no, do you really believe you will get to the
     project? What is holding you back? Is it time to let the
     project go and pass along all the yarn for the afghan you
     really don't want to crochet? Quilt pieces you won't get
     to? Draw a line in the sand and decide. Send all that
     guilt and negative energy out the window along with the
     components of the projects you aren't getting to, while
     adding space in your home and your mind to where
     those projects were previously occupied.

Your Relationships

There are loads and loads of books wholly dedicated to finding the right romantic relationship, weeding out those who are "not it" for you, or improving your current relationship with your partner or spouse so that you don't feel it's "not it." Here we're just spending a chapter looking at relationships and ways to make them better; you may want to consult with your pastor, your twelve-step sponsor, or a counselor if you want more guidance in that area.

Books that helped me were *If the Buddha Dated: A Handbook for Finding Love on a Spiritual Path* by Charlotte Kasl and *The Soulmate Secret* by Arielle Ford for dating relationships. *Boundaries: When to Say Yes, When to Say No-To Take Control of Your Life* by Dr. Henry Cloud and Dr. John Townsend and *9 Things You Simply Must Do to Succeed in Love and Life* by Dr. Henry Cloud are good for all relationships. Some of my best sources of inspiration and information regarding relationships come from church sermons and a weekly Bible study group I attend. For general tips on improving your relationship with your spouse (or how to find the right partner), and having stronger relationships with your children, parents, friends, and more, keep reading here.

One thing that applies across the board when it comes to a relationship, whether with a spouse or significant other, parent, child, or friend: for it to be pleasurable, you need to be centered, to know yourself and your desires and how to express them, and to set boundaries when needed. Earlier in the book we worked through the ways of acting ugly, and identified needs that were not getting met. Hopefully, by now you have had time to digest that and know yourself really well. You may have recognized some relationships that are not healthy for you. When you discover your dreams and pursue your passion, you may learn that there are people in your life who have taken you down a wrong path, or you are on their path and it's not where you want to be. Once you recognize this, the relationship doesn't need to end; instead communication must happen to get you on the path that will take you to your dreams. How the other person reacts will tell you if or how the relationship will continue. If you have been helping someone else build a dream and now want to build yours, that person may believe you are jumping ship and abandoning him or her. You may be surprised once you are firm in following your path about the lack of support you receive back from others.

Sarah Ban Breathnach writes in *Simple Abundance: A Daybook of Comfort and Joy* that, as in gardening, pruning your life strengthens rather than weakens you, but that doesn't mean you will like it:

> When we don't prune in the garden, nature does it for us through wind, ice, hail, fire, and flood. One way or another, the boughs will be shaped and strengthened. If we don't prune away the stress and plow under the useless in our lives, pain will do it for us. But after pruning, preferably voluntary, we're able to discern what's real, what's important, and what's essential for our happiness. Be of good cheer. Study your plants and study your lifestyle. When the right time arrives, go into the garden with sharp shears. Prune back and plow ahead.[82]

Expressing your desires is all about communication, one of the main areas that often affects relationships. No one can read minds. Ban Breathnach shares this about using communication to set boundaries:

> For most women, creating boundaries is excruciating, so we don't do it until we're pushed to the outer edge of tolerance. To create boundaries we must learn to say, thus far and no further. This means speaking up. Expressing our needs. Indicating our preferences. These moments are tense and can easily escalate into confrontations complete with tears, misunderstandings, and hurt feelings. This is why many women stay quiet, rendered virtually mute by unexpressed rage and unable to articulate any needs at all.[83]

In other words, we shut down. But even if we're mute, we're not powerless to draw a line in the sand. Ban Breathnach continues: "Speaking the language of 'no' is a good place to start creating boundaries."[84]

No can be a beautiful word, every bit as beautiful as *yes*, writers John Robbins and Ann Mortifee declare in their book *In Search of Balance: Discovering Harmony in a Changing World*:

> Whenever we deny our need to say "no," our self-respect diminishes. It is not only our right at certain times to say "no"; it is our deepest responsibility. For it is a gift to ourselves when we say "no" to those old habits that dissipate our energy, "no" to what robs us of our inner joy, "no" to what distracts us from our purpose. And it is a gift to others to say "no" when their expectations do not ring true for us, for in doing so we free them to discover more fully the truth of their own path. Saying "no" can be liberating when it expresses our commitment to take a stand for what we believe we truly need.[85]

Another way to rethink your communication is to avoid using "you" statements in the heat of conflict—"You hurt my feelings," "You made me embarrassed," "You weren't very kind." These immediately put the person you're talking with on the defensive. Instead say, "I feel hurt when I hear you say…" "I feel embarrassed when this situation happens," "I feel like you weren't very kind to me when…," so you're still getting your thoughts communicated about your relationship, but in a more effective way. Also, you can gently say to someone, "When you do this, I feel…," or "Did you realize this is how you sounded?" Or "I noticed when you spoke to [your son], he hung his head and seemed withdrawn." Often when it comes to communication, it's not what you say to someone, but how you sound saying it. Keeping anger and hurt feelings in check when you're having a conflict can go a long way toward establishing a healthy relationship.

For more simple, quick ways to improve the communication in your relationships, consider the following:

- Eliminate noise pollution within your conversations. Having your TV on while talking on the telephone is a "not it" combination. Having the TV on while eating dinner with your family is a definite "not it." If you are the person making the call, respect the dinner-time hour and avoid calling; also consider whether the person you want to talk with might be engrossed in a favorite TV show and won't be able to talk. (I'm really not into sports and wasn't aware of game schedules. When I called my son on a Monday night, I learned that *Monday Night Football* was on and learned not to call at that time in the future.)

- When hanging out with someone, it isn't necessary to fill up quiet with meaningless conversation. This is an energy-sucking activity. Allow for some quiet time if you're riding with someone in the car, or just hanging out on a lazy weekend afternoon.

- Send cards, emails, texts, or make a call when those close to you have a birthday or you're aware of a special occasion in their lives. By acknowledging these milestones, you can make them feel special by showing you care.

- Go shopping with friends and family, as was described in the clothing and home chapters, plan a wardrobe day, shop for paint colors, furniture, home accessories.

- Work on home projects with family and friends; enlist help painting the living room and make it fun.

- Go on a treasure hunt with your favorite buddy; shop antique stores, secondhand shops, and garage sales. Stop for treats or, better yet, bring your healthy treats with you and have a picnic somewhere.

- Cook together with family and friends, cooking big portions to share healthy recipes.

- Host a potluck or gourmet dinner with those you love to hang out with.

- Movie night, game night—you name it, make it fun.

- Get out and walk together, or go sailing, skiing, out for a run, to the gym. Invite those who share your passion to join you.

Understand that you might only be able to be around some people for three minutes; others you can handle for three hours; and some you can be comfortable with for three weeks or longer, as I learned through attending PSI Seminars. That's okay; it's part of life. If you feel one of your friends or acquaintances can only handle talking with you for three minutes, you might want to think about that and see if you might want to change something about your behavior. I'm not saying it's your issue, but it might be. The person might just be busy, but all you can do is change you, so start there. Most likely, the other party has no idea that you see your relationship might have a "time limit." So don't read too much into the amount of time others are spending with you. Instead use this "time limit" concept as a tool to protect yourself from harmful, negative, and toxic relationships, as well as to identify what relationships you want to work on.

Instead of spending time with people and situations where I don't fit, I can look for the ones where I do.

FOR COUPLES

There are so many things for a couple to do to keep their relationship strong. But one of the most important is to be present with one another and have an "I'm here for the long term" attitude. Be your spouse's friend, be his or her rock, the person he or she wants to turn to after a bad day or when times are tough with career, finances, or family.

Have alone time, just the two of you, with date nights and picnics together so you get quality time to share with each other. When you need to, spend your date night becoming united as a couple in your financial plan and spending habits. This will cut down on the number of arguments you have, guaranteed. Spend time looking at the next season of your life together; discuss travel plans, family obligations, or what sports or activities your children might be involved in next. This is a great way to plan ahead to get all the "to-do" items for these activities divided between you, so you can finish them with ease. It's also the time you can establish household rules or chores, whatever you need to make your household run more smoothly. Don't allow all your alone time to be spent here; you want to make sure to have fun and intimacy too. I'm not suggesting you monopolize your alone time with tasks; just make sure to have a balance of both, communicating what is going on and being on the same page.

If you have children, you can set up your rules for summer vacation, like if you'll be allowing your children to bring their bikes or friends to the lake. Let's say you decide to bring all the bikes. Someone needs to make sure they're in good working order. Maybe little Suzie had training wheels last year and they're still on the bike, though she's outgrown them, or maybe little Johnny has grown six inches in the last year and requires a bigger bike. When you do these evaluations in advance, and openly communicate, you save a lot of headaches. Instead of a last minute, "Oh, but Mom, I really wanted my friend Jimmy to come with..." or a last minute situation where someone has a hissy fit as you're packing and you have try to squeeze the bikes in without checking them, learning once you arrive that there's a flat tire and no bike tire pump packed, you can plan ahead.

Listen to each other's goals and dreams when you are one on one and support those, as well as the plans to achieve them. When you work as a team on these things, it will bring you closer together, strengthening your bond.

Realize now that you are a couple; you are your own family unit (even if you don't have children yet). Your spouse is now your top relationship priority. It's time to pull away from your childhood family unit and be united in a new family of you and your spouse. Your extended family gets to honor this, realizing that you as a family are now setting your own priorities, rules, and customs.

See each family unit you're close to as a planet in the solar system, on their own path. While one family may want to get together with their extended family weekly or for certain holidays or celebrations, they also may want to spend time on their own. That's okay; you can all catch up without emotional guilt "penalties" for taking time to establish your life with your spouse and children.[86]

Not setting up these kinds of boundaries can really cause problems for couples. Dr. Henry Cloud and Dr. James Townsend, authors of a book called *Boundaries: When to Say Yes, When to Say No–To Take Control of Your Life*, relate this story about a couple, Dan and Jane: "You wouldn't believe how she is with him," Dan said about his wife in a session. "She totally focuses on his every wish. When he criticizes her, she tries harder. And she practically ignores me. I'm tired of being the 'second man' in her life."[87] Dan wasn't talking about Jane's lover. He was talking about her father. Dan was tired of feeling like Jane cared more about her father's wishes than his.

This is a common sign of a lack of boundaries with one person's family of origin: the spouse feels like they get the leftovers. They feel their mate's real allegiance is to their parents.

Also, the spouse who has a problem with boundaries with their family of origin can become depressed, argumentative, self-critical, perfectionistic, angry, combative, or withdrawn when they interact with that family, Cloud and Townsend add. And then those "not it" behaviors can be passed like a virus onto their spouse or children. "His family of origin has the power to affect his new family in a trickle-down effect," Cloud and Townsend write—a definite "not it."[88]

If this is a problem in your couple relationship, you or your spouse hasn't completed the "leaving before cleaving" process. God has designed the process whereby a "man shall leave his father and his mother and shall cleave to his wife; and they shall become one flesh" (Genesis 2:24)[89]. The Hebrew word for *leave* comes from a root word that means "loosen" or "to relinquish or forsake." For marriage to work, a spouse needs to loosen their ties with their family of origin and forge new ties with the family the couple is creating in their marriage.

Cloud and Townsend have an excellent chapter in their book on marital boundaries, particularly on the controversial topic of submission. I highly recommend this book to married couples and engaged couples, so they can set up a healthy relationship before their marriage begins.

For those of you who may be a new couple, especially those of you who have come out of a divorce, realize that creating a new family unit may be hard for your family of origin. While they may be happy for you, they may have gotten used to having you enmeshed in their lives and they in yours, helping you make tough decisions as they've supported you. When separation occurs as a new couple begins to create its own unit, there's often difficulty in reestablishing healthy boundaries. Your family of origin may be used to having you available all the time because you did not have a life while you were grieving and recovering from heartache, so they became your life. Now, as we rebuild our lives, when the new family is created, new boundaries must be established to create a healthy system for all families involved. This can be a time of confusion and conflict if everyone doesn't see it as a natural part of the process of becoming a couple. It's going through the "leaving before cleaving" process all over again.

Sometimes, one person in a relationship might realize someone in their family or a close friend has a "herd mentality"—giving out unhealthy penalties of guilt when someone doesn't mesh with the herd (in other words, doing what the controlling parent, sibling, or friend wants). This isn't healthy and sucks the life out of relationships. If you find yourself in a herd mentality relationship, set and hold consistent boundaries with that person. Hold firm to your solar system family against the herd's opposition. Being a new member of a herd family is a bit like an old *Star Trek* episode where they attempt to assimilate you into the Borg collective (or, in this case, the family collective). If you don't set up consistent, clear boundaries right away, you could have a major fight on your hands when you get fed up with all you've been tolerating.

Also, take the time to keep the spark alive in your physical relationship with your spouse. Schedule a weekend getaway to get more alone time, do a couples massage, have a "bedroom" night where watching TV and reading are off the table. And don't forget what 1 Peter 5:14 says: "Greet one another with a kiss of love." This last one is a good practice to do each day.

FOR PARENTS

To keep your relationships with your children strong, let them pretend, play, dream, and make believe when they are young. Don't schedule every minute of their day. Let them have time to just be kids. You don't have to watch them like a hawk in these moments; in fact, letting them navigate playing on their own or with a sibling is a good practice. Make sure they're safe, but don't control their every move.

Set clear household rules for your children with your spouse and expect your children to follow them. A couple of your rules might be: respect others and their belongings, don't lie, don't tease or hit your siblings, listen to and respect your parents, and use appropriate language. Have consistent consequences if they do not follow the rules, as Dawn Eichman touts in her book *Let's Make Parenting Easier*.[90] Make sure those consequences are delivered soon after the misbehavior occurs, so your children understand why they are being disciplined.

Children flourish more if they have a defined structure they can live within. Discuss the rules at family meetings. If you're a single parent, you'll have to collaborate on these rules with your child's other parent, if they're involved in raising the child; if that parent is not involved, decide on your own how much freedom and how many responsibilities your children can have.

In *Let's Make Parenting Easier,* Eichman notes:
> Once your kids know that you mean what you say, they will rarely
> push you to the next step of the misbehavior ladder unless they
> are hungry or tired (and in these cases just feed them or put them
> to bed). If you stand firm and follow through on your word, the
> misbehavior will eventually occur less and less.[91]
>
> As your kids grow older, what they misbehave about changes.
> You must persevere. Kids seem to test parents from time to time
> just to make sure they are still paying attention to them.[92]

Also keep in mind that "when parents rely on threats, commands,
and physical force to discipline, children are exposed to models of
aggressive behavior, experience high levels of fear and anxiety, and
learn to avoid the punitive adult."[93] You are not destined to parent
your children as you were parented, if this is what you experienced
in your family of origin. Eichman adds: "Most certainly take the
good that your parents did in raising you, and for the areas that
didn't work so well, seek out new information. As long as you have
a willingness to change, you can acquire new parenting skills for
the challenges your children present."

Here's another tip Eichman shares in her book:
> When children are squabbling over something, you can give them
> time to resolve the conflict on their own. They do need practice
> on how to work through their problems. Fixing the problem for
> them prevents them from going through any resolution process
> for themselves. Not every disagreement calls for a consequence.
> Giving children time to work things out builds their social skills for
> the future. You can step in if you see an injury about to occur.[94]

Avoid labeling your children in a certain way, such as "Susie, you
are naughty" or "Johnny, you are so shy." Labeling is really dangerous business, because "you never know when the label you use will

become a part of who your child believes they are," Eichman says. "Kids will eventually believe that they are lazy, stupid, shy, dumb, mean, or whatever negative label you choose for them."[95] They will fulfill the prophecy that you have designed for them. Instead, describe what you see or what you want to see in your child. Let's say your child is pulling your cat's hair. Instead of saying he or she is being naughty, try: "You need to be gentle with the kitty." You describe what you want them to do. It's as easy as that.

"There is a way we as parents can maintain our authority and allow our children some personal power: offer them choices," Eichman shares.[96] Let them decide if they want a banana or an apple in their lunch, which of three outfits they want to wear to school, or if they want to participate in a basketball league or swimming lessons this year. Eichman says:

> By offering choices and allowing our children to choose one of those choices, they will feel more powerful in their lives. If we make all of our children's decisions, we are being too controlling. When we provide choices, the kids will also get some practice in making decisions. It doesn't matter what choice they make because the choices you give are all acceptable to you.[97]

You can also get your children to help clean up around the house. Teach them to put away the dishes from the dishwasher, how to make their beds, clean their rooms, and dust and vacuum. Not only will you get help getting the household chores done, but if you were doing all these things for your children, you would be "care-taking in a way that is not healthy for them," says Dawn Eichman in her book *Let's Make Parenting Easier*. "Care-taking like this robs children of their independence."[98]

Take time to have fun with your kids; enjoy them as they grow. Do fun activities (hikes, skating, biking, bowling, skiing, or sledding) with them, and find joy at home. Families can become so busy doing and running and buying, they suddenly find themselves under an avalanche of disorder and chaos. Relax. Build quiet time, team cleaning, and game and movie nights into your schedule. Have fun as a family.

Remember that as your children grow, they will develop their own interests. They won't be exactly like you, or love the same activities, sports, or hobbies that you do. As Kahlil Gibran writes in *The Prophet*:

> You may give them your love but not your thoughts for they have their own thoughts. You may house their bodies, but not their souls, for their souls dwell in the house of tomorrow, which you cannot visit, not even in your dreams. You may strive to be like them, but seek not to make them like you. For life goes not backward, nor tarries with yesterday. You are the bows from which your children as living arrows are sent forth.[99]

I raised my sons with the above attitude. I was the stable bow; my sons were the arrows. I loved, cared for, and guided them when they were with me, and then I let them go. Now I get to love, nurture, and guide my grandchildren, knowing that someday I'll let them go, while being there for them if they need me.

When we are responsible for minor children, that's one thing; once they become adults, and we want to continue giving input, it's not our job. To learn to give our opinions when we are asked can be a challenge. Dawn Eichman shares:

> When my adult children call me, I need to figure out how to talk to them in a different way. I must listen to them and not offer advice (unless they ask, of course). I must trust them and not try to persuade them to do things my way. I must accept them and not judge. I must simply love them.[100]

EXTENDED FAMILY RELATIONSHIPS

Our extended families can provide much joy in our lives. It is wonderful to maintain relationships with those we have grown up with. Participating in family traditions when it works for your own family's schedule, like going to the annual family reunion where you can visit with your parents, grandparents, aunts, uncles, and cousins, is great. With Facebook and other social media, it is easier to stay in touch with family, especially those who are a distance away, by sharing photos and stories with each other. I've heard it said from many extended family members that they only see one another at weddings or funerals. That does not have to be. Make it a point to keep in touch with those you have loved all your life.

Having holiday traditions with parents and siblings is a great way to consistently spend time together. Maybe just block off time in your calendar to have regular visits, go out to dinner and a movie, or bake holiday cookies or go on annual holiday shopping trips. Send out the holiday photos and letters.

What about pulling out the old family photo albums or playing the reel-to-reel home movies or slides to show your children and grandchildren what your family was like when you grew up? That can make for an evening of family fun.

One way to preserve family memories can be a journal of wishes. In this journal, older family members can share their wishes when it comes to the end of their life on earth. It may sound morbid, but we can also learn much about them and their lives in this process, which we can share with our children and grandchildren.

A JOURNAL OF WISHES

No matter how close your relationship is with your parents, grandparents, or other older family members, talking about death and what they might want out of life before then isn't always easy. To facilitate that, have your elder parent or family member create a Journal of Wishes, in which they write out a list of what they want to do while they're still able, what their funeral and burial wishes are, and if they have any wishes about their end-of-life care.

When you find out what they would like to do, you can support them in taking action. You'll also know Grandma's favorite hymn that she wants sung at her funeral or Grandpa's favorite Bible verses that he wants read at the service. This information helps reduce stress at an already stressful time—when you've lost a loved one. When you go through the journal, ask about their lives and have them share stories of their childhoods and youths, their early years as adults, whatever you might not know about. You'll learn a lot about who they really are. Also go through practical questions, such as the following:

- Do you have a living will and a medical power of attorney (regarding medical procedures in the event you are unable to make that decision at the time)?

- Do you have a minister or religious advisor?

- Have you made arrangements for the disposition of your personal belongings (in your will or in another document, or with a certain family member)?

- Whom do you wish to contact your creditors?

- Do you have a will or a trust?

- Who is your executor?

- Who are your physicians and dentist?

- Have you selected someone to be guardian for your minor children?

- Are there people you want to be notified when you die? Longtime high school or college friends? Military friends? Coworkers you have kept in touch with?

- What is your preferred funeral home?

- Do you have a prearranged and paid funeral plan?

- Do you have instructions regarding services and a budget for final expenses?

- Do you have a preference regarding memorial gifts?

- What are your favorite flowers?

- What songs/hymns would you like to have played?

- Is there a particular musician, soloist, or organist you would like to have?

- Are there readings or scripture passages that are especially meaningful to you?

- Do you have six or eight people you would like to designate as pallbearers?

- What are your wishes regarding disposition of your remains?

- What are your wishes regarding disposition of your remains?

- Do you have a cemetery plot? Location/plot/deed #?

- Do you have a preference about clothing in which you would like to be buried?

- Do you want a tombstone or memorial plaque?

- Do you want a particular inscription?

- What are your community involvements/achievements?

- What is your full name, including maiden name?

- What is your date of birth?

- Who was your spouse(s)? What were their full names and dates of birth?

- What was the date of your marriage?

- What are the names of your children, grandchildren, and great-grandchildren?

- What occupations did you hold?

- Are there special memories you want to share?

- What were your hobbies?

FRIENDS

One of the easiest ways to gain friends and deepen your relationships with the ones you already have is to be a good listener. That means really listening—not thinking of what you might say next, but waiting until your friend has finished talking and then still asking a few follow-up questions.

David J. Schwartz, in his book *The Magic of Thinking Big*, sees building friendships in this way: "The average person would rather talk about himself than anything else in this world. When you give him the chance, he likes you for it. Conversation generosity is the easiest, simplest, and surest way there is to win a friend. Don't be a conversation hog. Listen, win friends, and learn."[101]

Yet don't be so desperate for friendship or approval that you'll do anything to get it. If you feel like you need to expand your friend circle, try to find friends who like the things you do. Like to cook? Take a cooking class. Like to read? Join a book club. Do you feel like giving back is important? Volunteer for an organization you believe in and meet others who may have that same interest. If you love to work out, join a gym or special fitness class like Nia or yoga. If you like exercising outdoors, join a biking club or a ski club. You'll meet like-minded people in these places, making it easier to really connect with them.

Just like remembering our families, it is fun to continue relationships with friends. As our lives change and we move from high school to college and from job to job and location to location, we meet a lot of people. Some stay and some go. I have a collection of various friends from a lifetime of experiences. Many now live out of the area that I do, yet we stay in touch with phones, emails, and texts. Just because we no longer attend school together or just because our children were playmates at one time and are no longer in our homes does not mean we cannot maintain our friendship. I have friends from elementary school, friends from various workplaces and workout places, those who are parents of my children's friends, and so on and so on. I have moved many times over my life and I have friends from all over. It is fun to reconnect with friends who now live far away, even if it's a couple times per year, or maybe once every couple years. Regardless, we can pick up where we left off. We can meet for lunches, shopping, sporting events, or have each other over for a gourmet dinner. We can be on the phone and have our "coffee" together. When it comes to imagination, the sky's the limit.

Sadly, just as it is necessary at times to divorce a spouse, there are times when it is just as important to close a friendship. Some people are just toxic. Some people latch onto us—they found us and we did not necessarily choose them. If you meet someone who is that way, or realize one of your old or new friends is that way, it's okay to dump that person just like a bad date. Let your focus on that friendship fade. If you stop watering that weed, it will die eventually. While it may be difficult, you need to disconnect from those who are not healthy for you to be around. If you find yourself going down a path with a friend that is not healthy for you, stop the unhealthy behavior and see what happens to the friendship. It may endure with the changes, or it may not. Does your friend have an addiction that is getting in the way of your relationship? Again, you may need to take time off from that friendship, or end it completely. If your friend has a real problem with any of the following, so much so that it is getting in the way of what you want out of the friendship or you reaching your goals, that friendship may be in trouble:

- Overeating
- Overspending
- Gambling
- Keeping up with the Joneses
- Drinking too much

- Hanging out at the bar or club scene when you don't want to

- Being overly inactive

I'm not saying everyone who drinks is an alcoholic or everyone who overeats is obese and in bad health. I'm just saying, all things in moderation. Ask yourself how their bad behavior is impacting you. Or maybe *you* have the problem with one of these areas, and your life is out of balance or unmanageable. Then you might need to get help and focus on getting your life back on track.

Remember: we are all just doing the best we can.

Reasons and Seasons

People come into your life for a reason,
a season, or a lifetime.
When you know which one it is,
you will know what to do for that person.

When someone is in your life for a REASON,
it is usually to meet a need you have expressed.
They have come to assist you through a difficulty,
to provide you with guidance and support,
to aid you physically, emotionally, or spiritually.
They are there for the reason you need them to be.

Then, without any wrong doing
on your part or at an inconvenient time,

this person will say or do something to
bring the relationship to an end.
Sometimes they die.
Sometimes they walk away.
Sometimes they act up and force you to take a stand.
What we must realize is that our need has been met,
Our desire fulfilled, their work is done, and
now it is time to move on.

Some people come into your life for a SEASON,
because your turn has come to share,
grow, or learn.
They bring you an experience of peace
or make you laugh.
They may teach you something you have never done.
They usually give you an unbelievable amount of joy.
Believe it; it is real. But only for a season.

LIFETIME relationships teach you lifetime lessons,
things you must build upon in order to have a
solid emotional foundation.
Your job is to accept the lesson,
love the person, and put what you have
learned to use in all other relationships
and areas of your life.
It is said that love is blind,
but friendship is clairvoyant.
Thank you for being a part of my life,
whether you were a reason, a season, or a lifetime.

—UNKNOWN

DEALING WITH DIVORCE

It's no secret that divorce is a part of life for many people, and moving forward from it is often no easy task. Deciding you really need to end your marriage is tough. It was for me; I often thought I should try to save my relationship with my husband and, at other times, I thought I should just give up. I went back and forth, back and forth, about it until while attending a divorce support group a fellow participant asked me, "What has to happen for you to decide?" That was a pivotal point for me, yet I did not know the answer for several more weeks. Then when my spouse asked me to compromise my integrity, I knew. That was what had to happen for me to decide. I was able to draw the line in the sand, close the door, and not look back.

And once the door was closed, I had to learn to remember: that was then, this is now. By letting go of the past, by forgiving, we can move forward more easily. When we hold on, even in a small way, we still have a string attached that sucks energy from us whenever we think about it.

For my client Jo, a crisis spurred her to realize her marriage was "not it" anymore. "That was a pivotal point in my life," she told me. "I realized where I would have ended up had I not left the marriage. I could see the train wreck coming and was able to jump off the train before it crashed."

Yes, some relationships have an expiration date, where you just realize it's past its prime. Like food gone bad, it not only fails to fortify you, but it can even make you sick. And while you may, for a time, in the guise of compassion, make excuses to avoid that reality, you then just reinforce rationalizations to stay in a relationship that is no longer healthy.

**"If he needs changing, God, you'll have to do it.
I can't."**

When you focus on the truth, and speak it, you move from tolerance to accountability. Our spouses must know where they stand to properly assess their situations.

To let go of the situation is to permit former mates to face reality, not to protect them. For those of you who might be leaving behind a partner whose addictions or behavior fostered codependency in your relationship, now is the time for tough love. In using tough love, we allow others to make mistakes. They must have this freedom to affect their own destinies without unwelcome interference from us. Let them learn. Do not soften the blow of consequences flowing from any bad decisions. It is sad to see others make wrong choices in life, yet we can't always protect our loved ones from themselves. We are not responsible for other people's actions. These are all important lessons I learned from being involved in Al-Anon.

Exercising tough love includes the following:

- Making brief, specific, and firm requests about problems without indulging in insults, accusations, or blaming.

- Addressing the conduct in a positive manner without using absolutes, overgeneralizations, labels, and without second-guessing motives.

- Finding qualities and actions of others to compliment and reinforce.

- Not hesitating to apologize for one's own mistakes.

A common trap in avoiding practicing tough love or giving serious ultimatums is that we fear the angry response we believe will follow. However, as Dr. Henry Cloud relates in his book, *9 Things You Simply Must Do to Succeed in Love and Life,* just because a patient screams does not keep the doctor from administering the shot: "As long as you stay on course, he is only in control of himself and whether or not

> "Don't look back, always look forward and forgive."
>
> —**BOB PROCTOR,** *YOU WERE BORN RICH* [104]

he gets with the program," Cloud writes about a marriage plagued by addiction or abuse. "His anger cannot dictate what his options are going to be. Even if he is angry, the rest of you can still tell him the way it is going to be, what he has to do to keep living in your home, or whatever consequences you and your support team have decided upon."[102]

When we decide to walk away, "we must be certain that we'll be content whether we get to have a relationship with that person or not," says Melody Beattie in *Make Miracles in Forty Days*.[103] (For more on recovering from divorce, codependency, and an unfulfilling life, look for my next book, *It's Time*. For those who have addictions, or someone in their life struggling with them, I recommend the twelve-step programs associated with Alcoholics Anonymous and Al-Anon; both offer wonderful fellowship where you meet with others in similar situations.)

Let go of your spouse's power over you. Angie, a client, realized after her divorce that her ex-husband was still trying to rattle her, to push her buttons, and she was letting him. She got her inspiration to move out of that trap while watching *The Wizard of Oz* with her daughter. When Glinda the Good Witch said to the Wicked Witch of the West, "You have no power here," Angie realized she could say the same thing in her mind every time her ex tried to upset her. It worked; she stood in her power and no longer allowed him to have power over her. Yeah!

For many of us, our marriages may have failed because we did not learn to show mature love, which means loving yourself for who you are and loving someone else for who they are. Maybe we didn't receive unconditional love growing up; instead we earned love by being good. So we adopted immature forms of love toward others.

That's a tough history to overcome. Nevertheless, we can come to realize that mature love allows us to be ourselves with our loved ones.

One way we can learn to love ourselves more is to look at our liabilities and then find a positive way to view them. For example, if you see yourself as sometimes bitchy, you can view that as being assertive, sticking up for what you want. You can also decide that, if you want to pursue a future love relationship, this time you'll make sure to invest as much (or more) time in yourself as in your relationship.

By taking care of you, you show yourself and everyone around you that you love yourself. Then you fill up your bucket first and let it overflow to everyone else, instead of allowing others to siphon from your bucket before it can be filled or, worse yet, blowing holes into your bucket to become a constant drain. Learn what fills you up and what drains you. Do what fills you and eliminate what drains you, as I learned in a sermon from Pastor Bob Merritt while attending Eagle Brook Church in Lino Lakes, Minnesota.

How Warm Is Your Love?

Here's a meditation exercise that I learned in a Beginning Experience divorce support group that may get you thinking differently about love and how to share it with others:

First, close your eyes. Bring your flow of energy through the different levels of your body until it reaches the top of your head. Often, you may feel the flow of energy going out of your chest and not up to the top. If so, imagine a cover over your chest so the warm flow of energy goes to the top and fills you up. Also, if you feel energy leaking out of your chest, it may be related to a belief that love is doing something to or for somebody and is other-centered rather than centered within yourself.

When the flow of energy leaks toward others, you emotionally drain yourself by putting love onto others rather than filling your own bucket of life. The goal then can be to learn to love yourself in a more adequate manner. Your love for yourself can be full to the top, a warm glow burning within you, warming you and the people you come into contact with. Your friends then would be warm without having to prove they were lovable. They simply would feel warm by being close to your fire. In a committed love relationship, your significant other gets an extra flow of warmth from your fire. It is important to care for the fire within you and make sure you have a glow that warms you and allows those around you to be warm.

Letting Go

When you're worrying about someone, as I mentioned in earlier chapters, you are in fear. We fear when we cannot control or cannot foresee a positive outcome on the path our friend or loved one is going down. Here's an example of something you can personalize and send to let someone know you are letting go and putting him or her in God's hands. It's challenging, especially when thinking about adult children. You can give this to them, or read and hold onto it as you let go of the outcome.

For a dear one for whom I am concerned:

I behold the Christ in you.
I place you lovingly in the care of God.
I release you from my anxiety and concern.
I let go of my possessive hold on you.
I am willing to free you to follow the dictates of
your own indwelling God.
I am willing to free you to live your life according to your
best light and understanding.
I no longer try to force my ideas on you, my ways on you.
I lift my thoughts above you, above the personal level.
I see you as God sees you, a spiritual being,
created in his image, and endowed with qualities
and abilities that make you needed and important...
not only to me and my world, but to God and his larger plan.
I do not bind you. I no longer believe you do not have
the understanding you need in order to meet life.
I bless you; I have faith in you; I behold the Christ in you.

— HERVE MARXOUX, OMI

DATING

Whether you're heading back into the dating game after the end of a marriage or long relationship, or still single and wanting to find your soul mate, focus on exactly what you want when it comes to finding that special someone. If you have complete intention with what you want, the universe will make it happen.

You can start by creating your ideal: "I want a soul mate who is drug free, sexually exclusive, committed to our relationship, smart, adventurous, fun, financially and physically fit, and outdoorsy." Whatever it is for you that's important to have in a spouse, write it down.

Then trust your feelings as you wade your way into the dating scene. God gave us our feelings to guide us, to help us with our choices. One night a client struggling with what to do about a relationship called me. She felt she was tolerating a lot, settling, because in her area, the men were slim pickings. She later decided to break it off, but he came back with promises and they tried again… until the inevitable happened, more promises broken and another breakup. Her feelings told her the first time what the right move was.

Another client had been dating a string of men; she was "considering the possibilities," like in car shopping, looking for the best one. When she realized one was "not it," she closed the relationship, or online profile, and moved on to the next. She trusted herself to know what would work for her, with what she could live with. Because she had written down exactly what she wanted in her dream man and knew herself so well, when a "not it" situation appeared, she made quick assessments and moved on. When I was online dating, I knew you could not pay me to get on a motorcycle. Anyone passionate about motorcycles was an automatic "not it," a no-brainer for me; it was something I knew I would have no tolerance for. It was easy for me to trust that.

I found myself in a transitional relationship shortly after my divorce, when I was still in the boo-hoo stage of losing my marriage, but it ended quickly. Because I felt disappointed about that, a friend told me to look at it as practice for something better, something I benefitted from in making me ready for something more. He compared me to a little red sports car that had been stored in the garage for a long time and was out on its first drive, just getting the carbon burned out of the engine. I was now ready to cruise.

> "Sometimes it takes darkness and the sweet confinement of your aloneness to learn anything or anyone that does not bring you alive is too small for you."
>
> **—POET DAVID WHYTE**[105]

I now wanted my dream man in my life, and as I identified the qualities I was seeking in that person, I realized I really wanted someone honest and trustworthy (Mr. Transition Man had lied to me, so I saw the values in these). Now, over two years later, I have my dream man in my life and he was worth the wait. The experience of the transitional relationship helped me get clearer on what I wanted.

Knowing what you don't want helps you know what you do want. Thinking back to my single days after my divorce, I realize that some of my online dates led me to some very perfect findings. I met one date at the café of a fitness center, The Marsh, and while he was "not it," the fitness center was an amazing find. I joined after finding out they held the Nia classes I was searching for, and shortly thereafter, I met a group of friends who became my family away from home. After that, I lived at the gym when I wasn't working, and what a blessing it turned out to be. Another relationship I had during this time ended because I realized I would rather be out in the sun, journaling and writing my book instead of dating this guy.

I was allowing this relationship to continue because it felt good to be pursued, even though I was not attracted to him. I realized

I would have ended up compromising if I continued this. I knew I wanted to focus on my career at that point and to be open and available for my dream man once he arrived (a year later). I ended the relationship, felt better, and happily focused on my family, career, fitness, and home.

Lynette, a client, dated a fellow who at first treated her very well, wining and dining her. Their conversations were focused on his business, though, and she eventually realized he was in financial difficulty, looking for her to bail him out. She knew he was "not it" and broke off the relationship a short while later. We discussed his qualities and she stated he reminded her of a friend's husband, whom she admired. She also talked about how, after being back in the dating world again after twenty-plus years, she had been focusing on watching other couples, seeing what was working for them, how their personalities meshed. She prayed for clarity, shifted her thinking, and is now attracting exactly the type of man she wants. She chose the parts that fit into what she really wanted and released the rest, saying "not it." She also realized that she had been growing through her divorce and reentry into the dating world, putting her in the place where she was ready to attract her desires.

Remember that when you're in a bad relationship, you're not free and available for a good relationship. The man or woman of your dreams could be waiting for you. Don't endure a broken road; let God lead you to your dream.

One other thing to keep in mind as you date: be confident enough to take action and initiate a date or a new activity. Remember, it's crucial to make a specific request and suggest a time: "I'd like to cook dinner together next Friday evening." "I'd like to plan a camping trip for next weekend." By making requests and seeing if the other person is receptive, you find out where you meet and where you don't, as Dr. Charlotte Kasl shares in *If the Buddha Dated: A Handbook for Finding Love on a Spiritual Path*. You will know the positive aspects and limitations of being with this person so you can make an informed choice. While you might feel awkward

 **⚠ TIP**

Your online dating profile needs to include current photos, both close up and full length of you doing what you love, and descriptions of what you love to do, especially if you want to share these activities with your special someone.

or silly trying something new, you also might have a good laugh, open up your heart, move beyond your prejudices, and end up dancing closer to your beloved.[107]

BRINGING A BUDDHIST PERSPECTIVE TO DATING

What would it mean to bring a different perspective to dating? To approach it using Buddhist ways of thought? That's what Dr. Charlotte Kasl considers in her book, *If the Buddha Dated: A Handbook for Finding Love on a Spiritual Path*. Here are some of her thoughts:

- Instead of feeling a sense of urgency, we would be fascinated by the process of meeting and getting to know new people. Compassion, care, and kindness for others would supersede "getting someone to be with us."

- We would never want to control another person. We wouldn't put others on a pedestal, nor would we set them below us.

- We would enter into a shared union where we would cherish and give to each other, love unconditionally.

- We would accept that the process can be awkward, unpredictable, challenging, and surprising.

- When we would want to run away, be deceptive, tell lies, or put on a mask, we would need to walk right into our fears, sit down, and talk to them until they became our friends.

- We would commit to knowing and accepting ourselves, so we are better able to surrender to loving another person because we have nothing to hide and nothing to feel ashamed of.

- We would attune to a higher vibration of energy through becoming clear and open and would more quickly see when there is potential for a good relationship. We then would be attracted to others who are growing and stretching and those more likely to be a worthy companion.

- We would experience that entering a relationship and living in the heart of the beloved means our lives will change, our shells will crack open, and we will never be the same.[108]

 TOOL

It's never a bad idea to spend some time reflecting on what makes your spouse special. It helps you keep your attitude of being in this for the long haul and reminds you why you love this person and have made him or her such a big part of your life. Create a list like the one below, thinking about how you could fill out this thought: What I love and appreciate about my loved one is that he/she is:

Honest	Affectionate	Clever
Ambitious	Well dressed	Witty
Discerning	Careful to maintain stuff	Sensitive
Goal oriented		Protective
Entrepreneurial	Interested in buying good quality	Fun
Kind	Interested in enjoying the outdoors	Playful
Giving		Adventurous
Sweet	Business savvy	Family oriented
Sensual	Cute	

KEEPING SCORE

Whether in a relationship with a spouse, friend, or family member, "keeping score" (keeping a record of wrongs for that other person) is certainly a "not it" behavior. Instead, keep the slate clean, communicate, and let it go. Letting resentments build up will cause an avalanche (where acting ugly takes over) later on. Communicating right away may be uncomfortable for a moment, or even several moments, but it's better than waiting for a big blowup. Taking care of something as soon as you realize there's an issue gets everything

> *Let everything you say be good and helpful, so that your words will be an encouragement to those who hear them.*[110]
>
> EPHESIANS 4:29

cleared up, and keeps your relationship running smoothly.

One client, Malinda, realized she was keeping score one night. Her guy was watching a game on TV, and she went up to bed. After a while, he was still downstairs, watching that game, and Malinda became irritated—until she realized she was keeping score, a definite "not it."

A client who keeps score recently shared a story that happened twenty years before, when she was keeping score with almost everyone around her. She had been doing this for years, maybe most of her life, and putting up walls in her relationships. She did not communicate to those she had issues with; she just kept repeating and remembering the stories of how she was hurt to others, often calling the offenders names. She would remember comments people made, or when they did not do things she had expected them to. The ones she believed hurt her had no idea why she treated them so coldly or that she gossiped about them in that way.

Instead of keeping a record of wrongs, why not remember instead how grateful you are, what you appreciate about or enjoy about your family and friends?

=== **HOMEWORK** ===

1. Complete the "What I love and appreciate about you is" exercise, shown on page 251. Write it all down. You can do this for anyone, and it will improve your relationship when you focus on appreciating that person and not complaining about him or her.

2. Keep a gratitude journal for all the things you appreciate about your family, friends, neighbors, coworkers, and especially yourself as an act of love.

3. Press pause and think about your relationships. Are there things that come to mind after reading this chapter that you want to act on? How are things going with your children? Your spouse? Are you spending as much time as you want with them? Are you communicating with love or are you acting ugly with them? Are there critical conversations you want to have with someone?

4. What fills your bucket and what takes away from it? Want more time with your friends? Are you a people pleaser allowing your bucket to be siphoned from? What changes would you like to make? Are there ways you can fill your bucket with your friends and family?

Your Financial Goals

When it comes to your finances, especially if you're on a limited income, think about spending on yourself first—your basic personal needs/essentials. Be frugal; get what you need to take care of yourself nutritionally, physically, and mentally. Make sure to get your haircuts, the food you want, a comfortable home to live in, and a reliable option for transportation. With the tips already given in the preceding chapters, you're well on your way to watching your spending. Now move out to the next circle (see graphic below) of needs by making sure your home and vehicle are properly maintained.

From there, make sure you get out of debt. Make a plan to pay off debts if you have them, and start saving so you can stay out of debt in the future. Establish an emergency fund so you don't get slammed by payments for unexpected car repairs or broken appliances. Then establish short-term savings for things like holidays and vacations, so you don't feel deprived. Even if you just want to visit a local campground for your vacation, that still costs money. So budget for it. Then focus on your long-term savings, like for retirement (yeah!).

How you save and how you spend can make all the difference.

Finally, make sure to have some money for entertainment. It may be a low-cost option (using Netflix, visiting your local library often and checking out books and movies, eating in more than eating out) until you have your basic needs met, with an emergency fund and retirement funding in place. As you cover your basics, more dollars can be designated to any category you choose, be it additional clothing, upgrading your car, or increasing your savings. Maybe instead of a weekend camping trip nearby, you now have enough money to take off for a week to Yellowstone.

Pay yourself first. Have an automatic transfer whenever you get paid so a percentage goes into a savings and/or retirement account right away. You will not see this money, so it's out of sight, out of mind, and tucked away for you to spend later. If you do not have a consistent regular income, take a percentage of each dollar the moment money comes into your hands and make a transfer or deposit directly into your savings or retirement account. Then you'll have it there, rather than planning to fund these and then running out of money to do so.

PAYING DOWN DEBTS AND ESTABLISHING SAVINGS

When establishing your savings, adopt a lifestyle that allows you to transfer 10 percent of your earnings to savings. Then try to up that amount slightly each year, until you get to 80 percent spending, 20 percent savings, or 70 percent spending and 30 percent savings. Create the habit of saving first and spending last. Use the inner circle as shown above to take care of your immediate self-care needs first and work out from there. If in debt, get back to the poor college budget mentality and realize you might want to break out the peanut butter toast-meals for a while until you get things under control. Shop your pantry and home first. When you need to change the percentages of your savings plan, you will know. Something will come into your awareness and you will make the change. Consider what amount you give tithing to your church, or any other area of donation. Factor this into your percentages.

Know where you're at with a balance sheet. Very simply list your assets on one side, liabilities on the other. Subtract your liability total from the asset total to see where you stand. It may not be so bad after all, as I have found when coaching others who are afraid to even look at their balances. Once you know, start where you are; do what you can with what you have.

The goal is to live simply and elegantly, without spending boatloads of money, to be debt free with a goal of financial freedom, to retire early and do the fun things you want to do.

If you are married, be united with your spouse in your financial choices. Spend according to the plan you agree on.

If you are in debt, here is a basic repayment plan:

Item	Balance	Payment	Jan	Feb	Mar	Apr	May	Jun	Jul
Car	$25,000	$500	$500	$500	$500	$500	$500	$888	$1,000
Visa	$1,562	$150	$150	$150	$150	$500	$500	$112	0
Macy's	$850	$85	$150	$350	$350	0	0	0	0
Medical	$200	$50	$200	0	0	0	0	0	0
Total	$26,297	$785	$1,000	$1,000	$1,000	$1,000	$1,000	$1,000	$1,000

In the above example, the minimum payments required were $785 a month; however, the couple paying them decided they could pay $1,000 per month to pay off debt faster. They took their debts and listed them in order of largest balance to smallest. Starting in January, they took the smallest debt (the medical bill) and paid it off and then added the remaining extra money to pay the next lowest debt (the Macy's credit card). The car and Visa payments were kept the same as usual. In April, they split the $1,000 monthly budgeted amount between the car payment and Visa, paying off the Visa in June. Beginning in July, they were able to take the entire $1,000 to pay off their car in another twenty-one months, way ahead of schedule. They did this without incurring more debt and then were debt free, except for their mortgage. This concept, paying off your smallest debt first, then paying your next smallest debt, is championed by financial guru Dave Ramsey (although I was following it before taking his seminar at my church).

So if you find yourself in a hole of debt, stop digging and work on how to get out of the hole.

During this process it may be tempting to take money from one designated fund (your emergency fund or short-term savings) to fund something else. This only leads to trouble and should be avoided, unless an emergency situation arises. If you continue to pull from savings, you will not reach your goal. Keep some "envelope" money (a certain amount stashed away in an envelope) or petty cash for things that come up. Don't use savings for unintended purchases. You may need to say, "No, I will not be going to the movies or out for pizza" to your friends. You do not have to share with them why you aren't coming along.

When it comes to establishing your retirement savings,

> ### ⚠ TIP
>
> Establish a piggy bank plan. Put all your loose change in a piggy bank (you can pick up one at Target for about ten dollars, a good investment in a new habit). Designate a time frame when you will cash it in for a definite purpose you're saving for. My plan is that when the piggy bank is full, the money goes for souvenirs on my next trip. If I cash in before the trip because the piggy is full, I save the cash either in my home safe or in my savings account, depending upon how soon I will travel. This practice is less about saving for a small item; rather it is about looking at yourself as a saver.

discuss with a financial advisor how much money you might need when you decide to stop working. Go over what kind of retirement lifestyle you envision. Some folks plan to go fishing and live at their cabin when they retire, while some want to take extended vacations, often. What will you want? Will you downsize your home? Will you buy an expensive RV to travel in? Take the number of days you will travel and compare that with the cost of a hotel for that many nights. It may be more cost effective to rent an RV or just stay in hotels if you travel. RVs are expensive.

A very simple way to see if you have enough saved to retire is to divide the amount you have saved by the annual income you believe is needed. That will show you how many years the money you've saved will last. Factor in about 3 percent inflation to be even more accurate. This calculation does not factor in any earnings from interest or the stock market, or income from pensions or Social Security. See your financial advisor for a true picture.

BUDGETING

There are many great computer programs out there for budgeting. Taking the time to set one up is well worth it. It will make tracking your expenses and putting your money to work where you want it to easier. Want to travel more? Spend the money there and not at the mall in mindless recreational spending. You'll also be able to see how saving and paying down debt is affecting your overall personal wealth.

When setting up your budget:

- Think about short-term goals—one year or less (maybe saving for vacation).

- Move on to your mid-term goals—ten years (maybe saving for your next car).

- Then plan for your long-term goals—ten years and beyond (your retirement savings).

On building wealth, I have seen in my practice what Chris and Marlow Felton, authors of *Couples Money: What Every Couple Should Know About Money and Relationships* discuss: people who have an underlying thought process of unworthiness when it comes to having money.[111] Most don't even realize they feel unworthy of wealth in their life. It is one of the most destructive beliefs anyone can have and causes people to under-earn their potential and sabotage their own wealth. Judging yourself as undeserving is poisonous to your energy and your goals, and the biggest root of self-sabotage. You will never out-earn your self-image. What prices are you and your loved ones paying for your feelings of unworthiness? Accept yourself for who you are; focus on the great things about you, and forgive yourself. Get the picture of who you want to become, make the changes, gather support, move in that direction, and enjoy the journey.

BAD SPENDING HABITS

Spending on unnecessary things can quickly become a gushing wound, where you need to get the tourniquet out and stop immediately, then press pause and get your spending back in line with your goals. Learn to resist the urge to splurge on gifts and treats for yourself and others.

When it comes to spending, here are some "not it" financial choices:

- Spending your retirement money before retirement to support a lifestyle that is above your means

- Spending out of guilt (This doesn't right wrongs and recipients can learn how to push you to feel guilty if there's a reward at the end.)

- Spending in a delusional way, turning a blind eye to it, not watching what's in your account and charging more than you know you have

- Spending just because you have a coupon (Only buy it if you really want it—remember coupons are marketing ploys to get you to spend more money.)

- Have a current will to give the probate system directions on how to distribute your assets at the time of your death, or avoid probate by having a trust.

Far too often people use shopping as therapy—to give themselves a boost in mood and feel better about themselves and their lives. Unfortunately, the uplift from shopping only lasts a short while, and if you become a regular recreational shopper, you can quickly rack up debt and have a house overflowing with stuff. I've helped plenty of people clear their closets and cupboards because their shopping had created headaches in the long run.

While shopping as an outing may seem harmless, think about what you could be doing instead. Working on a project? Going to a movie? Going to the gym? Cleaning your house? Going for a walk? I know several families, couples, and, particularly, girlfriends who shop together on a regular basis and complain about a lack of money, a lack of space in their homes, or their large credit card bills. I worked with a couple who wanted to take a vacation and could not see a way to come up with the money. What I uncovered while working

Accept my blessing that is brought to you, because God has dealt graciously with me, and because I have enough.[112]

- GENESIS 33:11

261

⚠ BUDGET-CUTTING TIPS

Here are some more ways to be smart with your money, so you'll end up with more of it in the long run:

- Use low-rate or zero-interest credit cards and pay them off each month; do not carry credit card balances.

- Pay off all debt before spending more. This includes remodeling, so pay off your credit card first and remodel the kitchen later (pay for the remodel in cash if you can).

- Don't let college expenses take away from retirement savings. Your kids can get jobs in the summer and at school and take out loans for their education.

- Find extra money each month by:

  o Reducing the number of meals you eat out; cook at home instead.

  o Renting a movie instead of going out to the movies.

  o Drinking the coffee at work (or bringing your own travel mug from home) instead of swinging through a drive-thru for an expensive mocha on the way there.

- Ask how much is enough and identify your needs.

  o Can you get by with a $25,000 car instead of a more expensive SUV?

  o How much house do you really need?

  o Are you spending money on a storage unit to store your stuff to declutter your home? Do you really need what's in there? Consider selling your extra stuff and putting the money toward paying down your debt (and the monthly cost of the storage unit also can go directly to your monthly debt repayment plan).

- Make sure you are adequately insured.

- Pay the max toward your retirement savings if you have paid off your mortgage.

- Watch out for "mental blind spots" when spending, like using a credit card without paying off the balance and not watching the interest you're paying, or even neglecting to pay your credit card minimum in the first place because you're overwhelmed with paying all your bills.

- If you really want a vacation, think about the concept of a "staycation," where you visit local sights, museums, and parks. You can get the canoe out, go for a bike ride, and take local trails you haven't tried. Or you can take time to complete projects around your house (like painting the garage or living room) and do a thorough cleaning of each room. You can read, watch movies, and go to restaurants you've wanted to try. Staying home means saving money without being boring.

---

with them was that they had an overabundance of stuff based on shopping habits. They ended up clearing their home of all the undesired, unused stuff, sold it, and took a much-wanted vacation with the money. Once they arrived home, reconnected, they updated the look of their home with fresh paint and new storage

⚠ TIP

Protect yourself by adding overdraft protection on your checking accounts, and scheduling automatic deposits and payments so you're always on top of your finances. Check your account balances: daily for checking accounts and weekly for credit cards and savings and investment accounts.

> ### ⚠ TIP
>
> What would you do if your wallet or purse were stolen? Do you know what's in them? Are you carrying credit cards? Have you copied your cards or do you have the card numbers and the company's 1-800 numbers written down to call in case they're stolen? Did you know that you can place a call to the Social Security Administration fraud line if someone steals your Social Security card? Having your credit card numbers and company info stored in a safe place can save you time and stress in a situation like this. Do not store this information on your computer!

options. They were recharged and united as a couple. Yeah! What a win-win-win!

Take the money you were spending on recreational spending to save for your emergency fund and pay off debt. Take the extra time you're saving to really connect with your family, friends, and environment.

ORGANIZING YOUR FINANCIAL PAPERS

Once you've set up your budgeting plan and begin to get your finances in order, you can also take time to safeguard important financial papers. Part of getting your financial papers organized means deciding which can go into the safe and which you can keep in a file drawer. A bank safe-deposit box is the safest place you can have—it's free of risk from at-home fires and also from tampering. But there are certain documents you need to keep on hand, and many papers you can get copies of in case of fire. Here is a list of what to keep where:

Home Fireproof Safe or Bank Safe-Deposit Box

- Deeds and titles
- Marriage licenses and divorce decrees
- Birth certificates
- Home inventory

- Social Security cards

- Stock certificates

- List of bank accounts, brokerage accounts, certificates of deposit, and credit cards with account numbers and branch locations

Locked Home File

- Insurance policies

- Passport

- Tax returns

- Wills and trusts

- Power of attorney designation

- Medical directives

- Funeral and burial instructions

- List of bank accounts, brokerage accounts, certificates of deposit, and credit cards with account numbers and branch locations

Also create a personal inventory so, if needed, it will be easy for someone to see what investment, retirement, insurance, and savings assets you have. This can be put in a locked file and you can give a notice to anyone who needs to know where to find it in the event of your death.

Personal Inventory

Description	Account	Company	Amount	Owner	Notes	Contact Phones
Pension	HN34A	General Mills	$3,000/mo	Ken		
Social Security	SSN		$1,100/mo	Ken		
Social Security	SSN		$600/mo	Barbara		
IRA	333-4567	LPL Financial	$300,000	Ken		LPL advisor phone
Bank Accounts	Various	Local bank	$50,000	Joint	Checking	Bank phone
NQ Annuity	9789498	Prudential	$25,000	Barbara		Prudential phone
Credit Card	CC #	VISA	$5,000	Ken	0 balance	VISA phone
Life Insurance	177507	MetLife	$250,000	Ken	Whole life	MetLife phone
Life Insurance	778800	Prudential	$100,000	Barbara	Whole life	Prudential phone
Long-Term Care	111222333	John Hancock	$150/day	Ken		John Hancock #
Long-Term Care	111222345	John Hancock	$150/day	Barbara		John Hancock #

Include the following with the above personal inventory:

- Your home address

- Your vacation home address

- Your property and casualty insurance agent and contact information

- Your insurance coverage, with the deductible on home and vehicle policies, including umbrella details

- Financial advisor contact info—company name, address, email, phone

- Details of your wills, including date of will

- Trust agreements—name of trust, type of trust, beneficiaries

- Attorney contact info—address, email, phone

- Accountant contact info—address, email, phone

- Trust officer contact info—address, email, phone

- Personal representative contact info—address, email, phone

Make a list of where you can find your important financial documents. It could look like this:

Where's It At?

Tax returns, last three years	Home office file, bottom file drawer
Supporting tax documentation	Home office file, bottom file drawer
Life insurance policies	Home office file, bottom file drawer
Long-term care policies	Home office file, bottom file drawer
Disability income insurance policies	Home office file, bottom file drawer
Medicare supplement policies	Home office file, bottom file drawer
Homeowners insurance policies	Home office file, bottom file drawer
Vehicle insurance policies	Home office, third file drawer
Checking account statements	Downloaded to Quicken on laptop
Savings account statements	Downloaded to Quicken on laptop
Money market statements	Downloaded to Quicken on laptop

Certificates of Deposit statements	Downloaded to Quicken on laptop
Mutual fund statements	Home office, third file drawer
Stock certificates	Safety Deposit Box #202 U.S. Bank
Bonds (savings & others)	Safety Deposit Box #202 U.S. Bank
Credit cards	Frozen in a block of ice in the freezer
Credit card records	Downloaded to Quicken on laptop
Mortgage papers	Box on the top shelf of guestroom closet
Auto loans/lease papers	Home office, third file drawer
Home equity loan papers	Box on the top shelf of guestroom closet
Personal loan papers	Home office, second file drawer
Profit sharing statements	Home office, second file drawer
Pension statements	Home office, second file drawer
IRA statements	Home office, second file drawer
Keogh statements	Home office, second file drawer
SEP statements	Home office, second file drawer
401(k) or 403(b) statements	Home office, second file drawer
Copies of designation of beneficiary	Home safe with will
Forms for retirement accounts	Home office, second file drawer
Social Security statements	Downloaded to laptop with login info
Trust statements	Home office, second file drawer
Power of Attorney documents	Home safe with will
Annuity contracts	Home office, second file drawer
Passwords to computer programs	Home office, back of pencil drawer
Deed(s)	Home safe, office closet
Land contracts	Home safe, office closet
Buy/sell agreements	Safety Deposit #202 U.S. Bank

Right of First Refusal agreement	Safety Deposit #202 U.S. Bank
House keys	Home safe, office closet
Vacation home keys	Home safe, office closet
Vehicle keys	Home safe, office closet
Commercial property keys	Home safe, office closet
Investment property keys	Home safe, office closet
Vehicle title	Home safe, office closet
Coin collection	Under the bed
Gun collection	Gun safe, basement storage closet
Fine jewelry	Hat box, top of master BR closet
Birth certificates	Home safe, office closet
Passport	Home safe, office closet
Current financial statement	Office file, top drawer

Remember as you continue to pay down debts and get your finances in shape that there's plenty of money out there for you. You cannot receive it when you have a closed fist. Have fun with it; get the whole household involved. Now let's look at your career and see how you can make the most of it.

HOMEWORK

1. See exactly where you are financially, to the penny. Press pause with this information and ask yourself, "Is this where I want to be?" "What changes do I want to make to quickly move to my dream?" Maybe you decide it's time to quit smoking! Ask yourself, "Are my needs being met?" (Think of the circles graphic at the beginning of the chapter.)

2. Copy the contents of your wallet after you evaluate what's in there and if it really needs to be there, like credit cards—carrying them makes it more likely you will use them. Store copies in a safe place.

3. Where's it at—complete your inventory and store in a safe place.

4. Contact your financial advisor for a review of your accounts and goals.

Your Career

In the introduction of this book, I shared a story about taking a Bible study on vocation in the boo-hoo stage of my divorce, and through tears, I took these notes:

Do what you love...
Do what you are most passionate about...
Don't let your buts get in the way...
Don't let anyone stop you!

Think about these notes yourself as you consider what might be next for you and your career. Really focus on what might be the right next thing. In Sarah Ban Breathnach's *Simple Abundance: A Daybook of Comfort and Joy*, she writes that taking time to focus on such things is really essential, especially for women, who are often rushing through life while trying to meet the never-ending demands of work, family, and home:

> As we get nowhere fast, we lose focus and clarity, existing in a perpetual state of confusion. Many times during the day we'll speak of feeling out of kilter—describing a lack of centering within. When the center isn't holding, it's because we've lost touch with

the tremendous healing power of our Vesta aspect. We have wandered far away from the sacred hearth and don't know how to find our way back to heat, light, and warmth. In order to regain focus, women need to restore a sense of "at-homeness" to their lives.[113]

Taking the Bible study on vocation helped me focus on what I really wanted in my career, as I was bored with my job and had always wanted to complete my college degree. So I decided my first step toward that goal was to go to the local college to see if my credits from a technical school twenty-five-plus years ago would transfer. While there, talking with a career counselor, I realized that I had downshifted my career in the past few years, stepping back and taking a lower-paying secretarial-type job while dealing with my divorce. I felt I had lost skills due to this downshift and also felt bored and stagnated.

The counselor said I should pat myself on the back for getting to where I was, that I had done well for myself through the years, and that many people who came into his office would want what I had. He told me I had made great decisions and to give myself credit for those. And taking a step back when I did was what I needed to do to take care of me. Blaming myself for that would only cause me pain.

He also talked about the potential burnout if I knocked myself out getting a degree and then quickly went into a high-pressure career. Did I want that? Did I want to have to adjust to living on an entry-level pay scale again? Did I want to push hard to get that degree, get a new job for about ten years or so, and then retire without any guarantee I would have earned more money along the way?

The answer to all of his questions to me was no, so he suggested I go to the hardware store and "buy a shiny new hammer and smash your fingers really hard until they bleed because that is what you are doing to yourself every time you beat yourself up for not having a degree." Stop hitting your fingers with the hammer, he added; in other words, stop placing judgments on what you've done and where you are.

He then suggested I work a regular non-stress job, take classes for fun, volunteer, or teach fitness classes. Whatever I consider fun, I can focus on that because I've earned it.

Some of us did not have the opportunity to obtain the degree—so what! Build on what you have; start where you are and work with your skills in new areas. Just because you do not have the coveted degree does not make you less than someone who has one, so stop beating yourself up about it. When I negotiated a salary, I learned ten years work experience in an area is considered equivalent to a college degree in many industries when calculating pay. This may not be true for all professions (for instance, you cannot become a nurse without getting a nursing degree), but you decide what's right for you. For me, going back to get my degree became a "not it" as I realized I could make more money as an entrepreneur.

What about you? Is there a place in your life where you can buy a shiny new hammer? Do you beat yourself up over your career, education, as a spouse, parent, and friend? Did my story resonate with you anywhere in your life?

When it comes to your career, one of the first things you can consider is if you have a *career*. Or is what you're doing just a job to you? Are you working just to earn money or are you on a career path too? If you're feeling stuck, start looking at your job as your career, or as a stepping stone on your career path. Then opportunities will just start showing up.

Also consider that you may be working a job you hate to pay for things you don't really need. By doing this, you are sacrificing your true desires just to pay for more and more stuff. A big house, a full garage, and the latest and greatest in tech gadgets may give you a sense of place for a while, but in the end it's all just stuff. Remember, you can't take it with you, right? Revisit the "Your Financial Goals" chapter to see how you can reduce your spending so maybe you can take a job you love, even if it doesn't pay as much. I recommend reading *Your Money or Your Life: 9 Steps to Transforming Your Relationship with Money and Achieving Financial Independence* by Joe Dominguez and Vicki Robin for an in-depth look at this topic.

If you feel torn between work and home, now is the time to think about how you might better manage that. Do you really want to be a stay-at-home mom? Can you readjust your budget to make that work? Or are you torn because you really love your job, yet really want to be there for your family? Consider some of the tips in the preceding chapters and on page 275 to help you find balance at home and in your work life. And don't forget to press pause to unplug from the chaos and determine what changes you want to make.

For those of you moms considering transitioning back into the workplace after having children, remember your time at home has given you skills you can transfer to the workplace. If you've been organized at home, you can be organized at work—organizing is organizing. Juggling tasks at home and juggling tasks at work require the same skills. I have coached several women who, after staying home with their children, have felt a lack of confidence about resuming a career. They felt out of the loop and out of practice by not utilizing their skills. Once we looked at all they had done at home with their family, we saw how these skills could transfer.

Sometimes it makes sense to ease back into work part time if you've spent years being a stay-at-home mom. You decide what is best for you. Just because you have a friend or family member who really knocks herself out trying to do it all does not mean that's for everyone. Your friend may be on the straight path to burnout. Want that? One key I have found with my coaching clients is that when they are out of debt, they feel they have more choices when deciding to pursue a new career.

Balancing Work and Home

Here are some tips for those of you struggling to balance your work life and home life, or for those of you reentering the workforce after being home with children for a while:

- Put your time and money into your priorities. If your priority is your family, your fitness, and your faith, make sure you aren't working so much that it keeps you from these priorities. Sometimes it's necessary to work a holiday, or to work late and miss a workout. Or sometimes a work function happens when you want to attend a worship service or a Bible study. But if these instances become the norm, you aren't living your priorities, and your life won't keep moving smoothly. When things are not going well at work, you bring it home, whether you realize it or not, and when things are not going well at home, your work suffers right along with that.

- If you're considering working at home, or you have a work-at-home job, realize that you will struggle to keep your work and family life separate. It's all too easy to have these worlds collide. To keep them separate, have a designated work time and stay focused on work during that time. Do your best to keep your home distractions at bay during this time so you get work completed.

- Rather than commuting for an hour or more a day in high traffic, reduce your commute if you can by going to an office business center (OBC) in your neighborhood. Even if you can only work this out with your employer to do a few days a week, it will make a difference.

- Plan some transition time from work to home. Whether that includes picking up the kids, getting groceries, picking up dry cleaning, or going to a hair appointment, there are a lot of things to do between work and settling in at home for the night.

- Avoid scheduling something every night; even if you don't have a family to care for at home, being overcommitted in the evenings can become overwhelming. Otherwise, you may not have time to keep your home, finances, and eating plan organized.

- What about working part time? Is it an option for you? How about working thirty-two hours per week (which most companies start as full time)? This may be a good way to ease back into the working world or keep your home life more balanced.

- Maximize your time by having an errand day. Lumping as many errands as you can into an hour or two saves time in the long run. If you have a consistent day in which to run errands, you'll reduce stress because you will always know that is your day to get your errands done. It doesn't have to be on the weekend either. Maybe your spouse or Grandma takes the kids for the evening so you can get this done on Wednesday and avoid crowded stores.

- Online shopping is a great option. You can buy what you need, at your convenience. If you buy a lot at once, you often can get free shipping and other discounts. You save money, time, and avoid hassles—a win-win-win, for sure.

When looking at career options, play "not it." For example, I was invited by several companies to work with them as an insurance agent or an investment rep when my two-year lease was up on my insurance office and I decided to make a career change. When I investigated these offers, the jobs just did not feel right. I was able to confidently say "not it" to them because I had already identified and put out what I was looking for. I knew 100 percent I would get that, without a doubt. It was a very exciting time as options flew at me. I said to myself, "I wonder how this will all come together," and was amazed as I watched and took the necessary steps as the opportunities appeared.

 TOOL

When thinking about where you want to go with your career, ask yourself: What do I want to be doing one year from now? Five years from now? What is your ultimate career vision? Start writing it down.

Not long after the third-bridge episode, which I described in Chapter 1, I contemplated pursuing my consulting business Systems For Change, and then I was offered a position with a company to do what I wanted to do in the business I had envisioned launching. Instead of opening the consulting part of my existing coaching business, I accepted the position, worked until the project's completion, and then began consulting. This process reminded me of the third bridge. I didn't go where I thought I wanted to, but it ended up a better opportunity by allowing me to practice my business before I began out on my own.

As Napoleon Hill writes about in *Think and Grow Rich*, when the opportunity came, it came in a different form and direction than expected, but it still came:

> That is one of the tricks of opportunity. It has a sly habit of slipping in by the back door, and often it comes disguised in the form of misfortune, or temporary defeat. Perhaps this is why so many fail to recognize opportunity.[114]

GOAL SETTING

In the early 1980s, I learned Management by Objectives, which I've used throughout my career. When I became a life and career coach, I learned SMART goals and discovered the two work well together. I use this in my consulting practice where I begin by observing and assessing a work flow, process, team, or individual to identify best practices and where processes get backed up or blocked, and find where handshakes aren't happening. Once I identify issues, with the management objective in mind, I create solutions, implement them, train staff, and am there to maintain as the business grows. I use SMART goals when I work with individuals and teams to reach their objective/goal.

SMART stands for Specific, Measureable, Achievable/Attainable, Relevant/Realistic, Time-based.

Here's how you can use the SMART system for establishing those goals:

- Realize the process can seem daunting, especially if you or your employees haven't done it before. But it can be simple if you look at your department objectives and then ask yourself and/or your employees what can be done to meet those objectives. For example, if the departmental objective is to improve the customer satisfaction score, the team can work on providing more self-service information to reduce the number of calls and call-wait time or offer tools to improve customer service levels by clarifying how to communicate with a customer.

- Remember the S in SMART is for Specific: your objectives (or your team's) can describe specifically the result that is desired

- Make the goals measurable (M for Measurable): in order to use the objectives as a part of a review process, it needs to be very clear whether you or someone on your team met the objective or not.

- Make the goals achievable or attainable: (A for Achievable/Attainable)

- Make the goals realistic or relevant (R for Realistic/Relevant): realistic objectives are objectives that recognize factors that can't be controlled. Said another way, realistic goals are potentially challenging but not so challenging that the chance of success is small. They can be accomplished with the tools that you or your team members have at their disposal.

- Make the goals time-based (T for Time-based): the final factor for a good objective is that it is time-based. In other words, it's not simply, "This is the final piece in making the objective real and tangible. The implied date is the date of the next review, when you or your employee will be held accountable for the commitments made through these objectives.[115]

Pastor John Arnold, in "Why SMART Goals Aren't Always So Smart," says, once or twice per year, find a goal that is not realistic, something outside your norm that may not even be achievable. Use the SMT, Specific and Measurable with a deadline (Time). Making a quantum leap will step up the baseline—it may make me the best me by giving me a sense of accomplishment by intentionally pushing out past the edge of my comfort zone. SMART goals are the norm, our baseline. A quantum leap is going for it with everything we've got.[116]

SETTING UP YOURSELF AND YOUR OFFICE FOR SUCCESS

Whether you are the manager of your whole office, the manager of your department, or even a middle-level or entry-level employee, there are ways you can set up your day-to-day tasks and your office space so that you are set up for success in your career.

First, select simple efficient tasks to practice consistently, such as:

- I check my voicemails and emails first thing in the morning.

- I do my filing at the end of the day when I clear my desk for the day.

- I do my transfer tracking on Tuesdays.

- We hold our weekly meeting every Wednesday morning.

- I file the regular monthly claims first, getting them out of the way, and then focus on any rejected claims, looking at sequential billing cycle and coding issues, resubmitting oldest first to clean up my accounts receivables.

Then, consider what your "best practices" may be in getting your job done. Is there a better way to handle a certain task? Do you see where having a step-by-step method to a certain process ensures it is done correctly time after time? Implement these so you and your office colleagues are doing your best work, day after day.

Concentrate all your attention on any given task until you have mastered it. If you need to write down how you did it, if the task is something new to you, do so. Then you'll remember how to do it the next time. For processes you may do infrequently, such as mail mergers or printing labels, make a binder or file of instructional how-to's so you can refer to it the next time you do one of these tasks.

File new information or paperwork that crosses your desk where it should go right away so you aren't looking for it when you need it again. If your office is high-tech and you get a lot information transmitted without being printed out (paperless info), make an organizational system to file this information on your computer. Then back up your files often and print out important documents that you may need if you have a systems failure (and a backup failure). Remember which documents must be printed and put in a client file to be in compliance with industry and company rules.

Also, block off your time for certain tasks or projects. Look at your week ahead and estimate how much time you will need to get a certain job done. If you complete your task early, what's next on your priorities list? Be realistic about what you can get

> **⚠ TIP**
>
> Cleaning your desk before vacation or a holiday is like cleaning your house before company comes. It feels really good to come back home or back to the office when it's clean and organized. Why leave yourself a mess to not look forward to?

Are you ever on the road with your business? Think about how to organize all you will need while you're away. What basics do you need in your traveling office? Common forms? Pens? Paper clips? Files? Notepads? Stock up on these; have extras in your car's trunk or briefcase. Think about if there's something consistently missing that you need. If you had it with you, would it save you and others time and energy? If the answer is yes, make sure you bring it along on your next trip.

done and flexible if other important tasks come up.

Determine if your activities are red-time activities that produce no income or green-time activities that generate income. Now, we all know that you will need to spend some time on red-time activities (filling out time cards, invoicing, filing, filtering through all the emails to focus on the ones worth pursuing), but be as efficient as you can with these so green-time activities get more of your focus. Some of these red-time tasks can be done while you're on hold for a call or waiting for computer downloads.

Remember, communication is key. Being out of sync doesn't make for a good impression, so keep things consistent, even for things as simple as how you and your employees answer the phone, or what your phone systems standard voicemail messages are. Here are the standard voicemail options for my business, Systems For Change. Notice how they're consistent, while designed for a specific purpose:

- General: "This is the office of Systems For Change. We are currently assisting another client. Please leave your message and we will return your phone call by the end of the next business day. We thank you for your call and appreciate your business."

- Office closed: "This is the office of Systems For Change. The office is currently closed from [date] to [date]. Please leave your message and we will return your call when we return. We thank you for your call and appreciate your business."

If you are going to have employees make calls to set appointments for you, let them know whom they are calling before they pick up the phone. Keep in mind that having them read from a script may not work well until they've practiced some and know they need to keep the call sounding like a conversation, rather than someone just reading something word for word, according to realtor Alicia Romano.[117] Let your employee know that they may have to veer off the script based upon what the person on the other end says.

THE Time Management Grid

Stephen Covey's Time Management Grid which is found in his book "7 habits of highly effective people;" which looks similar to the Johari Window can be used at work to prioritize tasks that come across our desks:[118]

- Important/Urgent I: crisis, pressing issues, deadlines, meetings
- Important/Not Urgent II: preparation, planning, prevention, relationship-building, personal development
- Urgent/Not Important III: interruptions, some mail
- Not Important/Not Urgent IV: trivia, some phone calls

	URGENT	NOT URGENT
IMPORTANT	**I** • crisis, pressing issues, deadlines, meetings	**II** • preparation, planning, prevention, relationship-building, personal development
NOT IMPORTANT	**III** • interruptions, some mail	**IV** • trivia, some phone calls

⚠ TIPS FOR RUNNING YOUR BUSINESS

Dorcas Kelley offers many great tips for running a business in her book, *The Business of Coaching*. Here are a few of them:

- "Businesses are like houses, they both need periodic attention and maintenance; otherwise they fall apart."

- "The life of your business is a process, an evolution, just as your life is a process; your business will change over time, just as we all change over time. Expect the changes and welcome them. With each change, take time to determine which aspects of your business are impacted, and adjust accordingly."

- "Have a business vision. Keep a journal about your business vision so you can review its revolution. Visions don't have a final destination because they are constantly unfolding. Visions often get juicier as you dig deeper, asking yourself a series of 'whys' or 'because of…' or 'in service of…' questions to uncover the next layer."[121]

When we are blocked at work and our projects are stuck, other things will just keep distracting us. If you find yourself in that spot, consider the four quadrants; Are the distractions important? Is your project not urgent? My friend Deb Lansdowne, an interior designer, tries to get just one thing done if she is in that situation. "If that's all you do, it's something," she says. "Usually more gets done because you get on a roll."

If something isn't getting done, is it because it's boring to you? Do you not like it? Do you not know enough about it? Do you have to have an unpleasant conversation with a customer or team member? If you're procrastinating, that's a clue that you're really resisting that task. One way to deal with that is to block time weekly for such tasks, or delegate them to someone else. If you can't delegate

⚠ TIP

When you're stuck on a certain task or project at work, you can do one of the following to move past the resistance:

- Splash water on your face.
- Declutter your work area.
- Listen to music.
- Do some deep breathing.
- Do a good deed.
- Wear a power outfit when you take on this task again.

Day to Day on the Job

To save energy and reduce the stress on your body at work, here are a few tips:

- Evaluate the work to be done ahead of time.
- Break your tasks down.
- Eliminate unnecessary steps.
- Break up heavy tasks with lighter ones.
- When working on an activity, make frequent position changes and take breaks.
- Allow enough time to get your work done.
- Organize work areas with everything you need for your project.
- Create zones in your office space for specific tasks or projects.
- Alternate sitting and standing while working on a project.

the task, how can you make it fun? Have a reward in place when you complete it.

Also, if you find yourself procrastinating, beware of the "as soon as syndrome," as described by Dorcas Kelley in *The Business of Coaching*: [119] "I'll go to a networking event as soon as my website is done" or "I'll offer sample sessions as soon as my intake packet is complete." This is a trap! You don't need a website to network and you don't need an intake packet to offer sample sessions. Get out of the trap by doing those tasks now. Don't wait!

Tolerations and distractions at work are like mosquitoes buzzing around us, sometimes stinging us, and diverting our attention away from our focus. This is not the time to quit. Just get back to focus.

You can also use the Gordon Training International "Four Stages for Learning any New Skill" concept when learning new tasks at work. Remember the four steps of learning discussed in the "Making Your Dreams a Reality" chapter? Here they are again:

Unconscious incompetence:
Don't know what you don't know

Conscious incompetence:
Know you don't know

Conscious competence:
Know what to do and have to think about it—takes effort

Unconscious competence:
Automatic—doing without thinking

Just because you're doing something new doesn't mean you're going to be good at it right away (conscious competence). Cut yourself some slack, and be confident based on the skills that have gotten you this far, knowing you will learn this too (unconscious competence); whatever it is, you are growing. Just like learning a foreign language, it takes practice; practice sets the skills in place. Even if learning gets uncomfortable, it doesn't have to diminish your confidence. When frustration hits, and it may, don't let it shake you. As Price Pritchett writes in *You 2: A High Velocity Formula for Multiplying Your Personal Effectiveness in Quantum Leaps,* "Turn the negative energy to positive energy, and let that energy propel you like jet fuel."[120]

Even if you find yourself overwhelmed by a work deadline, not necessarily because you're practicing new tasks, you can change your energy from negative to positive. I press pause, taking a deep breath and doing a quick assessment. I break down what is left on the project into steps and pat myself on the back for what I have already accomplished. As I recognize how much is already done, it helps me to move forward. Just a quick one-minute assessment can get me back on track. I start where I am and get done what's fresh and fast before delving into the tough stuff.

BURNOUT

Sometimes being unmotivated at work or feeling stuck while trying to do certain tasks is really about being burned out. Another sign of burnout is constantly getting sick (you get the flu, then a cold, then pneumonia, then an ear infection, etc.) or struggling with depression. If you go to bed exhausted every night and wake up tired every morning, when everything becomes too much effort, you might be burned out. If you are cranky all the time, often burst into tears, and go into fits of rage at the slightest provocation (acting ugly), again you might be burned out.

> "Burnout is what we do to avoid surrendering. Yet in the end we need to surrender to the burnout itself."
>
> **—DR. DINA GLOUBERMAN,** *THE JOY OF BURNOUT* [122]

Work can be so seductive that we can find ourselves completely caught up in its rapture, unable to resist. In fact, work can be a distraction from whatever is disappointing in your home life, as Sarah Ban Breathnach notes in *Simple Abundance: A Daybook of Comfort and Joy*. "When you simply can't deal with life, a fax that needs to be answered immediately can be a fine friend," she says.[123]

Burnout is all about unbalance: you have too much work or responsibility, too little time to do it, over too long a period. It comes from living unbalanced for years, when what was supposed to be a temporary situation becomes a lifestyle.

If you find yourself burned out when it comes to your job, you are the only person who can change that, by making the lifestyle changes you need to.[124]

This includes calling everything to a halt, to take a slower path, to make a detour.

Other ways to avoid burnout include the following:

- Exercise, doing cardio and lifting weights.

- Eat breakfast.

- Eat five-plus fruits/veggies per day and limit processed foods.

- Sleep.

- Have pets so you have something to come home to.

- Build your social support (i.e. friends and family you can talk to when you need to).

- When asked to do something, you can stop, look, and listen, and go:
  o Stop: I will let you know if I can.
  o Look: Look at calendar.
  o Listen: Listen to your gut.
  o Go: Say no without excuses.

THE PERFECTIONIST'S TRAP

Being a perfectionist also can lead to burnout. The pursuit of perfection is the opiate of choice for millions of women, because we are creatures that live by our senses and because the response we get for perfection feels so wonderful, even if it's for only ten seconds, that we want to repeat the experience. So we commit to doing everything perfectly, setting in motion a cycle of self-destruction.

Aspiring to be Little Miss Perfect is an addiction of low self-worth. Maybe when we were young, nothing we did was ever good enough, so we just kept on doing until doing was all we could do. When doing more and more didn't make any difference, we thought if we did our work perfectly, we'd hit the mark. When we did, suddenly voices other than our own sang our praises. Champagne or chocolate couldn't even begin to compare with the ecstasy of genuine compliments. But here's one thing to keep in mind, as Sarah Ban Breathnach notes in *Simple Abundance: A Daybook of Comfort and Joy*, "Upon completing the universe, The Great Creator pronounced it 'very good.' Not 'perfect.'"[125]

NETWORKING

It's no secret that networking is important for your career, not only if you're in the market for a new job, but also if you're launching a business and need promotion, or you need your contacts to help you brainstorm and solve problems at your business.

Think of it this way: you know about three hundred people personally, and they know about three hundred personally. When you reach out to your friends and ask them to refer you to their circle, you go out another circle of three hundred each. Multiply this out and see how many people you can reach out to: 300 x 300 = 90,000 x 300 = 27,000,000. Wow, now that's a lot of potential!

To reach that initial three hundred number of your own contacts, think of FRANCE—reaching out to Friends, Relatives, Acquaintances, Neighbors, Coworkers, and Everyone. As you begin to build your network, list out the people you meet and think of your contacts as a family tree that is branching out. It's amazing to watch the tree branch out in ways you wouldn't expect. Then think about who you can target on this list during your job search. Or if you're running your own business, where are you getting your business from in these contacts? Make sure you reach out to them and thank them if they're helping you build your business. This was a strategy I used often as a Mary Kay consultant.

As an insurance agent, I spent a lot of money on a networking group and received no results; I had better results on a no-cost method of getting out there and seeing the people face to face, handing out my business card. Don't doubt a no-cost or low-cost option because it doesn't appear to be very sophisticated; try it. A designer friend of mine put up a small before-and-after display on the entrance bulletin board at my insurance office and got a great client—you just never know. Put yourself out there where people will see you, whether that means starting a website, blog, or social media presence or handing out brochures and business cards.

> ⚠ **TIP**
>
> Remember that once you've networked and built a base of clients, it costs you more in time and money to bring in new clients than to keep existing clients. The same is true for keeping employees: it costs you more in time and money to find a new employee than keeping an experienced one happy in his or her job and with your company.

If you decide to attend a networking event, there are a number of things you can do before, during, and after it. Beforehand, prepare, especially if you start going to a lot of events. Otherwise you may not remember your cards, your brochures, your story, and your elevator speech. Going to a lot of these events will mean you'll become more familiar with your pitch, so you can just wing it if you have to. If you've been to a certain networking group before, or are a member of a club or organization where you can often pitch your business, remember to offer something new and current when you do your spiel. Otherwise, these people will have heard your base presentation, over and over again. Also remember personal appearance matters at these events—look professional, throw out that piece of gum, and make sure you've brushed your teeth.

At the event, make a point of meeting as many people as you can before everything begins. You can also reconnect with people you've met at past events because repetition, repetition, repetition matters. The more people get to know you, the more they will automatically think to call you for their business. Stay after the event so you can talk to more people and show them examples of your work. Consider becoming a presenter at one of these events, or at least a discussion leader, so you can showcase your skills more. If you do end up speaking or serving as a moderator, remember to let others have time to talk. Think about a ball bouncing between the group, from one person to the next, across the table, each person getting a chance to speak. No one should monopolize the conversation in a question-and-answer time or an open discussion.

After the event, take all your contact cards and do a brain dump of notes as you look at each business card; write down who this was and how you might help them. Note the date and place of the event, so you can use that information when you contact these people again. Start writing follow-up notes or emails to these contacts, giving them your next available time for an appointment or sharing ideas on how you can help them. Don't hesitate to reach out to them by phone either, or following up your initial contact with another note, email, or call. Remember repetition, and use a tracking system that works for you.

STARTING A SMALL BUSINESS

Maybe in one of your dream-building sessions, the idea of starting your own business came to the forefront, but you really have no idea of where to begin, or even what that business might be. You can start by thinking about what you're passionate about or a hobby that you might turn into a job. Maybe you have skills from your current job that you can transfer into building a business of your own.

Remember what I said in Chapter 1, "Getting Started on Dream Building": you wouldn't get the idea if you couldn't do it. To build on that concept, Sarah Ban Breathnach shares in her book *Simple Abundance: A Daybook of Comfort and Joy:*

Dreams are gifts of Spirit meant to alter us. Trust that the same power that gifted you with your dream knows how to help you make it come true. Courage is fear that has said her prayers. In order to hear your calling and answer it, you must generously give yourself the gift of time. The bottom line is not how fast you make your dream come true, but how steadily you pursue it.[126]

Once the subconscious mind accepts an idea, it begins to execute it, says Dr. Joseph Murphy in his classic work on metaphysical principles, *The Power of Your Subconscious Mind.* Ban Breathnach adds:

It works by association of ideas and uses every bit of knowledge that you gather in your lifetime to bring about its purpose. It draws on the infinite power, energy, and wisdom within you. It lines up all the laws of nature to get its way. Sometimes it seems to bring about an immediate solution to your difficulties, but at other times it may take days, weeks, or longer... its ways are past finding out. [127]

If you can find something that you can build a business from, think about if you have the resources to do it, and how much time you want to commit to it. Then make business plan, as Dorcas Kelley suggests in her book *The Business of Coaching.*[128] Your business plan needs to include any legal, tax, and insurance considerations, as well as marketing and networking plans. Think of your business plan as a tool, not just a formal document to obtain a loan. It's a management process designed to make your business better, and your plan will change as your business changes; it needs to be fluid, a compass to keep you going in the right direction. Keep it simple in describing your business to help drive your decisions. Use dates, details, and deadlines as you manage with your long-term objectives.

As you craft your business plan and consider moving forward, continue your research, looking at options and following leads. Consult a book like *The Business of Coaching* that goes into more detail about starting your own business; look for seminars, classes, or career centers that may be able to give you more information to make your dream a reality. Be careful to have your legwork done; jumping in too quickly increases the potential for failure, which is "not it."

Also make a written description of what you would like to be, do, or have when it comes to launching your own business. Write out your ambition in as much detail as possible and in the present tense. Do not write it out as something you are planning to do. Write it out as something you are currently doing. Write *I can*, say *I can*; drill it into your subconscious mind, and then share your idea with someone who has confidence in you and is compatible in your thinking, someone who will build you up with respect to your idea. "Whatever it is, you must step out and boldly pursue it. Figure out how, not whether or not you can," Bob Proctor writes in *You Were Born Rich*.[129]

Remember that it takes most new companies at least three years before they become properly established. Some individuals don't give their businesses three weeks or even three months before they give up. So if you feel scattered or fragmented at some point early on, focus on what's important. Focus on your plan and feel accomplished for what you have done so far.

If you chase two rabbits,
both will escape. Focus, focus, focus!

There will always be situations that will pull us off focus. When I began my coaching business Systems For Change, I ordered business cards and bookmarks for this book with my new phone number on it. I spent a lot of money on these and ordered a large quantity. The new phone number had issues, and after weeks of calls to the phone company, I had to get a new phone number. My new business cards and bookmarks were no longer accurate. Talk about pulling me out of focus, briefly; yet as the diversion presented itself, I treated it like a mosquito and swatted it away, and took the proper action to resolve it. When something gets in your way that pulls you out of focus, that frustrates or challenges you, feel that frustration, feel that fear, feel whatever it is you're feeling, and move forward anyway. Stay focused despite whatever else is happening.

> "Leaders transfer what they know to others, helping them grow."
>
> —AUTHOR UNKNOWN

When I was a new insurance agent working strictly on commission and had a bad month, I often let fear take over and talked with my friends during work hours about how I didn't think I could live on these small checks. I continued complaining, and the results were the same. Once I turned it around and focused on the positive, I spent my phone time calling clients and prospects, setting more appointments. Then I began seeing bigger and bigger checks. By the time I closed my office, I was doing very well. The point is that the more I complained, the more I had to complain about.

It's at the point where we say "I can't" that we give up and quit, telling ourselves our dreams will never come true. This is when we say, "Why try? It'll never happen for me." Recognize that this is a trap. Just say, "Step aside, Satan; I have the power of God and with God all things are possible." If you can dream it, you can do it.

Consider finding a business mentor to help you navigate the path of launching your business. Mary Kay Ash, the founder of Mary Kay Cosmetics, often touted this method of hooking yourself to a star, someone who is where you want to be, and see what he or she did to get to this point. How did this person's business start? What did he or she do when at the stage you're at? You can get a lot of good ideas for starting your business by finding a good mentor.

Also, when formulating what your business will be, you can use the Play the Movie technique I shared in the "Making Your Dreams a Reality" chapter. It comes from Dr. Henry Cloud's book *9 Things You Simply Must Do to Succeed in Love and Life* (and I learned a version of it in coaching). In the book, Cloud uses the example of a construction business as he "plays the movie" of how business would be affected if certain things happened.[130] For instance, what if interest rates went up? How would that affect a construction business? What if land costs increased? By considering what scenarios could negatively affect your business, you can anticipate how to deal with those, and how you could succeed in spite of them.

GAINING CLIENTS

When it comes to gaining new clients for your upstart business, review the networking section earlier in this chapter, and then build on gaining contacts by focusing on making appointments with these potential clients to let them know about your new venture. It all starts with appointments, so designate time every week to make connections, place phone calls, and write emails. Once you've come up with who is your ideal client, target those people for your appointments first and prepare a presentation about your business for them. Think about how to add to your sales funnel (see chart) to see if potential clients really are just that, or are "not it," not worth pursuing.

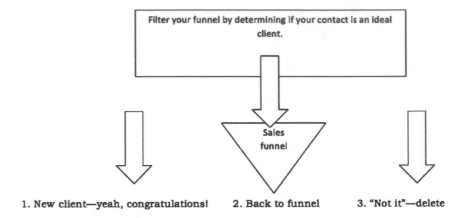

1. New client—yeah, congratulations!   2. Back to funnel   3. "Not it"—delete

When your prospects go through your sales funnel they either become new clients, go back to the prospecting funnel where you expend your marketing efforts, or you determine they are "not it" and delete them.

Think of pursuing and servicing your clients and prospects by the opportunities they present:

- "A" clients are ideal clients; spend your time with them, serving their needs and prospecting for more clients like them.

- "B" clients are good clients and have potential to be more than that, which make them A prospects.

- "C" clients are inherited clients; service them and they may become A or B clients, or D clients.

- "D" clients or prospects don't have much potential to be more than that; either take them off your prospect list or spend minimal time serving them. D = Delete.

One thing that helped me as an insurance agent was having a "hot list" of potential clients to call. I would add and subtract names from the list as I played "not it" (when I would get a no, or a disqualified prospect). Get good at setting appointments from this list. As I learned being a Mary Kay consultant, book ten of these appointments and hold three to five to keep your business on track. If selling your business services is something you aren't always comfortable with, see yourself as a giver of your time and talents, as benevolent. Think this: "I am not bothering anyone by offering services, rather I am creating value for them"—another tip I learned while selling Mary Kay.

People hang around in the same crowds; like attracts like. If you find yourself in a bad crowd, meaning meeting with would-be D clients, change the crowd. Quit booking with those who are not your target. It wastes your time and energy, leaving you in a negative state that can create a downward spiral. Want that?

When you do meet with potential clients, keep the get-together simple. Have a focal point, a goal for the meeting. Don't act needy or give off the impression you may be too busy to actually provide the service you are promoting to them. Neither of those will attract clients.

Remember it's a numbers game, so don't quit if things don't go well. Instead learn to laugh at your mistakes. Keep at it and you'll get better. Getting "no" sometimes means "I don't know enough about it," or "not now." It may not mean a "no" forever, unless you determine the client is disqualified. Sometimes

> ⚠ **TIP**
>
> Track the name of your prospect, what you cover in your discussions, and the results. Consider purchasing a customer-relationship management software if you don't have one so you can easily monitor this. Then keep an activity log for a glance at how you're spending your time when it comes to balancing getting new clients versus serving the ones you have.

it takes repetition, getting in front of potential clients multiple times to develop a relationship with them and for the information to sink in. It's like planting seeds in the spring to harvest in the fall. If the sale doesn't happen right then, it isn't time yet or not meant to be. During the presentation, you may decide this is not someone you wish to work with, but then by all means, let the person know by suggesting something else that may work for him or her. No matter what your potential client decides, make sure to say thanks for his or her time and do the appropriate follow-up. The key is to keep moving—don't sit and wait; keep holding more appointments, making more calls. Keep your momentum, keep moving, and stay focused.

If you find yourself continuing to struggle, look back at your approach. Have you done appropriate follow-ups? Have you shown clients that you care, instead of just what you know? If you realize there are things you wish you had done differently over the last few months or the last year, take those "not it" moments to change things for the year ahead.

As you begin to gain new clients, think about using client intake forms or a new client checklist so you can keep on top of what you'll need to do next for these clients. What needs to happen next for you to make your client happy? Document as you complete these tasks. If you grow your business to add employees, get them in on using the forms and checklists so everyone on the team knows what the goals are for that client.

A Typical Sales Call

Here are the steps you can take as you go out on your initial meetings with potential clients, when you're selling your business to them:

- Establish a rapport with them by briefly introducing yourself, the services you offer, and asking them what

298

they would like to accomplish if they employed
your services.

- Determine their needs, not necessarily their wants,
before fully presenting your product or services.

- Recommend a product or service you provide that meets
their needs by using feature and benefit statements
about the product—that means telling them what's in it
for them.

- If they object to what you're offering, deal with those
objections. Their objection may be not having enough
money for what you're offering. When I sold insurance
and Mary Kay, I got that objection often. So overcoming
an objection may sound like this, "I know this policy is
more that you're wanting to spend compared to your current company, but this is the additional coverage you're
getting for those dollars and you're actually getting more
coverage than you currently have, as you requested."
Check for their acceptance by doing a trial close like,
"How does that sound to you?" Or "Is there anything
else I can tell you about this account or product?"

- Use the feel/felt/found method when promoting what
you're selling—telling them "I feel, have felt, and have
since found" when talking about the benefits of your
product or service. For example, "I understand you feel
this policy is more expensive than the one you currently
have. I felt that way when I increased my limits too,
but found that the feeling of security and peace of
mind I had once I added the coverage was worth the
extra money."

- Lastly, ask for their commitment right now, to sign
on the dotted line if that's needed. If there is another
objection, like "I need to talk with my spouse," ask,
"When can the two of you come in?"

TIME MANAGEMENT

As discussed in the "Your Personal Image" chapter, how you manage your time affects how you show up in life. This is especially true at work. So using a time management system when it comes to your career is especially important. This can easily be done on your work calendar on your computer, but you also can do it the old-fashioned way: using paper. I like having a paper calendar to jot things down on while on the phone or if I have multiple sessions open on my computer. Do whatever works best for you. The point of this book is to get you to stop sleepwalking and think about what you're doing. Is what you're doing now working? If not, what can you change so it will work?

In the book *Simple Church* by Thom S. Rainer and Eric Geiger, the authors talk about how our world is not simple. Not even close.[131] Daily we experience information and decision overload. As the world is getting smaller and smaller (because of globalization through technology), things are just getting more and more complex. In the midst of all the noise, all the rush, all the change, all the busyness, and all the uncertainty, people long for simplicity. People respond to simple because things are so hectic and out of control. The busyness and complexity of life makes simple a great commodity, something desired.

> "Professional development and personal development go in hand in hand."
>
> —**BOB PROCTOR,** *YOU WERE BORN RICH* [132]

Keep your calendar simple so it isn't something that overwhelms you. The first step in doing that is to get your tasks on your calendar as soon as you realize you need to. Otherwise notes go floating in and out of notice by being tucked here and there, sometimes found much later and too late.

For an easy, inexpensive time-management system, on a spiral notebook or clipboard with scrap paper (recycled from the mail), draw the grid below, leaving room to list the tasks you need to get done during the week:

September 19 to 25

M 19	T 20	W 21	TH 22
Early a.m. run Call clients to schedule reviews	Transfer tracking follow-up Meeting prep	Weekly meeting Noon yoga class Meeting follow-up	Early a.m. run Review prep
F 23	**S 24**	**S 24**	
Filing Prep for next week appointments	Remove Saturday and Sunday if you do not work those days and use space here for additional notes.	Remove Saturday and Sunday if you do not work those days and use space here for additional notes.	

You can list extra tasks that could be done if you have time in the space you left blank from Saturday and Sunday (if you don't work those days). Some of these tasks could include the following:

- Review prospectus; discard dated and order new.

- Schedule client annual meetings for….

- Send birthday cards to clients.

- Order holiday cards and calendars.

If you do not wish to create your own planner, one can be purchased on my website, www.systemsforchange.net.

Establish great daily habits in your planner, such as:

- Staying on top of client reviews

- Working out before work by using the gym in your office building

- Bringing lunch to work to save money and eat something with healthier ingredients

- Planning fun into your day (taking breaks)

Add your great habits to your calendar.

Author John C. Maxwell shares in his book *Leadership 101: What Every Leader Needs to Know* that "what matters most is what you do day by day over the long haul. The secret of our success is found in our daily agenda."[133]

LEADERSHIP

Maxwell also shares the following about leadership and having success in your career:

- Leadership is complicated. It has many facets: respect, experience, emotional strength, people skills, discipline, vision, momentum, timing, and influence.

- No matter where you're starting from, you can get better.

- Without the help of the body, the mind cannot go as far as it can. You must take the approach Theodore Roosevelt did, who spent time every day building his body as well as his mind, throughout his life.

- Don't quit, because if you get into that mode of quitting, then you feel like it's okay.

- Nearly all our faults can be forgiven more easily than the methods we come up with to hide them.

- Any time you concentrate on the difficulty of the work instead of its results or rewards, you're likely to become discouraged. If you dwell on it too long, you'll develop self-pity instead of self-discipline. The next time you're facing a must-do task and you're thinking of doing what's convenient instead of paying the price, change your focus. Count the benefits of doing what's right and then dive in.

- Think about how planned neglect might actually help you move forward. One young violinist found herself making her bed, straightening her room, dusting the floor, and doing whatever else before practicing. But then she found she wasn't progressing and reversed things. She started practicing first, deliberately neglecting everything else. That program of planned neglect accounted for her success.

- Too many priorities paralyze us.

- If you have only one letter to write, it will take all day to do it, as is Parkinson's Law (work expands so as to fill the time). If you have twenty letters to write, you'll get them done in one day. Our most efficient time to work is the week before vacation. Why? That's when we have a lot on our plate and get it done. Why can't we always run our lives the way we do the week before we leave the office, making decisions, cleaning off our desk, returning calls? Under normal conditions, we are efficient. When time pressure mounts or emergencies arise, we become effective. Efficiency is the foundation for survival. Effectiveness is the foundation of success.

- Leaders earn respect by making sound decisions, admitting their mistakes, and putting what's best for their followers and the organization ahead of their personal agendas.[134]

To be a great leader or successful as an entrepreneur, taking risks is essential. As Bob Proctor shares in *You Were Born Rich*, risk to one person may not represent risk to another.[135] But those who find success make major business decisions, ones that could affect their personal wealth or future success, without considering these as especially risky—they're just living their lives, as though it was impossible to fail. "Risk takers are knowledgeable people who study situations carefully, have confidence in their own abilities, and have a very healthy self-image," Proctor adds. "Becoming a risk taker means you act courageously, which is considerably different than acting foolishly."[136] You might encounter a few situations where the line separating these two concepts becomes extremely narrow, so be careful that you never cross over that line inadvertently or otherwise.

Remember, you will meet resistance as you move forward with your career or business, you will face challenges, but look at them as if you are pregnant with possibilities. Giving birth is a challenge, but there is no turning back once you start the process. Work through the resistance you're facing to reach success. Good luck! Today is the day to start your journey.

HOMEWORK

1. When considering your career, ask yourself:
   "What do I love?"
   "What am I most passionate about?"

2. Take time to focus on your career in a dream-building session. Afterward, make some decisions on some of

those dreams—when you can begin working on them, who you can tell about them. Then eventually tell everyone you know about your goals.

3. Press pause, check in, and celebrate your successes. Determine if you desire changes in your career, and then identify the steps to get there and take the first steps to make these changes.

4. Ask what's next and write it all down in as much detail as you can imagine.

5. Practice replacement beliefs—repeat these until they become reality:

    *   "I accomplish my work quickly, easily, and accurately."

    *   "The answers I seek come quickly to me."

    *   "Balancing work and home is effortless."

6. Create your own new beliefs, write them down, and repeat them until they are set in your mind, replacing the old negative beliefs.

7. Brainstorm: What's on my plate that I can finish today? A pending sale I can close? Someone on my prospect list to contact? What is left hanging that I can take care of?

Conclusion

Today I am writing from a dream space, a balcony filled with beautiful plants, flowers, and wicker furniture; with beautiful views of nature, of water and woods; very tranquil and serene. I have the flexible schedule I have long wanted, more time for family and friends, faith, and fitness, which I am able to share with my dream man. We have taken many incredible trips together, near and far, and plan to do more. I just purchased new furniture to finish our romantic bedroom, new clothing to fit my outdoor active lifestyle, and a new car that has everything I wanted—all in the last week.

Thank you God for providing!
I have enough.

Today I was able to take a nice, long run; yesterday we put our bikes on the car rack and biked a nearby trail for a couple hours in glorious sunshine. Today I made nutritious salads for lunch together on the patio with a healthy dessert. For dinner, we're making homemade pizza. I feel truly blessed to have the time and money to take care of myself and enjoy those I love.

Life is as good as I dreamed it would be. As you know by reading this book, it did not always look this way for me. Knowing what I *did not* want, what was "not it," has allowed me to dream of exactly what I *do* want, and achieve it. It feels great to be a sought-after consultant and coach. But now that I have made these life changes, does that mean I will stop dreaming? No, this is only the beginning of new dreams for me (and the same can go for you). My dream life now is focused on enjoying those I love, taking extremely great care of myself while dreaming of what retirement might look like. Dreams really can come true; if you can dream it, you can do it! So what are you dreaming of?

Remember, your time is so precious on this earth, so don't waste a moment living someone else's dream. Support others to reach their dreams when you can. Don't forget that we're all just doing the best we can, and to take and do everything in moderation. If you have a habit you can't shake, get help if it's making your life unmanageable or your life revolves around it, like my coffee addiction (and cigarettes many years before that); I had to let go of the outcome and the need to have my own way.

A few years ago, I wanted to travel to Europe, starting with visiting France. I put it on my list and let go of any details. It was a someday thing. I had no passport, did not speak French, and had a spouse who was not interested. A few years later, I was divorced and my fiftieth birthday was upon me. I wanted to do something ostentatious to celebrate this milestone. I loved going sailing, so that was on my radar, but what could I do to treat myself for my birthday? A note I found said:

"I will do it at all costs... no one will stop me!"

Because I realized I was playing small in life, I thought about France and got butterflies! I had no money saved for travel and had no one to travel with. I borrowed a book from the library about a couple that purchased a home in the Dordogne River valley of France; there was a castle in their backyard and many castles in their region. This really spurred me on to want to go, so I purchased a map of France and put it on my office wall for inspiration. I put Post-it flags on all the areas I wanted to go. I began telling people I planned to go, even though I still lacked funds and a traveling companion.

I had no idea how I could possibly do it, but that did not stop my desire. One day a girlfriend shared that, after my mentioning it for the past four months, she would like to go. We began planning, even though I did not have the money to do it. I let her know about my lack of funds and we researched ways to travel on a budget while sharing expenses. Once we investigated, it didn't seem so expensive after all. Although it was more work to plan the trip on a budget, we made it fun with almost a year of weekly dinners and wine after work. We had great girlfriend time and ended up deciding on three regions in France we really wanted to go to.

> "See yourself living in abundance and you will attract it. It always works; it works every time with every person."
>
> **—BOB PROCTOR**[137]

Three months after making the decision to go, I received my twelfth month of my townhome lease rent free, which was not designated anywhere in my budget. This covered my plane ticket. I knew the rest of the money would show up from somewhere and continued planning. We settled on the dates before the "high" season hit. A few months later, I learned because of a successful year, my bonus at work would be enough to cover the travel expenses of our two-week trip. In fact, along with the money I saved while in the planning stage, I had enough and more. It all happened magically.

I signed up for French classes in the fall only to learn the class was not offered for whatever reason. Then, to my surprise, another French class opened up in January, ending in April. While I missed the last class because we were in Paris, it was still perfect timing.

From Paris, we traveled to the Dordogne River area and finally to the Mediterranean coast, returning to Minneapolis from Marseilles. We had a great trip! Lesson learned: believe in your dreams even when you have no idea how they will come together. Let those dreams evolve; put them on the back burner if you have to.

And what about the sailing? I got to do that too, on my fiftieth birthday, six weeks after the trip!

Once I learned I could let my dreams evolve, I applied the technique to other areas in my life. The coaching term is manifesting; when I am in a church group, we say, "It's a God thing." I know it is not coincidence. You decide what you believe. I believe God puts these desires in our hearts and allows them to happen in our lives. I believe God puts each step of the way out there for us to do the next thing.

But the passionate traveler looks for something. What? Something must change you, something ineffable, something or nothing happens. "Change me," Ed, a character in Frances Mayes's *Bella Tuscany*, writes in a poem. "Change me into something I am." Mayes adds, "Change—the transforming experience—is part of the quest in traveling."[138]

It's about enjoying the journey
and finding joy in everything we do.

As you realize something is "not it," the sooner you close the door, the sooner what *is* it will arrive. Take time to pause when you realize your journey has led you to live the life of your dreams. That's what life is about!

When you've reached your goals and are living your dream, what's next? You decide. What are you dreaming of now? What's giving you butterflies when you think of it? Once you find your path and follow it, everything else falls into place.

If it wouldn't have been for looking for treasure from trash, kicking tires, and the "not it" concept, I may not have been so inspired to write my book. I am now in a sense of wonderment watching it all unfold.

So let the old life fall away and cherish your new beliefs, your new life!

Coaches love to give assignments. When you notice a tool you want to implement, give yourself an assignment and stick to it. Maybe it's something as simple as writing your chief aim, seventy times per day for seven days.

Maybe you aren't able to implement this assignment today but know you can on Monday, so block off time on Monday and for six days afterward. Make sure you do the assignment before you go to sleep. Try to complete the assignment first thing in the morning, as you will feel accomplished knowing it's done for the day. Do what works best for you.

I have felt the fear in building a new life and dreams and done it anyway; the victory is sweet. When I am faced with fear now, I no longer tell myself to "buck up little camper," as I know once I decide and act, I am no longer afraid. Yeah!

I have exactly what I wanted... well, except maybe this little dippy thing isn't just right, or maybe what I wanted earlier isn't quite right for now; so now what? Tweak. Press pause. Identify what you want now.

Maybe you dreamed of travel and aren't quite happy with your hotel because you tried to save fifty dollars. I found myself in a cheap hotel room with an unbearable smell. There was no way I could have slept there, so happily I was able to show management, cancel the room with no charges, and find a better one in a short time, which enhanced how I was able to be with those around me, leading to a happier me. It was well worth the extra money.

Sometimes we are tempted to give into temptation for immediate gratification, which is almost always "not it." When we are tired, lonely, and hungry; when we want others to like us; when we seek approval at the cost of our needs, we are not on the right path. We make relationship compromises and sabotage our boundaries. The sooner we say no to that which is not right, the sooner the right thing will appear.

Today I am grateful for my feelings of dissatisfaction and envy. They have spurred me on to the next right thing for me. When I identify I'm feeling that way, I don't stay in it; I press pause, identify, decide what I want to change, and move on. I realize I wouldn't be where I am today had I not been prompted by my feelings in an earlier part of my life. Now I live my life on my terms.

Stop resisting what will release you: the truth will set you free—your truth. As you start putting the pieces together, think of the big picture—envision the puzzle done as you put it together!

Remind yourself: I will know when the time is right; I will just know.

Remember that in order to move to something new, it was necessary to move away from something that was comfortable.

Sometimes we need to take action, to push against the resistance we're feeling. Sometimes the external pressure is quietly shaping and forming us into what we're about to become. Those times of not feeling guided, not feeling led, not knowing what to do next can be as powerful as taking clear action, says Melody Beattie in her book *Choices: Taking Control of Your Life and Making It Matter.*[139]

When visualizing your new life—whether you are using a vision board, a secret board on Pinterest, gathering items in a box or a binder, whatever method it is—draw a line and step across it. How does it feel? Process those feelings. You have arrived, it is here, start.

Go. You have everything you need and whatever else will be there perfectly on time. Trust that. Trust God.

Do today that which will cause you to feel better tomorrow, as Tom Wilhite, co-founder of PSI Seminars, once said.[140]

Napoleon Hill, in his book *Think and Grow Rich*, writes, "The starting point of all achievement is DESIRE. Keep this constantly in mind. Weak desires bring weak results, just as a small amount of fire makes a small amount of heat."[141]

You're not trying to "get;" you're allowing it to happen. Make your dream welcome, let it happen, allow it to arrive.

Think of this illustration, which Richard Bach uses in his book *Illusions*:

> Once there lived a village of creatures along the bottom of a great crystal river. The current of the river swept silently over them all—young and old, rich and poor, good and evil, the current going its own way, knowing only its own crystal self. Each creature in its own manner clung tightly to the twigs and rocks of the river bottom, for clinging was their way of life, and resisting the current, what each had learned from birth. But one creature said at last, "I am tired of clinging. Though I cannot see it with my eyes, I trust that the current knows where it is going. I shall let go and let it take me where it will. Clinging I shall die of boredom." The other creatures laughed and said, "Fool. Let go and that current you worship will throw you tumbled and smashed across the rocks and you will die quicker than boredom!" But the one heeded them not, and taking a breath, did let go and at once was tumbled and smashed by the current across the rocks. Yet in time, as the creature refused to cling again, the current lifted him free from the bottom and he was bruised and hurt no more. And the creatures downstream, to whom he was a stranger, cried, "See a miracle! A creature like ourselves, yet he flies!"[142]

God gives us experiences in life we do not expect, but he also provides solutions and ways for us to grow.

313

When you find yourself in a situation you are not pleased with, stop, be quiet, and pray; let the answers come to you. You may get them right away; you may get them later. Just know your answers will come when it is time and no sooner. God has not forgotten you; he has great things for you. Ask, have faith, and believe he wants to give you everything you desire. Believe he puts these desires in your heart, and then receive and be grateful. Gratitude and feeling the best you can are keys.

In a 2005 speech at Stanford University, just six years before he died, Apple entrepreneur Steve Jobs said this: "Your time is limited, so don't waste it living somebody else's life. Don't be trapped by dogma, which is living with the result of other people's thinking. Don't let the noise of other people drown out your own inner voice. Have the courage to follow your heart and intuition."[143]

I pray I can reach out to someone else and help them. If I can just change one life by writing this book, I believe I can potentially change many lives. Doing what I love is truly a gift; I am so blessed. I want you to feel the same.

Best wishes on your journey to the life you seek. Remember you are not alone, but sometimes you need to be alone to hear God's voice to show you the way.

I hope you have fun saying "not it," and finding, "That's it!"

Recommended Resources

If you want to find out more about the topics covered in this book, the author recommends reading the following:

Changing for Good by James Prochaska, John Norcross, and Carlo DiClemente

Choices: Taking Control of Your Life and Making It Matter and *Make Miracles in Forty Days*—by Melody Beattie

Couples Money: What Every Couple Should Know About Money and Relationships—by Chris and Marlow Felton

French Women Don't Get Fat and *French Women for All Seasons: A Year of Secrets, Recipes, & Pleasure*—both by Mireille Guiliano

If the Buddha Dated: A Handbook for Finding Love on a Spiritual Path—by Charlotte Kasl

Leadership 101: What Every Leader Needs to Know—by John C. Maxwell

Let's Make Parenting Easier—by Dawn Eichman

The Magic of Thinking Big—by David J. Schwartz

9 Things You Simply Must Do to Succeed in Love and Life by Dr. Henry Cloud

Boundaries: When to Say Yes, When to Say No-To Take Control of Your Life—by Dr. Henry Cloud and Dr. John Townsend

Positive Energy—by Judith Orloff

The Precious Present—by Spencer Johnson

See You at the Top—by Zig Ziglar

Simple Abundance: A Daybook of Comfort and Joy, *Something More: Excavating Your Authentic Self*, and *Romancing the Ordinary: A Year of Simple Splendor*—all by Sarah Ban Breathnach

The Soulmate Secret—by Arielle Ford

Think and Grow Rich and *The Law of Success*—both by Napoleon Hill

You 2: A High Velocity Formula for Multiplying Your Personal Effectiveness in Quantum Leaps—by Price Pritchett

Your Money or Your Life: *9 Steps to Transforming Your Relationship with Money and Achieving Financial Independence*—by Joe Dominguez and Vicki Robin

Real Wealth—by Bruce Helmer

You Were Born Rich—by Bob Proctor

Simply Beautiful: Inside and Out—by Jill Krieger Swanson

When Life's Not Working: 7 Simple Choices for a Better Tomorrow—by Bob Merritt

You can learn more about PSI Seminars and sign up to attend them at the PSI Seminar website, www.psiseminars.com.

You can learn more about Nia dance classes and find classes in your area by visiting www.nianow.com.

Learn more about wardrobe planning from Jill Krieger Swanson. Her website is www.jillswanson.com.

Financial Peace University—The Dave Ramsey Program: www.daveramsey.com/fpu/home

You can learn more about twelve-step programs at these websites:
Al-Anon: http://www.al-anon.alateen.org/
AA: www.aa.org
Overeaters Anonymous: www.oa.org

Check on your credit score free at:
Experian.com
Transunion.com
Equifax.com

The Marsh A Center for Balance and Fitness is a unique facility promoting a healthy attitude toward life. Membership-based it is also open to the public with comprehensive services and programs including fitness, studio/pool classes, spa, restaurant, retail, meeting spaces, overnight guest rooms and more. It is located in a western suburb of Minneapolis at 15000 Minnetonka Boulevard, Minnetonka, MN 55345. Contact: 952-935-2202 or email communications@themarsh.com. Web site: TheMarsh.com and on Facebook and LinkedIn.

About the Author

Lori Douglas Rehnelt is:

- the founder and CEO of Systems For Change, a business consulting and coaching practice

- the president of the parent group for Head Start/Home Start preschool from 1984 1986

- a women's advocate with the Victims Crisis Center from 1985–1986

- a public speaker

- the mother of disabled Iraq War veterans

- a member of Beginning Experience Divorce Support Group from 2009–2012

- a member and leader within Jaycee Women/Women of Today in the 1980s

- a technical writer

- an American Cancer Society volunteer

- a member of We Care Divorce Support Group from 1985–1987

- a member of Al-Anon

- insurance-and-securities licensed: Life/Health, Series 6, 63, and 7

- a practicing Christian

- a graduate of PSI Basic, PSI 7 Team 511, PSI WLS Class 115

- a former business office manager in hospitals and nursing homes

- a Mary Kay consultant

- a Channel One Food Shelf volunteer

- a former member of NAIFA (National Association of Business and Financial Advisors)

- a member of Lakes Area Women in Business

- a former member of the Chamber of Commerce Women's Entrepreneurial Roundtable

- a certified life coach/group coach

- a published author

- a Habitat for Humanity volunteer

- a leader of workshops and retreats

- someone with extensive experience in change management within hospitals, nursing homes, insurance, and financial services business offices.

Endnotes

Introduction

[1] Breathnach, Sarah Ban, *Simple Abundance: A Daybook of Comfort and Joy* (New York: Time Warner, 1995), foreword.

[2] Breathnach, Sarah Ban, *Something More: Excavating Your Authentic Self* (New York: Warner Books, 1998), "The Silent Hemorrhaging of the Soul" reading.

Getting Started on Dream Building

[3] This verse is paraphrased from The Message Bible.

[4] Ruth Stricker, *The Marsh Monthly Volume 28, Issue 1*, January 2013

[5] Rhonda Byrne, *The Secret* (movie adaptation of the book), Prime Time Productions, 2006.

[6] This verse is from The MacArthur Study Bible, New King James Version.

[7] This verse is from the Living Bible.

[8] Napoleon Hill, *The Law of Success* (New York: Dover, 2012), 78.

[9] Paraphrased from Price Pritchett, *You 2: A High Velocity Formula for Multiplying Your Personal Effectiveness in Quantum Leaps* (Dallas: Pritchett Publishing Co., 1990).

[10] Judith Orloff, *Positive Energy* (New York: Harmony, 2005), 22.

[11] This verse is from The MacArthur Study Bible, New King James Version.

[12] This verse is from The MacArthur Study Bible, New King James Version.

[13] Leo Buscaglia, *Living, Loving, and Learning* (New York: Ballantine Books, 1982).

Acting Ugly: A Case of Unmet Needs

[14] David J. Schwartz, *The Magic of Thinking Big* (New York: Simon and Shuster, 1959, 1966), 30.

[15] James O. Prochaska, John Norcross, and Carlo DiClemente, *Changing for Good* (New York: HarperCollins, 1994).

[16] This information about the Five Stages of Grief comes from the Beginning Divorce Support Group.

[17] Buscaglia, *Living, Loving, and Learning.*

[18] This verse is from The MacArthur Study Bible, New King James Version.

[19] This verse is from The MacArthur Study Bible, New King James Version.

[20] This verse is from The MacArthur Study Bible, New King James Version.

[21] From Dr Deborah Kern's "Acting Ugly: A Case of Unmet Needs" workshop.

[22] Ibid.

[23] Pritchett, *You 2: A High Velocity Formula for Multiplying Your Personal Effectiveness in Quantum Leaps.*

[24] Michael Neill, *Supercoach* (Carlsbad, CA: Hay House, 2009), xii.

[25] Joel Osteen, *Become a Better You* (New York: Free Press, 2007), Chapter 19, "Keep Yourself Happy."

Self Care: Putting Your Needs First

[26] Ban Breathnach, *Simple Abundance: A Daybook of Comfort and Joy.*

[27] Neill, *Supercoach.*

[28] Debbie Ford, *Dark Side of the Light Chasers* (New York: Riverhead Books by the Penguin Group, 1998, 2010), xix.

[29] Bob Proctor, from author's coaches' training notes.

[30] Neill, *Supercoach*, 110.

[31] Talane Miedaner, *Coach Yourself to Success* (Chicago: Lincolnwood Contemporary Books, 200), 97–98.

[32] Schwartz, *The Magic of Thinking Big*, 47.

[33] Marianne Williamson, *A Return to Love* (New York: HarperCollins, 1992), 165.

[34] Schwartz, *The Magic of Thinking Big*, 60.

[35] Osteen, *Become a Better You*, Chapter 19, "Keep Yourself Happy."

[36] Ban Breathnach, *Something More: Excavating Your Authentic Self*, 97.

[37] Joseph Luft, *Of Human Interaction* (Palo Alto, CA: National Press, 1969), 177.

[38] Henry Cloud, *9 Things You Simply Must Do to Succeed in Love and Life* (Nashville, TN: Thomas Nelson, 2004), Chapter 5, "Play the Movie."

[39] Pritchett, *You 2: A High Velocity Formula for Multiplying Your Personal Effectiveness in Quantum Leaps.*

[40] Ford, *Dark Side of the Light Chasers.*

[41] Melody Beattie, *Make Miracles in Forty Days* (New York: Simon and Shuster, 2011), 4.

[42] Byron Katie, *A Thousand Names for Joy* (New York: Three Rivers Press, 2005), 4.

[43] Ibid, 111–112.

[44] Orloff, *Positive Energy*, 29–30.

[45] Hill, *The Law of Success*, 37.

[46] This verse is from The MacArthur Study Bible, New King James Version.

[47] Adam Phillips, *Missing Out: In Praise of the Unlived Life* (London: Hamish Hamilton, 2012), prologue.

[48] Napoleon Hill, *Think and Grow Rich* (London: Penguin Books, 2005), 49, 51.

[49] Cloud, *9 Things You Simply Must Do to Succeed in Love and Life*, 62.

[50] Ralph Waldo Emerson, "Spiritual Laws," in *Essays: First Series*.

[51] Ford, *Dark Side of the Light Chasers*.

[52] *Paths to Recovery* (Virginia Beach, VA: Al-Anon Family Group Headquarters, 1997), 327, 330, 335.

[53] This sidebar comes from Lori Bestler's newsletter. The trigger words listed are taught to numerous individuals working in the cognitive behavior therapy, NLP, hypnotherapy, and other mind-shifting fields. The structure of trigger words used is not new. However the explanation and examples are original. For more insight on this sidebar, reference these other books:

- *The Structure of Magic, Vol. 1: A Book About Language and Therapy*, by Richard Bandler and John Grinder

- *Feeling Good: The New Mood Therapy*, by David D. Burns

- *The Biology of Belief*, by Bruce Lipton

[54] Orloff, *Positive Energy*.

Making Your Dreams a Reality

[55] Gordon Training International www.gordontraining.com

[56] Frances Mayes, *Bella Tuscany* (New York: Broadway Books), 208.

[57] This poem comes from materials that Elisabeth Elliot distributed at an event the author attended.

[58] Prochaska, Norcross, and DiClemente, *Changing for Good*, 38–46.

[59] Orloff, *Positive Energy*.

[60] This verse is from the New International Version (NIV) Bible.

Your Nutrition

[61] Mireille Guiliano, *French Women for All Seasons: A Year of Secrets, Recipes, & Pleasure*, Ouverture.

[62] Kanika Khara, "Bowel Problems," www.buzzle.com.

[63] Mayes, *Bella Tuscany*, 133.

[64] Carolyn Dean, *The Magnesium Miracle* (New York: Ballantine Books, 2006).

Your Health and Fitness

[65] Dorothy Hulst and James Allen, *As a Woman Thinketh* (Camarillo, CA: DeVorss and Company, 1982), 34–35.

[66] Suzanne Somers, Ageless: *The Naked Truth about Bioidentical Hormones* (New York: Harmony, 2007).

[67] Ibid.

[68] Ibid.

[69] Janice Novak, *Posture, Get It Straight* DVD, HGT Media, 2011.

Your Personal Image

[70] Mayes, *Bella Tuscany*, 179.

[71] Sarah Ban Breathnach, *Romancing the Ordinary: A Year of Simple Splendor* (New York: Simple Abundance Press: Scribner, 2002), 137.

[72] Ibid.

[73] *Whole Living Magazine*, October 2012, 41.

[74] American Dental Society, *Healthy Mouth, Healthy Body*, www.ada.org/sections/professionalResources/pdfs/ADA_PatientSmart_Healthy_Mouth.pdf

Your Home

[75] Ban Breathnach, Romancing the Ordinary: *A Year of Simple Splendor*, 207.

[76] Ibid.

[77] Ban Breathnach, *Simple Abundance: A Daybook of Comfort and Joy*, June 29 reading.

[78] Kathryn Robyn, *Spiritual Housecleaning: Healing the Space within by Beautifying the Space around You*, in Sarah Ban Breathnach's *Simple Abundance: A Daybook of Comfort and Joy*, 197.

[79] Ban Breathnach, *Romancing the Ordinary: A Year of Simple Splendor*, 210–211.

[80] Guiliano, *French Women for All Seasons: A Year of Secrets, Recipes, & Pleasure*, 197.

[81] Ban Breathnach, *Romancing the Ordinary: A Year of Simple Splendor*, 212.

Your Relationships

[82] Ban Breathnach, *Simple Abundance: A Daybook of Comfort and Joy*, June 29 reading.

[83] Ibid, October 7 reading.

[84] Ibid.

[85] John Robbins and Ann Mortifee, *In Search of Balance: Discovering Harmony in a Changing World* (Navato, CA: H. J. Kramer, 1991).

[86] I learned about this from Pastor Rance Settle.

[87] Henry Cloud and James Townsend, *Boundaries: When to Say YES, When to Say No to Take Control of Your Life* (Grand Rapids, MI: Zondervan, 1992).

[88] Ibid.

[89] This verse comes from the New American Standard translation.

[90] Dawn Eichman, *Let's Make Parenting Easier* (Turtle Lake, WI: Self-published, 2008), 10.

[91] Ibid, 13.

[92] Ibid, 13.

[93] Ibid, 9–10.

[94] Ibid, 12.

[95] Ibid, 17.

[96] Ibid, 27.

[97] Ibid, 28.

[98] Ibid, 30.

[99] Kahlil Gibran, *The Prophet* (New York: Plimpton Press, 1937), 18–19.

[100] Eichman, *Let's Make Parenting Easier*, 60.

[101] Schwartz, *The Magic of Thinking Big*, 162–163.

[102] Cloud, *9 Things You Simply Must Do to Succeed in Love and Life*, 228.

[103] Beattie, *Make Miracles in Forty Days*, 6.

104 Bob Proctor, *You Were Born Rich* (Scottsdale, AZ: LifeSuccess Productions, 1997).

105 David Whyte, *The House of Belonging* (Many Rivers Press, 1997).

106 Orloff, *Positive Energy*, 26.

107 Charlotte Kasl, *If the Buddha Dated: A Handbook for Finding Love on a Spiritual Path* (New York: Penguin Compass, 1999).

108 Ibid.

109 This verse comes from the New Living Translation Bible.

110 This verse comes from the New Living Translation Bible.

Your Financial Goals

111 Chris and Marlow Felton, *Couples Money: What Every Couple Should Know About Money and Relationships* (Denver: Self-published, 2011), Chapter 4 "Unworthiness."

112 This verse comes from the English Standard Version Bible.

Your Career

113 Ban Breathnach, *Simple Abundance: A Daybook of Comfort and Joy*, November 5 reading.

114 Hill, *Think and Grow Rich*, 20.

115 Robert L Bogue, "Use S.M.A.R.T. goals to launch management by objectives plan," www.techrepublic.com/article/use-smart-goals-to-launch-management-by-objectives-plan/#.

116 Pastor John Arnold, "Why SMART Goals Aren't Always So Smart."

117 Realtor Alicia Romano.

118 *The 7 Habits of Highly Effective People: Powerful Lessons in Personal Change.* (New York: Free Press, 2004) 151

119 Dorcas Kelley, The Business of Coaching (Sunnyvale, CA: Self-published, 2009).

120 Pritchett, *You 2: A High Velocity Formula for Multiplying Your Personal Effectiveness in Quantum Leaps.*

121 Kelley, *The Business of Coaching*, 8, 9, 36, 37.

122 Dina Glouberman, *The Joy of Burnout* (Makawao, HI: Inner Ocean Publishing, 2003), 62.

123 Ban Breathnach, *Simple Abundance: A Daybook of Comfort and Joy*, October 2 reading.

124 Ibid, October 1 reading.

125 Ibid, October 3 reading.

126 Ibid, September 9 and September 10 readings.

127 Ibid, August 20 reading.

128 Kelley, *The Business of Coaching*.

129 Proctor, *You Were Born Rich*, Chapter 7 "The Risk-Takers."

130 Cloud, *9 Things You Simply Must Do to Succeed in Love and Life*, Chapter 5, "Play the Movie."

131 Thom S. Rainer and Eric Geiger, Simple Church (Nashville, TN: Broadman & Holman, 2006), 8.

132 Proctor, *You Were Born Rich*.

133 John C. Maxwell, *Leadership 101: What Every Leader Needs to Know* (Nashville, TN: Thomas Nelson, 2010), 158.

134 Ibid.

[135] Proctor, *You Were Born Rich*.

[136] Ibid, Chapter 7, "The Risk-Takers."

Conclusion

[137] Bob Proctor, www.all-famous-quotes.com/Bob_Proctor_quotes.html.

[138] Mayes, *Bella Tuscany*, 177–178.

[139] Melody Beattie, *Choices: Taking Control of Your Life and Making It Matter* (New York: HarperCollins, 2002), 48.

[140] Quote was part of a PSI Seminar presentation.

[141] Hill, *Think and Grow Rich*.

[142] Richard Bach, *Illusions* (New York: Bantam Doubleday Dell, 1977), introduction.

[143] Quote was part of a PSI Seminar presentation.